FROM A RUINED EMPIRE

LETTERS—JAPAN, CHINA, KOREA
1945–46

Edited by Otis Cary

Correspondents:

Donald Keene
Wm. Theodore de Bary
Otis Cary
Frank L. Turner
Sherwood R. Moran
Hisashi Kubota
Richard K. Beardsley
Warren Tsuneishi
David L. Osborn

KODANSHA INTERNATIONAL LTD.

Originally published by Kodansha International Ltd. as
War-Wasted Asia: Letters, 1945–46.

Distributed in the United States by Kodansha International/USA Ltd., through Harper & Row, Publishers, Inc., 10 East 53rd Street, New York, New York 10022. Published by Kodansha International Ltd., 12-21, Otowa 2-chome, Bunkyo-ku, Tokyo 112 and Kodansha International/USA Ltd., with offices at 10 East 53rd Street, New York, New York 10022 and The Hearst Building, 5 Third Street, Suite No. 430, San Francisco, California 94103.
LCC 75-11395
ISBN 0-87011-638-X
ISBN 4-7700-1138-5 (in Japan)
First edition, 1975
First paperback edition, 1984

CONTENTS

6

To those who disappeared in the deep leaving only a diary
To those who died on land or in the sky for freedom's sake
To all—especially students—on both sides who did not return
from the Pacific War.

太平洋戦争に
いのちをささげたすべての人々──
　　一片の日記を残して「わだつみ」の
　　もくずと消え
「自由」のために、陸と空に散った
学徒兵その他太平洋の両側に帰り
来ぬすべての人々──に

FOREWORD

These letters were written thirty years ago during the months immediately following the end of World War II. The writers were all involved in intelligence activities using the Japanese language in which they had competence, either by contact at an early age or by study. All the writers, except Warren Tsuneishi and Hisashi Kubota, had been trained in the U.S. Navy Japanese Language School, which was started at the University of California in Berkeley but had to remove to the University of Colorado in Boulder when persons of Japanese ancestry were evacuated from the West Coast, since most of the teachers were of Japanese parentage. The other writers (except for Richard Beardsley who entered the school later) were among the thirty or so enrolled in the second class because of some ability in Japanese or background knowledge of Japan or China.

The routine at the language school was extremely intensive since an attempt was made to teach us all aspects of Japanese—conversation, and reading and writing from *katakana* to *sōsho*. Groups consisting of five students were reshuffled constantly, so that there would be cross-stimulation and different talents and competences would rub off onto others. Our teachers were dedicated and tireless, and their weekly examinations left us little time for relaxation. We started as yeomen, second class, a device that allowed us to be paid until we were commissioned at the end of the course. Our class started in February 1942, and after a few months was accelerated because of the critical need for language officers as the American drive gained momentum in the Pacific. By January 1943 we were summarily commissioned and given assignments, the scheduled fourteen months having been telescoped to eleven. Most of us went to Pearl Harbor for duty at ICPOA (Intelligence Center, Pacific Ocean Areas) of CINCPAC

(Commander in Chief, Pacific Fleet), the intelligence arm of Admiral Chester W. Nimitz's command.

Pearl Harbor was still of manageable size then, and the peacetime traditions of the regular navy were being maintained. We were not required to live on base in designated bachelor officers' quarters, and soon we were finding apartments and even renting houses in desirable parts of Honolulu. Our work was largely with captured documents and prisoners of war, but it was not long before we were sent out on temporary duty with marine and army units which were landing on one island after another. The remarkable talents of this group, the intensity of our training, the unusual materials with which we worked—all tended to foster considerable camaraderie and esprit. Indeed, many have since developed careers, usually academic, on the basis of this experience. This original pool of Japan experts has contributed so much that it should be the subject of some responsible survey and study while they are still active.

By August 15, 1945, all of us must have accumulated more than enough points to be released, but the navy was in no hurry to dismiss us. Of course, we were eager to see the object of our intense and enforced study, Japan and the areas Japanese forces had controlled. As we anxiously awaited our assignments, those of us who had lived together in a house in Manoa Valley promised to write each other letters depicting in detail our experiences and impressions. Although we were not professionally trained observers, we hoped there would be enough interest in our experiences to warrant publication, so on our return to Washington in the spring of 1946 we had these letters retyped and bound in two volumes. To our regret, publishers were not interested, claiming that the American public was tired of the war. We were disappointed, but establishing our careers—most of us in the field of Asian studies—was our prime concern.

In 1947, after completing Amherst and some graduate work at Yale, I was asked to come to Japan as a member of the faculty of Amherst College on leave to serve at Doshisha University, with which Amherst had maintained long ties. I found more interest in Japan in the experiences of the war years despite devastation and serious social and economic disarray. Since two books about my own experiences written in Japanese and including portions of my letters sold well, I thought our original collection translated into Japanese might be of some interest. I was able to put together a Japanese version, doing much of the translation myself, under the title *Ajia no Arechi Kara* (From War-Wasted Asia) published by Kaname Shobō in Tokyo in 1952. The two original volumes of edited typescript have remained with me all these years and I still think that these letters written at a unique period of history will find interested readers. Last year I sent to the writers, all of whom have kept up with each other, xerox copies of their letters from the two volumes, asking for approval to publish them again, this time in English. I received mixed reactions, but nobody vetoed the idea. It was my intention to publish them just as they were, "warts and all," despite the temptation to improve and correct them. These then are our honest efforts to tell what we saw and felt long ago, unglossed by hindsight-granted wisdom. It is my hope that these will add much human material not usually available from professional correspondents or in academic texts. They should be not only of topical interest but also useful to students who may wonder how matters would have looked to them three decades ago. Considering the academic and professional reputation of many of the writers, I appreciate their concession in allowing the publication of these, their less than mature professional thoughts. Youthful idealism and enthusiasm, however, need no apologies, and I hope that we will be rewarded by the reactions of our readers, whether they come to our attention or not.

The letters have been arranged chronologically, not by place or topic. The endpaper map and the dates afford, I hope, enough of a frame on which to follow the developments. In the original editing in 1946 an occasional personal paragraph was eliminated. These were not all the letters we wrote but were picked for interest. Some names were changed to protect privacy. Spelling, punctuation, and capitalization were standardized, and translations of Japanese words and other explanations have been added in brackets where they first occur. However, the reader would do well to note the following words which appear frequently: *gumbatsu* (the military clique); *zaibatsu* (a giant financial combine); *kempeitai* (the military police); *bushidō* (the warrior code).

There is no need to take responsibility for mistakes or misjudgments, the existence of which we freely admit. We only hope that others in their youth will be encouraged to record their experiences at critical times in historic situations. If these letters help to illuminate the events which occurred during those early postwar months in East Asia, we will be amply rewarded.

Our special thanks go to Betty Turner and Fanny de Bary, who transformed the original letters into neat and readable typescript in 1946. More recently daughters Ann and Ellen Cary have helped with typing and organizational chores.

August 15, 1975   OTIS CARY
Amherst House
Doshisha University
Kyoto

BIOGRAPHICAL INFORMATION

Otis CARY (b. 1921), Professor of History, Doshisha University (on leave from Amherst College) and Representative of Amherst College in Japan, living in Kyoto.

Born in Japan and schooled through fourth grade at Japanese primary school in Otaru, Hokkaido. Returned to U.S.A. in 1936 to attend Deerfield Academy and Amherst College. Attended the U.S. Navy Japanese Language School, first at Berkeley, then at Boulder's University of Colorado. Duty at Pearl Harbor's Joint Intelligence Center, participating in the Aleutians campaign (Attu and Kiska) and the taking of Saipan. Executive Officer in charge of prisoners of war. Attached to the United States Strategic Bombing Survey in 1945 and Civil Information and Education Section of SCAP in 1946 until return to U.S.A. Rank: Lt. (s.g.).

SINCE THE WAR: Graduate work at Yale and sent to Doshisha University as Amherst's representative in 1947. Author in Japanese of several volumes of wartime and cross-cultural experience including: *Nihon Kaigen, Jeepu Oku no Hosomichi, Nihon to no Taiwa,* and translations of Reinhold Niebuhr's *The Irony of American History* and *The Self and the Dramas of History* into Japanese.

Donald KEENE (b. 1922), Professor of Japanese, Columbia University.

Born and raised in Brooklyn. Attended Columbia College and the U.S. Navy Japanese Language School, first at Berkeley, then at Boulder's University of Colorado. Assigned to Pearl Harbor's Joint Intelligence Center, Documents Division. Participated in the Aleutians campaign (Attu and Kiska) and the Okinawa campaign. Rank: Lt. (s.g.).

SINCE THE WAR: Studied at Harvard and Columbia University; Lecturer at Cambrige University, 1949–53, then returned to Columbia University. Numerous publications and translations, including: *Battles of Coxinga, Japanese Discovery of Europe, Japanese Literature: An Introduction for Western Readers, Living Japan, Modern Japanese Novels and the West, Sources of Japanese Tradition, Bunraku: the Art of the Japanese Puppet Theatre, Nō: the Classical Theatre of Japan, Landscapes and Portraits.*

Wm. Theodore DE BARY (b. 1919), Horace Carpentier Professor of Oriental Studies, Columbia University.

Born in the Bronx. Studied at Columbia College and Harvard before attending the U.S. Navy Japanese Language School, first at Berkeley, then at Boulder's University of Colorado. Assigned to Pearl Harbor's Joint Intelligence Center and participated in the Aleutians campaign (Kiska) and the Okinawa campaign. Immediately after the war, duty with the Naval Technical Mission to Japan. Rank: Lt. Cmdr.

SINCE THE WAR: Returned to Columbia Graduate School; Fellow of American Council of Learned Societies, Cutting Traveling Fellow and Fulbright Scholar in China, 1948–49. President of the Association for Asian Studies, 1969–70, and former Vice-President and Provost, Columbia University. Author of numerous publications and translations, including: *Sources of Japanese Tradition*, *Sources of Indian Tradition*, *Sources of Chinese Tradition*, *Five Women Who Loved Love*, *Buddhist Tradition in India, China and Japan*, *Approaches to Asian Civilizations*, *Self and Society in Ming Thought*.

Frank L. TURNER (b. 1918), Senior partner, Pacific Projects, Ltd., Tokyo.

Born in China. Returned to U.S.A. to study at University of North Carolina and Fletcher School of Law and Diplomacy. Attended the U.S. Navy Japanese Language School, first in Berkeley, then at Boulder's University of Colorado. Assigned to Pearl Harbor's Joint Intelligence Center and participated in the Gilberts (Makin) and Marianas (Tinian) campaigns. Immediately after the war, duty with the Strategic Bombing Survey. Rank: Lt. (s.g.).

SINCE THE WAR: Returned to U.S.A. to work with AID, Stanford Research Center, and Ford Foundation as economic consultant in Pakistan, Japan and other places in Asia before returning to Tokyo in private business.

Sherwood R. MORAN (b. 1917), former Administrative Officer of Clark County Mental Health Program in Springfield, Ohio.

Born and raised in Japan. Attended Yenching University in Peking, 1935–36, then went to U.S.A. to study at Oberlin College. In the steel business in Pittsburgh until attending the U.S. Navy Japanese Language School, first at Berkeley, then at Boulder's University of Colorado. Assigned to Pearl Harbor's Joint Intelligence Center. Immediately after the war, duty with the Naval Technical Mission to Japan. Rank: Lt. (s.g.).

SINCE THE WAR: After discharge, started the *Newsweek* office in Tokyo. Continued in publishing with Crowell-Collier Publishing Co., 1946–56, and Springfield Gravure Company as co-owner; changed to securities business 1964–71, now retired.

Hisashi KUBOTA (b. 1915), Chemist, Oak Ridge Institute of Nuclear Studies, Tennessee.

Born in Hawaii of Japanese parents. Attended University of Hawaii, majoring in chemistry, 1935. After volunteering, learned military Japanese at the U.S. Army School at Camp Savage, Minnesota. Assigned to Joint Intelligence Center in Hawaii. Participated in the Palau (Peleliu) and Marianas (Saipan) campaigns. Duty in Japan for three months after the war before returning to Hawaii.

SINCE THE WAR: After graduate school at the University of Wisconsin, working at Oak Ridge Institute of Nuclear Studies.

Richard K. BEARDSLEY (b. 1918), Professor of Anthropology, University of Michigan.

Born in Colorado. Graduated from University of California at Berkeley. Attended U.S. Navy Japanese Language School at Boulder's University of Colorado. Duty at Joint Intelligence Center at Pearl Harbor and in Japan after the war.

SINCE THE WAR: After graduate school at Berkeley, continuous assignments with the University of Michigan. Numerous publications, including, as coauthor, *Village Japan*, *Twelve Doors to Japan*, *Japanese Culture: Its Development and Characteristics*.

Warren TSUNEISHI (b. 1921), Chief of Orientalia Division, Library of Congress, Washington D.C.

Born in California of Japanese parents. Attended UCLA and the University of California at Berkeley. Graduated from Syracuse University by way of Heart Mountain Internment Center in Cody, Wyoming. After volunteering, learned military Japanese at the U.S. Army School at Camp Savage, Minnesota. Assigned to Army Intelligence with MacArthur's XXIVth Corps headquarters. Participated in Leyte, Camotes Islands and Okinawa campaigns. Immediately after the war proceeded to Korea and Japan en route to U.S.A.

SINCE THE WAR: Attended Yale and Columbia Graduate Schools. Now at the Library of Congress, after many years at Yale's Sterling Library.

David L. OSBORN (b. 1921), former Ambassador of the U.S.A. to the Union of Burma.

Born in Indiana. Graduated from Southwestern University in 1940. Attended Harvard Graduate School before the U.S. Navy Japanese Language School, first at Berkeley, then at Boulder's University of Colorado. Assigned to Pearl Harbor's Joint Intelligence Center. Immediately after the war, assigned to Ponape. Rank: Lt. (s.g.).

SINCE THE WAR: Returned to Harvard Graduate School and entered Foreign Service, with tours in Tokyo, Taipei, Sapporo, Kobe, Geneva, Taipei (Counselor of U.S. Embassy), Tokyo (Consul General), National War College, Deputy Assistant Secretary of State for Educational and Cultural Affairs, Tokyo (Deputy Chief of Mission with rank of Minister and Acting Ambassador), Hong Kong (Consul General), and Rangoon (Ambassador), now retired.

Above left: Otis Cary
Below left: Ted de Bary
Below: Don Keene

Above left: Sherry Moran
Below left: Dave Osborn
Above: Frank Turner

Left: Ted de Bary, Otis Cary and Don Keene at a "waterhole" in Hawaii, Christmas, 1944, with Otis's aunt.
Below: Sitting on the left of the table are Don Keene, Ted de Bary and Otis Cary. Photograph by Sherry Moran in Hawaii, 1944

Above left: Otis Cary with Dr. Shikiba on his right and the other members of the Shikiba family, in Dr. Shikiba's garden, early 1946. *Below left*: Yukio Ozaki, the veteran parliamentarian, listening to a point made by Otis Cary (extreme left), while Dr. Shikiba looks on, at Ozaki's home, late 1945 in Atami. *Above*: Dinner at Dr. Shikiba's early 1946. Otis Cary stands behind Princess Takamatsu, and Dr. Shikiba stands behind Prince Takamatsu.

Facing page, above: A view of Hibiya corner in Tokyo, in the fall of 1946 when it was (comparatively) quiet owing to the postwar dearth of vehicles; *middle*: General MacArthur's headquarters, the Dai-ichi Insurance Company Building, with scaffolding in front in preparation for the Christmas 1945 decorations; *below*: Looking north from the "Electric Building" in Tokyo, in the fall of 1945. Many of the buildings appear intact, but are actually only gutted shells. Note right front.

This page, above left: In Tokyo's burned-out areas, jerry-built structures sprang up overnight, providing much needed shelter; *below left*: Some young survivors of the war in Kōfu, a heavily bombed city near Mt. Fuji; *above right*: American servicemen used to buy these baskets in the street for a nickel apiece; *below right*: Dr. Scheer in Tainan, together with some of the children he loved so well.

Left: Emperor Hirohito of Japan reading the *Stars and Stripes*, with a bust of Lincoln in the corner behind him. This photograph was published in *Life* magazine in early 1946. *Below*: One of the first candid family shots of Emperor Hirohito and his family. From left to right are: Higashikuni Morihiro, Higashikuni Shigeko (wife of Higashikuni Morihiro, formerly Princess Teru), Emperor Hirohito. Empress Nagako, Higashikuni Nobuhiko (the emperor's grandson), Princess Suga, Princess Taka, Princess Yori, Crown Prince Akihito, Prince Hitachi.

THE LETTERS

FROM DON KEENE IN GUAM
TO TED DE BARY IN HONOLULU

August 19, 1945

Dear Ted,

I heard from Beardsley that you are now back in Honolulu. You were probably surprised to discover that I left so soon after my return, especially in view of my determination to get back to the mainland as quickly as possible. It was the decision of a moment, one that I now fully regret but which I am sure I would make again, did I not foresee the consequences. At the moment I am sitting in an office in Guam. It is mercifully cool this afternoon, which means that I am not glued against the back of the chair by my melting flesh. I am waiting, a not unfamiliar practice.

The day I left Pearl, or rather its morning, determined me. I was out at Otis' camp talking at once idly and seriously with the men there. One of the prisoners congratulated me with a broad smile on the news of the night before—Japan's proposal of surrender. Most of them, however, seemed quite preoccupied and I soon found myself alone in the large workroom. One fellow came in whom I did not know. We talked a few moments and then introduced ourselves. It was Matsusaka. His father had owned a large factory, but Matsusaka wanted now to engage in some sort of trade which would help strengthen international relations. He was obviously enthusiastic about what he said, and spoke with jerky little gestures of his hands and a smile which seemed to punctuate the sincerity of his words.

"I surrendered thinking that I might be the only one, but determined that there would be at least one. Defeat may prove the best thing possible. It will level all distinctions in common shame and sorrow. That must happen or Japan will be lost in a

25

sense worse than military defeat. . . . I want to go back at once myself to start, to do anything. Won't you help, you who understand us?"

"No," I answered, "I am going back home. It is not for me to help in any case. It is your country; you must do the work yourselves."

"But, in the meantime, during the occupation at least. . ."

Perhaps it was philanthropy in the narrowest sense, the personal friendship I felt for this person I had met not twenty minutes before, but I suddenly felt a desire, a desire more than an obligation, to help. I mean to help him, and to help others like him, rather than to help a government which interests me very little or a vast proletariat with which I would be embarrassed. For what reason I cannot say—perhaps the hope of a smile of gratitude.

In any case, I volunteered to leave Hawaii for the Western Pacific again, rather than return to the States. On the plane trip to Guam my head was full of ideas, wild adventures involving foiled brass hats, young people saved from the depths of ignorance, prejudice and regimentation—a world in my own image if you like. A man of goodwill, selfish undoubtedly, but desirous of helping, of winning the war.

Since my arrival here I have felt increasing disillusionment and depression. I am still as anxious as ever to do what I originally planned, but now it seems as though I am doomed to wait indefinitely. One has to be very circumspect here when assignments are being handed out, flatter and be jolly or else one will discover oneself prowling about the Bougainville jungles.

Please let me hear from you as soon as you can write.

Don

◆ ◆ ◆

FROM WARREN TSUNEISHI IN SEOUL
TO DON KEENE IN GUAM

September 12, 1945

Dear Don,

Now that I have some time for writing, I thought that I would tell you a little about what has happened to me since my arrival a week or so ago from Okinawa. The first day, of course, was the most vivid and exciting.

From our ship lying at anchor in the yellow-green waters off western Korea, the harbor city of Inchon appeared like any other modern seaport town: on the waterfront, long, low corrugated steel warehouses; and on the pine-covered hills beyond, the red brick of schools and churches and the white concrete of government houses and commercial establishments. Until our convoy of troop transports, cargo ships and small escorts arrived from Okinawa, the harbor itself had been sheltering only small, wooden fishing luggers and diesel craft, while here and there the hulks of rusting merchant ships lay half-submerged in the water.

We waited with a growing restiveness while the landing barges made the long trips from ship to shore with the first echelon troops. The brilliant September sun moved steadily across the blue sky.

I felt personally a sense of trepidation. There are about thirty of us Japanese-American interpreters and translators attached to the XXIVth Corps, and additional teams of five to ten attached to the various divisions, the Counter Intelligence Corps, Military Government and miscellaneous units. As I waited for my turn to go down the cargo net, and then ashore, I thought that Korea, after forty-odd years of Japanese misrule and oppression, would not be the healthiest spot in the world for us.

I felt I could only expect the very same questions which were often put to me during my period of training in the States: "What is your nationality (meaning 'race')? Chinese? No? Japanese! Then what are you doing in the army? An interpreter? Oh." I was afraid that, like Americans, the Koreans would be unable to differentiate between Japanese-Japanese, whom they have good reason to hate, and Japanese-Americans; nor would they be able to comprehend how completely American birth and life in the United States have made us. I felt, however, that perhaps we would be able to convince them with our bad manners, our hit-or-miss spoken Japanese, and our general inability to act like the polite and docile—and at times cruel—Japanese.

A week ago, on September 3, when an advance party of some

ten officers was being selected to be flown into Korea, a Nisei language officer's name was scratched at the last moment because of the development of bitter anti-Japanese outbreaks in Korea. Also, the Japanese had accepted the terms of surrender only two weeks previously. They still had their guns, and no one knew how they would react, particularly toward us. They might even consider us "blood traitors."

At long last came the order to debark. We scrambled down the cargo net into the rocking landing barges, and after circling around our mother ship, headed for the shore.

Inchon serves the capital city of Seoul as a port much in the same fashion that San Pedro serves Los Angeles. The Japanese call it "Jinsen," and still have their black-uniformed, saber-carrying police on duty.

Since our interpreter-translator section had been split up into smaller elements of three or four men and dispersed among numerous units, we were not particularly noticeable, but when we walked off the landing onto the streets, we immediately became the center of attention. The Koreans crowded around us, staring at us with frank curiosity. They shot questions at us in Korean and we kidded back in English. Dared we speak to them in Japanese? Already we had heard stories that on the preceding day Japanese troops had fired on a group of demonstrators killing two Korean students and wounding a third. The Koreans had tried to assemble on the docks to welcome us and demonstrate their joy over their liberation.

Since there was no immediate transportation to Seoul available, we were given an hour to tour the city. With a whoop we were off, not singly or in pairs, but in groups and with carbines slung over our shoulders. Before we had progressed one block, we had gathered about us a small entourage, which rapidly grew in size and gaiety, until by the time we reached the center of the city fifteen minutes later, it had grown into a crowd of immense proportions. The people were obviously in a gay mood, their faces burning with happiness and curiosity. "So these are Americans," they seemed to be thinking, "the fabulous Americans from the land of milk and honey. But that person. . ." and they looked at me. "He isn't American; he must be Korean!" Nudging each other, they pointed at me, turning their heads aside when I glanced their way. How long, I wondered, could I maintain the subterfuge?

It was dusk when we reached the outskirts of Seoul, two hours after we had set out from Inchon. The twenty miles of pitted, rutted highway had made greater speed impossible, even in our jeep. There in the suburban areas Koreans lined the streets, shouting their welcome to us, waving at us, cheering us on. We replied with cries of "*Mansei! Mansei!*"—the Korean equivalent of the Japanese "*Banzai!*"—trying in vain to catch the happy contagion and feverish excitement which seemed to pervade the crowds.

Farther on, in the darkened streets between business districts, we passed platoons and companies of Japanese troops marching in close formation, their backs bent under tremendous field packs, their leather shoes squeaking in the quiet autumnal evening.

"Jeez, look at them big healthy bastards!"

"What the hell, they're armed, aren't they?" Some of them were trailing rifles.

"Wonder where in hell they're going."

Not one turned a curious glance toward us. Instead, keeping their eyes on the ground, they plodded forward steadily, marching away into the darkness. Later we passed similar groups of fifty to two hundred men with perhaps two or three GIs carrying "tommy guns" marching along beside them. They were apparently being marched to prisoner of war enclosures.

It was quite dark when we found the Hanto Hotel where we were to be quartered for the night. The Hanto Hotel, we knew from our orientation lectures, was a modern, eight-story building with business offices on the first five floors, Japanese-style rooms on the sixth, and Western-style rooms on the remaining two. On the eighth floor, too, was the dining room. The Hanto Hotel had no ballroom.

Tired, grimy and dusty after the long ride, we dropped from our jeep, adjusted our packs, clapped on our steel helmets, and slinging our carbines, walked into the handsomely appointed lobby of the hotel. The marble floors glistened. Two potted palms flanked the elevator doors. An austere Korean gentleman stood behind the reception desk in a cutaway coat. Involuntarily my eyes went down to my own dirty, baggy fatigues. Someone breathed, "Girls," and we turned. Led by two suave-looking men, a group of some twenty astonishingly pretty Korean girls were silently filing into the lobby. They wore long, silk Korean gowns, dazzling in the beauty of their colors. I was overcome by an acute sense of unreality, as if I had been suddenly plunged into a wild dream. An elusive thought, which I could not capture at the moment, flitted through my mind. Later that evening I remembered and laughed out loud. Of course! We were the modern counterparts of the Vandals that had taken Rome. Barbarians marveling at and ashamed before the luxuries of civilized Rome!

Beauty, such as confronted us in the lobby, ought to be appreciated, but the troop billeting officer, a tall, grim man who appeared at that moment, apparently did not think so. He turned to the two suave-looking men and engaged them in conversation, snatches of which we overheard.

". . . but what are they doing here?"

"Big party . . . entertain . . . welcome U.S.A. soldier."

"Sorry. No girls. Regulations."

". . . party . . . welcome U.S.A. soldier . . . very grateful to U.S.A. soldier."

"Sorry. No girls. That's final."

And so the girls, obviously disappointed, had to depart. We, too, were unhappy over this turn of events.

The Korean managers of the hotel, who had only recently replaced the Japanese, were bound to entertain us, however, and this they did with a welcome banquet. My seat was next to a Mr. Kim, one of the managers. Mr. Kim was the austere gentleman in the cutaway whom we had first seen in the lobby. After a few toasts of "Rare Old Nippon Brandy"—which was neither rare nor old, though acridly Nipponese—his reserve broke down. Under his mask, it developed, he was not austere at all: he had simply been frightened by our uncouth appearance.

Because of the dictates of oriental politeness, he was hesitant about asking direct questions. But after making a remark in Korean and perceiving that I had not understood, he blurted out in English, "I am sorry; you are Korean?"

"No," I answered, "American."

"But . . . but . . . " He was struggling for words that he had learned years ago, words that he had forgotten through lack of use.

"If it's all right with you," I said in Japanese, "let's speak Japanese." He was startled.

"Ah, you speak Japanese!"

"Yes, that is so."

"I beg your pardon," he said perplexedly, "but where is your country?"

"America."

"But you are not like other Americans. You have oriental features."

"My parents are from the Orient."

"From Korea?"

"No, from Japan." He was so disappointed that I hastened to add, "But that was years and years ago. I was born and brought up in America."

"But you are of Japanese blood and in the U.S. Army?"

"Yes, I am an interpreter."

"Is that so?"

"Yes, that is so. I am an interpreter, but a rather poor one. I can't even speak your language, Korean. If you prefer, I won't speak Japanese." I gestured, pointing to the banners that hung on the walls proclaiming:

KOREAN INDEPENDENCE—MANSEI
KOREAN LIBERATION—MANSEI
ALLIED FORCES—WELCOME

"No, no, that's all right," he protested. "I am happy to find someone who can understand me." He recounted the difficulties he had had with the billeting officer. They finally had to resort to the age-old method of charts, diagrams, pidgin English and fingers.

"It is so difficult, not knowing English," he smilingly concluded, and then growing sober and pointing to the banners he said, "I did not think it possible even in my dreams. I firmly believed that Korea would become free in my lifetime, yes, but not this soon. And we have you to thank for our liberation. Deeply, deeply, I thank you. You have suffered so much to liberate us and make us independent." Tears welled up in his eyes. Embarrassed, I suddenly felt ill at ease.

The Koreans are deliriously happy over their newly gained freedom. But independence, which they believe to be automatically theirs now, is yet to be acquired. The years of Japanese occupation have not left them unaffected, for an intensive campaign was undertaken to wipe out all traces of the Koreans' national identity. This campaign resulted from a Japanese attitude which I shall try to describe by paraphrasing their own words. Although they had ruled Korea kindly, albeit firmly, for over a generation, though they had established fine public schools to educate the ignorant Koreans to be fit subjects of the emperor, though they had proclaimed the racial identity of Koreans and Japanese, and though they had done all these good things unselfishly and in the best interests of the Koreans, who were simply incapable of helping themselves, yet the obstinate peninsula people persisted in retaining their characteristic traits, in keeping their family names, in speaking and writing their own language and subversively acting like Koreans.

The problem eventually became acute during the war years, when it became desirable to have a good, round, hundred million Japanese subjects fighting the Greater East Asia War rather than just seventy million, the population of the home islands. By decree, then, thirty million Koreans became Japanese.

One by one, orders came down from the Governor-General:

All Koreans will learn the national language. Only Japanese will be used.

The tiny elevator girl, who always greets me with a smile and who has just turned sixteen, said to me, "And even old Grandmama, who had never spoken a word of Japanese in her life, had to go to night school and recite the Japanese ABCs. Grandmama learned to repeat words she didn't even understand."

The teaching of Korean is forbidden.

A graduate of the Keijō Imperial University—now Seoul University—said to me, "That is why, tragically enough, many Koreans, particularly youngsters, cannot even read and write their own language. Japanese, rather than Korean, is their native tongue. But you cannot abolish a culture by decree. More than one student was jailed for studying Korean secretly."

All Koreans will take suitable Japanese names.

A Korean who had studied abroad in Germany and Switzerland said to me, " 'Kim' became 'Kanemoto,' 'Bak' became 'Boku,' and 'Paek' became 'Shirata.' But here the Japanese made a great error; for if there is one thing we treasure above all else, it is our family names. You ask me why we have so many Kims, Lees and Baks as we do. The answer is that we are a homogenous people, closely interrelated by marriage and blood ties. No Korean can change his name without disgracing it forever. That is one of our beliefs. The Japanese thought the change would draw us closer to them; it only succeeded in alienating us and fanning our resentment toward them to a higher pitch."

The Greater East Asia War demands that Koreans devote their energies to the study of the Japanese qualities of frugality, austerity and self-sacrifice.

The elevator girl again, angrily, "The Japanese expected us to sacrifice. They weren't going to, though. Before the war ended, we were so short of food that Mother said she would kill us rather than see us starve to death. And if the war had lasted another year, we would have surely died. They took everything—our young men, our rice. They even took our brass spoons to melt into shells."

That the Japanese succeeded to some extent in the Japanization of Korea, however, is clear. This is most evident in the matter of language. I have met very few Koreans, at least in Seoul, who do not have a good command of Japanese. (This is not true, of course, in rural areas.)

The *Keijō Nippō* (Seoul Daily News), once the official organ of the Japanese Governor-General, still publishes daily in the Japanese language, although its publisher, editor and writers are now all Korean. The reason for the continued existence of the paper is that many of the people either find it impossible or too difficult to read the numerous Korean-language newspapers. Still, I believe it is generally understood that the use of Japanese will be restricted as much as possible. There even exists an official ban on spoken Japanese. I experience a shock, therefore, every morning when I hear the newsboys in the streets shouting, "*Keijō Nippō! Keijō Nippō! Kyō no* [Today's] *Keijō Nippō!*" Heard above the hubbub of Korean crowds, the Japanese phrases sound incongruous.

All in all, however, the Japanese were never able to win the confidence and friendship of the Koreans, let alone transplant Japanese culture to Korean soil. I do not think they ever realized that the respect they so greatly desired from the West was something they arrogantly denied their "fellow" Koreans.

I hope I can see you before too long.

Warren

◆ ◆ ◆

FROM DON KEENE IN GUAM
TO TED DE BARY IN OKINAWA

September 23, 1945

Dear Ted,

I am writing rather early in the morning with just enough of a bad taste in my mouth to remind me that last night I was drinking. Drinking out here is less the result of any desire than it is a universal social obligation. Another such obligation is one which involves the patience, fortitude, loyalty and courage required in hearing sung for the thousandth time one or another version of "Bless 'em All," a tune of which the chief glory would seem to be that any words chosen at random seem to fit its music without any noticeable fallings from the usual high standard. This being a marine outfit, what is more natural than to hear twenty-verse songs about General MacArthur?

> I've returned, I've returned, I've returned
> With fiery vengeance to burn.
> My air force is hitting them hard in the rear;
> My doughboys are all drinking Blue Ribbon beer.
> And my navy has swept the seas clean,
> Murmansk to the green Philippines.
> Against Jap statistics
> I'll hurl my logistics
> And then I'll call in my marines.

MacArthur has become for men all over the Pacific the legendary figure of attack, the traditional butt of thousands of jokes, most of which have only the slightest real relation to him. Occasionally a lone dissenter will say, "Well, you've got to admit that he did a wonderful job with what he had," but this remark is inevitably met with a barrage of invective and contradicting evidence. It will undoubtedly prove a great shock to those on the home front, long-schooled to the picture of gallant Douglas MacArthur, to hear of him treated so cavalierly. Certainly no person has ever been given better treatment at the hands of war correspondents, who see in him, perhaps, their military equivalent.

War correspondents! I think of one of them, on a ship anchored off Kiska, when he heard that there were no Japanese on the island. He was furious. His actions clearly showed that the fact that thousands of American lives (whose loss he would have rendered in terms of "American blood" or "the lives and hopes of American boys") had been saved, because we were able to take for nothing a difficult objective, meant nothing to him. The waste of his time in coming on a wild-goose chase in the "Grade B War" out in the Pacific was paramount in his consideration. However, just before I came out here to Guam I heard a broadcast with the same reporter giving a restrained account of the fighting in the Aleutians. "What did they do? Not much—just saved us from a Japanese attack on the United States itself!" Thus was his story metamorphosed for other money.

I suppose that before long there will be "inside histories" of all the campaigns in the Pacific, analyses by reporters of every phase of the fighting. If there is a little honesty, everything written may not be an entire waste, but it seems almost useless to expect the truth from a newspaperman. One of my most vivid impressions of the press was on the occasion of the famous Muraki wedding on Okinawa. As you must remember, when Muraki gave himself up, he asked to remain together with the Okinawan nurse with whom he was captured. Since we needed the information which he could give us, we agreed. At this point someone must have decided that it would be a wonderful idea if the two could get married. Perhaps it was even on moral grounds, for the two were sleeping in the same tent. In any case, the wedding was hardly Muraki's choice. On the day of the ceremony there was a great deal of fuss and excitement. An area was roped off in the XXIVth Corps command post and a *torii* [the traditional sacred gateway of Japanese shrines] hastily transplanted there. The crowd gathered. Lieutenant Muraki appeared in an army uniform lent him by another prisoner. The girl wore a beautiful Japanese bridal kimono. It was decided to have the bride walk in time with the Wagner "Wedding March" as rendered on an accordion. It was difficult to convey to the girl just what was desired and she was finally allowed to trot up to the *torii* in utter confusion and terror. The wedding ceremony was more or less the usual Christian one, recited by the chaplain in English and then translated by a Nisei best man. A ring was then handed to Muraki. He put it in his pocket. The wedded couple walked over to the place where General Buckner and all the other high-ranking officers were standing and bowed deeply, saying in English something like, "Thank you very much. I pray for your long military success."

The newspaper reporters, in the meantime, were screaming with rage. "That's not the way they'd treat one of our boys. . . . Just wait till the boys in the front lines hear about this. . . . They ought to kill 'em all. . . . Here we fight in the mud and they get married. Very nice." Photographers crowded around the two Japanese. "Smile. That's right, smile. Kiss her, go ahead. . . . What's the matter with him? Is he a sissy?" Pictures were taken from all angles by the photographers while the reporters continued to make penetrating comments. Is it any wonder that the articles which appeared on the wedding were all hopelessly inaccurate?

The reporters, as usual, were so busy listening to themselves talk that there was only an incidental value in the event. This I have found to be true: whenever I have known the actual facts of any happening and have seen a newspaper account of it, the latter has always been distorted or false. To picture Muraki's wedding as an act of magnificent generosity on the part of the Americans was what one would expect of them. It is largely as a result of the misinformation supplied by reporters that Americans have been led to think of themselves as the great saviors of the world. On certain local issues it is possible to check the reports which emanate from the oracles of our day, but the public is forced to swallow whole the idiotic stories of utterly uninformed men on so vital a matter as the enemy we have been fighting.

I wonder if these people writing "inside histories" will include all the dirty stuff that has marked our campaigns. A captain in my tent, who served with the First Raider Battalion on Tulagi, Guadalcanal, New Georgia, and Vella Lavella, told me the other night about a platoon sergeant he used to have who went around from "Jap" corpse to "Jap" corpse removing gold teeth. When the captain argued with him saying, "How in the name of heaven can you put your hand into a stinking Jap's mouth?" the sergeant produced a bagful of gold teeth and predicted that he could sell them for a lot of money. Another story the captain told was of three "Japs" who had fallen from a coconut tree near Munda and were lying on the ground dazed but alive. One marine took out his knife and said to the captain, "This is the way we used to do it in Nicaragua," thrusting the blade into the throat of one, the chest of the second, and finally, holding the struggling "Jap" down with one hand, into the abdomen of the third. The captain seemed revolted by these stories, but on the other hand was desirous of seeing every single Japanese killed, and would let out exclamations of disgust at the fact that Japanese prisoners seen mending roads here on Guam are permitted to remain alive.

On Attu, I myself saw some of our atrocities, in the form of bodies from which the ears had been cut as souvenirs to be sent back to homes in America, presumably, or other bodies into which the numeral "7" had been cut to commemorate the achievements of the 7th Divison. Before I left ship, a regular navy lieutenant commander begged me to get him a pair of "Jap" ears. He said, "I promised my boy before I left Honolulu that I'd get him a pair. When we were off Guadalcanal in my destroyer, I saw a great big 'Jap,' must have been one of the imperial marines, floating in the water, but we were going too fast to stop. Damn! They would have made a fine pair of ears. You'll get me one, though, won't you?"

There is the other side, too. One thing I won't forget is how Sergeant Peterson, who had been decorated both at Guadalcanal and Tarawa, the latter time with the Navy Cross, explained in sign language to a Japanese prisoner how to use an enema. The hospital corpsmen didn't care and there weren't any interpreters around, but the sergeant voluntarily did all the dirty work involved. Then, too, is the curious fact that even on Attu, when the prisoners were taken, they were usually showered with cigarettes, candy, and requests for autographs.

I think that the answer to the problem of such behavior is that the Americans are unable as yet to appreciate the Japanese as human beings, much like any others. It is inconceivable to me that Americans in Europe would value some old sock or filthy cap just because it had belonged to a German, yet that is what is regularly done with Japanese souvenirs. The curiosity attached to the Japanese prisoner is such that many Americans are amazed to find that some of them are reasonably well built, that others have had enough education to say "Thank you" in English (which is usually interpreted as, "He speaks fluent English!").

The captain, my tentmate, advocates extermination of the Japanese because of their innate wickedness, one example of which he cited being the cannibalism recorded of them in New Guinea and elsewhere. I had previously spoken of the matter to prisoners who, while expressing horror at the deed, said in return, "If your comrade, feeling himself dying, were to say to you, 'I beg you to eat me so that the rest of you can live,' what would you do? Wouldn't you be moved by the spirit of self-sacrifice which denied the individual for the survival of many?" Of course, it may be answered that the persons eaten in New Guinea did not so plead, but the fact remains that the Japanese are capable of the type of communal interest, if you like, that permits cannibalism for the sake of the group.

On this island there was recently a cannibalism case. The two defendants had been discovered as a result of their own confessions to other prisoners in the stockade, who were instinctively repelled by the account and moved to inform the officers in charge. By the time the trial came up, however, they had changed their minds and were anxious to serve as character witnesses. The trial itself was held under the worst possible circumstances, the official interpreter, a Guam Chamorro, being capable of rendering "Were you out on patrol?" only by "Were you out on a picnic?" It was generally conceded that the two prisoners would hang, and the trial was therefore not pressed as it might have been.

The story was that of a band of Japanese who had been hiding in the jungles of Guam, long since cut off from any organized units. The leader of this particular band was a certain Ohora. Ohora one day became incensed at an Okinawan civilian (who had been living on Guam) and killed him. The group had been wandering in the jungle for months, living on lizards and roots, so Ohora thought that it would be a good idea to eat the Okinawan as their first real food in a long time. They cut off the head, the hands and the feet and buried them. The fat and gristle were then also separated. Ohora cut up the flesh into chunks and fried it. Then, while the group sat around eating the Okinawan, others living in the jungle joined them, attracted by the smell of the cooking. The Okinawan lasted for several days. At one point, Shōji, one of the defendants, couldn't stand it any longer and started to throw away some of the gristle which had been stored in a bucket. Ohora caught him and accused him of eating the gristle himself. A few days later, Ohora told Shōji that he had to kill the Okinawan's son, a boy of twelve or thirteen. "But Shigeru is a nice boy. Let's not kill him. We can get along on lizards," Shōji protested. Ohora answered, "If you don't get

Shigeru, we will kill you and eat you instead." Shōji was sufficiently frightened. He went over to Shigeru's hiding place and
invited him for dinner. Like the terrible joke in *Hamlet* about
Polonius being at supper, not where he eats but is eaten, Shigeru
became the victim, the dinner itself. The other defendant actually
killed him, and they all sat around eating that night. Shigeru
proved to be a better dinner than his father. Shōji admitted having
eaten his testicles—"They didn't taste very good."

The defense held that this was the law of the jungle. My
tentmate, had he known the story, would have pointed to it as a
crowning proof of Japanese wickedness. I had known that the
Japanese had practiced cannibalism in New Guinea and in the
bypassed islands of the Marshalls, but so close a contact was
frightening. The first reaction of anyone on hearing of a case of
cannibalism is a nervous laughter. It is only on thought of the
particulars of the deed that one feels the real shock—the frying of
the flesh and the cleaning of the innards. Is the kind of horror we
experience a basic congenital one? Natives of the Southwest
Pacific lived for hundreds or thousands of years without feeling
it. I think that Herodotus recited the case of some tribe whose
members considered it a grievous sin if sons of dead fathers did
not eat their parent's body. The horror of the story of Atreus and
the banquet at which he ate his sons, or of Harpagon similarly
punished by a wicked ruler, must be based on something funda-
mental, as basic perhaps as the dread of incest. Yet, the prisoners
could ask me if eating a dead comrade might not be best in view
of his expressed wishes, and there was a defense of the admitted
cannibals on this island on the grounds that the "law of the
jungle" is not the law of ordinary man.

The problem is an extreme case of something with which we
shall have to deal in the Orient—the divergence of absolute
standards. Thus, for example, while a Japanese can consider
it absolutely bad to be taken prisoner, bad without qualification,
we do not agree at all. On the other hand, we are infuriated by
Japanese treatment of our prisoners, little imagining that it may
result more from a Japanese divergence of opinion on treatment
of prisoners than from deliberate evil, our absolute judgment.

All this brings up the question of war criminals. The other day I had a rather violent argument on the subject, finding myself one against many. The argument was rather circuitous and not especially memorable except in the idealism of my opponents. It is unusual for me to take the more cynical side of an argument, but in this case I found myself unable to agree with their more elevated theory—that fixing the onus of "war criminal" on the leaders of Japan would have the effect of establishing some kind of standard of international morality, at least, a first step in that direction. I have often had arguments with Japanese prisoners in which I insisted that Japan must adopt Western morality, if only because she is outnumbered in the world. That seems to be fairly obvious to me; Japan's defeat in the present war and her surrender must prove that the foundation on which the Japanese myth is based was unsound. It is one thing to insist on uniform morality. It is another to say that by killing off certain of Japan's military leaders we will have persuaded the Japanese of the validity of our ways. The people with whom I was arguing had the good sense at least not to contest my opinion that, regardless of the punishment meted out to war criminals, others in the future will not be dissuaded from a similar course. All it means is that no man will start a war if he is certain that he will be beaten. Punishing Japan's leading militarists and industrialists at this time would be an act of overwhelming self-deceit. We would be persuaded that we were acting on lofty motives and would actually be indulging in the cheap wickedness permitted the victor, as we would realize in later years.

Guilt for the war rests with the entire Japanese nation. If we could look into the hearts of each and every Japanese and find just which ones opposed the war, not because they thought Japan might be defeated, but because they believed that the war was wrong, we might understand more clearly where the guilt lies. How many Japanese, when they read of the attack on Pearl Harbor, thought of it as an act of aggression and evil? As many as there are we can say are guiltless, or possibly so, if they did not condone the successes of Japanese arms in China. The others, the seventy millions, are as guilty as any nation has ever been.

To punish the leaders would be meaningless. The others, if un-punished, will think, "Poor Tōjō (or poor Yamashita), he did his best, but we were beaten. If only we had worked a little harder!" To punish the leading Japanese under the brand of "war crimi-nals" would be to repeat what every nation has done since earliest history, but giving the act the benefit of a high-sounding name. If our finger of guilt were to point not only at the conquered countries, but also at the English in India or Hong Kong, or the French in Syria, or the Russians in Eastern Europe, or the United States for bombing Japanese civilians in undefended residential areas, the statement that the trials marked a beginning would have some meaning. As it is, they serve rather to mark an end to the war, an end marked as usual by recriminations and self-satisfaction.

As far as war criminals are concerned, I don't know how many are guilty of murder of our prisoners or of Chinese civilians. I think that these should be found out and punished as for civil murder. As for mistreatment, though, such as forcing prisoners to work in the broiling sun or to eat only rice and fish, I think that we had better forget the matter entirely. It would be too easy to make accusations and too easy for an American to feel that something was an outrage which was almost normal to the Japanese accustomed to severe marches and miserable food. For the Japanese prisoners on Okinawa to have been fed nothing but K-rations for months, long after the island was secured, was hardly excusable, but certainly not criminal.

The Japanese have been many times more cruel toward our prisoners than we have been toward theirs, but at the same time, Japanese civilians were told how well Americans were being treated at prisoner camps. Newsreels of prisoners playing base-ball, drinking milk (almost impossible to get in Japan) and attending church were shown throughout the country to convince the Japanese civilians of the justice of their treatment. Such attention would certainly not have been necessary in the United States; our civilians have no desire to be reassured that Japanese prisoners are being well-treated. The difference is that while the Japanese are religiously devoted to what they think is "just," even

though utterly mistaken in their conception, they are unable to
see what lies between the wish and its fulfillment. Thus, they could
see themselves the just and wise rulers of the world, capable of
generosity to their fallen foes, and solicitous about the welfare
of the "independent" Philippines or East Indies they set up.
When something gets in the way, however, they have no patience
with it. If there is not enough food for the prisoners and themselves, too, they will starve the prisoners, thinking of the justice
of their decision. It is hard to be generous with food when one is
a little hungry oneself. It is also hard to be considerate to American prisoners when it is not unusual for a Japanese soldier of
superior rank to beat mercilessly another Japanese soldier without
thought of anything but the justice of his wrath.

If it were possible, I think the best solution would be to forget
the past and to attempt a real reconversion of the Japanese nation.
I think that we have a good chance of arousing the interest and
active cooperation of many young Japanese. Intelligence on our
part can really win the war. I wonder if Americans won't find the
Japanese the most agreeable people in Asia from almost every
standpoint. The Japanese will certainly admire the Americans.
With this initial advantage we can create a powerful and meaningful friendship.

I noticed in the paper that we are having a great deal of difficulty finding reliable and efficient Koreans to help us. That,
I suppose, was to be expected. On the ship aboard which we
evacuated about a thousand prisoners from Okinawa to Hawaii
I talked with a Korean named Mun, a prisoner I had first noticed
when he was brought into the division stockade. I was feeling
rather irritated at the Koreans aboard ship and thought I would
tell Mun everything I held against his people. I told him first of
the hypocrisy which seems to characterize all Koreans with whom
I have had dealings. I used to go almost every evening to the
Korean prisoner of war stockade on Oahu, ostensibly for a
Korean lesson, but actually for the pleasure of talking to the
Koreans. Sometimes we would sit until late at night discussing
such unlikely subjects as "Virtuous Behavior," engaging in an
enjoyable, if sophomoric, argument. Or they would have im-

provised parties and sing long Korean songs, pretending to drink in between verses, and making elaborate gestures to convey the strength of the supposed liquor. On one particular night, however, we were sitting in one of the camp tents, watching the members of the "Korean Eagle Party" drill. Changwan Kim, the general, observed the great improvement in the formations with a pleased expression on his smooth face, convinced that he was readying the other prisoners for the day when they would accompany the American forces in an invasion of Korea. I was talking with Pokwan Shin, a handsome boy of great charm, and with the dark-faced Cho, whose expression was so intense when he told of the terrors of the Japanese. A few others as usual stood in the back of the tent, listening but not feeling equal to taking part in the discussion. Shin spoke up, "At last I have realized the great ambition of my life. Ever since I read a certain book in high school I have wanted to join an organization like the Korean Eagle Party."

"Of what book are you talking?" I asked.

"*Wa ga tōsō.*"

The Japanese meant nothing to me for a moment and then the words straightened out into *Mein Kampf*. I felt a sudden slap, the kind of slap one might feel if one were awakened that way. I stuttered something about this book having been the very symbol of all we hated and fought against.

"But we all read it. We all believed it. Japanese propaganda was very strong." This from Cho, whose face had been for me the passion of a free Korea.

And Shin thrust his fine features closer to me saying, "Everyone had to believe their propaganda. I was once thrown into a detention cell for questioning it just a little."

I should, I suppose, have been more sympathetic, but I felt that knowing the cause of their hypocrisy was one thing, and being victim of it another. The little admissions they had made to me that not all Japanese were fiends now made sense. The Koreans couldn't help it; they had collaborated, had made every possible positive step of collaboration in order to make a bare living. But it hurt me that they had lied thus, had been so hypocritical, had deceived me so with earnest words and faces.

When I had told Mun of this, I stopped and waited for an answer. A very sensitive person, Mun clenched his hands at the edge of the desk and cried, "Such persons must be killed!"

But among the Koreans we have captured I am afraid that such persons are the most numerous. Driven by various reasons to their present state, these Koreans now present a hopelessly complicated pattern of hypocrisy. They can be servile or brutal by turns, depending on what will get them the most. I wonder if my experience with Koreans will not be repeated many times by other Americans in Korea.

I should be leaving soon, but not for any place where I will be likely to meet you or any other close friends. Don't forget to look up Hisashi Kubota if you go to Sasebo. You will find him a bright and agreeable person with whom to talk if ever you grow weary of silence or patter about point-discharge systems and other methods of getting out of the navy.

Don

◆ ◆ ◆

FROM TED DE BARY IN TOKYO
TO DON KEENE IN GUAM

September 24, 1945

Dear Don,

We are in Tokyo now, which cannot surprise you much more than it does Otis and myself. In Okinawa, we were told there was no air service from there to Sasebo or to any other point in Kyushu, and very little even to Tokyo, at least not enough to handle the enormous traffic headed there from all over the Pacific. Yontan airfield is jammed with air travelers trying to get to Tokyo and Shanghai. Most of them are joy-riders. Some, like Otis and myself, had travel orders and air priorities, but no one even looked at them. Bribery with liquor or camera film was about the only means of getting aboard a plane for Japan. We worked it, finally, with a load of lumber, or rather the promise of one. The air passenger officer of a troop transport squadron wanted lumber for his tent floor, and I knew where some might be obtained at Tenth Army Headquarters. Otherwise, we would be still waiting there, sleeping as we did last night inside an empty plane. Even the transient barracks had been closed down, and we practically had to steal food.

It seemed like a bypassed island. Thousands of men, hundreds of planes, and shiploads of equipment were sent there to do the biggest job of the war. Then suddenly the job was called off, and now nobody gives a damn what happens. The big shots and many little ones are running off to China and Japan for sightseeing and souvenirs. Those who cannot do so well for themselves are just taking it easy, except for a conscientious few who struggle on with their jobs in the face of general confusion and corruption. Everything gave evidence of a terrific letdown. In front of the Air Transport Command quonset was the old sign: "Welcome to Yontan Airfield—Every night a Fourth of July," reminding one of last spring's air raids and the spectacular antiaircraft barrages they provoked; reminding me especially of a cold, wet dawn when we hugged the mud desperately as "Jap" shells screamed overhead toward the big C–54s a hundred yards away at the end of the airstrip.

There was one other relic of the campaign: the prisoner stockade, which Otis and I managed to visit late the night of our stopover. It was a wild trip in a heavy rain. Our jeep shook from one mudhole to another, over roads which had not been worked on since the marines first drove through in April, and truck traffic had torn the ancient surface to shreds. But our trouble was well rewarded by the reception given us. Apparently no one had visited the prisoners since the war ended and they were hungry for news of the peace, the occupation, plans—if there were any—for their return home, and of the language men they had met during the battle. Masuyama, the chemist, asked particularly about you. Unfortunately, we had only about ten minutes with them, but I could tell from the way they mobbed us, all talking at once without hesitation, that their spirit had changed little since I left in August. They are still as open and receptive as the day I first stopped by their tent in the officers compound and got to talking about the latest pony edition of *Time* magazine. None of the tension, suspicion or hostility that sometimes made things awkward for us at the Guam and Pearl Harbor stockades. Everyone was in exactly the same boat; the guilt or shame of surrender, of collaboration, was shared equally by all. And unlike your experience with Guam prisoners, there were probably no secret blacklists of those who talked with us prepared by fellow prisoners.

I wish Otis had been able to see more of my acquaintances there. He has had so much more experience with prisoners than I, and could judge better the difference between this lot and those captured earlier in the war. He was ready to believe them better adjusted to captivity than many of the others, his idea being that the attitude of most prisoners reflects the treatment we have given them—not the degree of physical comfort provided, but the consistency of our policy in handling them. And despite the poor living conditions on Okinawa, these fellows were not subjected to so many changes in policy, pointless interrogations, and political maneuverings as the earlier ones.

Still I think the Okinawa prisoners had this healthier attitude principally because they surrendered together and in such large numbers. No one was alone in his supposed shame, and the Japanese conscience (or most people's, for that matter) is not so easily disturbed when there is company to share the burden.

If you are still waiting for a ship at Guam, this letter is not going to make you any happier or quiet your restlessness. The more I tell you about our first adventure in Japan, the more you will regret not coming with us. I don't mean that this is a tourist's wonderland; if anything, it's far closer to hell on earth than any city should be. But one does not have to be a Baudelaire to find it fascinating.

This is a fine morning in Tokyo, sunny and cloudless. I expect I could see Mt. Fuji if the Marunouchi section did not have so many beat-up, burned-out office buildings blocking the view in that direction. As we flew in, we saw Fuji's summit rising above the clouds. Most of the passengers were disappointed to find it bare of snow in September. They took it for granted, from all the pictures they had ever seen, that Fuji was snow-capped the year around. Even so, it was imposing; "a considerable protuberance," as Johnson admitted to Boswell on seeing Ben Nevis. Its dark blue cone stood out above the whiteness of bulky clouds, not like the last step to heaven, but like a giant fortress over the land.

Our pilot took his time landing. For almost an hour we circled over the bay and plain, saw the pagoda-shaped battleship *Nagato* where she lay inside the Yokosuka breakwater with ships of our own fleet keeping her company. Beyond were hundreds of white-sailed fishing boats, the first I had seen in years. We came in low over the waterfront where many factories and warehouses still stood, though it was hard to tell in what condition. They may have been badly burned out inside, but it was ironic to see them standing at all, for inside this fringe of industrial and commercial buildings the residential areas were completely flat with destruction. Our bombing of Tokyo, and I suppose of most other cities, certainly hit the Japanese home, right where the average man would feel it most. One can hardly believe the reports in American papers that the Japanese do not know they lost the war. The evidence of it is everywhere, inescapable, and in many respects permanent; some temples and museums are gone for good, and the rest will take decades to restore.

We saw more desolation on the ride from Tachikawa airfield to the city. The outer suburbs were pretty well off. Frame houses crowded the road in a solid line, and behind them were truck gardens, neat patches stuffed with corn, taro and other vegetables which one could not identify through the pines and houses. Then, as we left the suburbs and approached the center of town, it seemed rather as if we were running out into open country. There was no city din, no crowding, no more restricted view from the street. There was practically nothing left; the rubble did not even look like much, though occasionally one noticed an improvised shelter dug out of the ruins and covered by a piece of tin. Again there were isolated factories, dark and lonely like New England mills in the early thirties, though they did not seem to have been touched by bombs. The finest structure along the route was a gas storage tank, a good bombing target, completely untouched. Fire bombs seemed to have destroyed everything but the obvious military targets.

But, after all, the scenery was not much different from what we saw at Naha and Shuri, so the Japanese themselves were the big attraction for me. The kids had not learned to call "Habba-habba" yet, but they waved and saluted for all they were worth. Some made the V-sign, some hollered, *"Banzai,"* and one little baby stumbled to the sidewalk screaming, *"Baka, baka, baka yarō!"* [roughly, "you bad, bad men!"]. A few older people saluted too, but the girls had apparently been instructed to take no notice of us. They looked away until our truck passed, then turned around to peek and giggle and nudge one another. Nowhere did I see any show of hostility. People were either openly curious or else they studiously minded their own business. It is probably the latter attitude which the news correspondents characterize as sullen and resentful, imputing to an expressionless face the emotions which can be most easily sensationalized.

The six of us who are here now and speak Japanese have spent a lot of time idling around the streets engaging these sullen-faced individuals in conversation wherever possible. None of us has yet run into one who did not open up like a flower when spoken to. If we stop on a corner to talk to one, immediately a dozen others crowd around to share the talk, to find out what they can about the Americans, the outside world, or anything else we will take the time to discuss with them. Generally they avoid talking about the war. Polite as they are, it probably seems improper to discuss something so controversial on such short acquaintance. It is too much to expect that they should have changed their opinions overnight, and I am just as glad to find them silent rather than hypocritical. But there are other reasons for silence too, and among them I would emphasize the fact that they are so damned tired of war. If we ask about the bombing, they answer our question but try to steer the conversation to American baseball: "Who is leading the leagues now?" There is little to be learned from talking to us about the bombing; they have lived through months of it, and still live in the ruins. Can you blame them for wanting to think about something more pleasant? Must we be pedantic about the lessons of the war, tell them to sit in their ruined corner and ponder their ruin endlessly?

One thing apparent from sidewalk gossip is the unpopularity of Tōjō. No one hesitates to speak frankly about the general: "A big faker, finished forever as far as the Japanese people are concerned." They particularly scorn his suicide attempt; a true samurai, they say, never bungles the job if he really wants to commit suicide. "It is pretty bad when the wife of Marshal Sugiyama joins her husband in suicide and Tōjō cannot do so well."

But there are also a few more thoughtful persons, who, while they have no sympathy for Tōjō, remember his tremendous popularity early in the war and have little sympathy for the loud curses of disillusioned admirers. I cringe a little, too, when I find these Japanese exhibiting a big weakness, their acceptance of the samurai code, while denying a lesser weakness symbolized by this fallen idol. There might be some justice in judging Tōjō by his own standards, but I am not sure that the samurai code meant very much to him, and in any case there are much better grounds for condemning him. I wonder how long it will take the Japanese to see Tōjō the way we do, particularly to understand the part which involves their own guilt. Now they are acting as the Italians did toward Mussolini, kicking a carcass contaminated by their own sins.

So far I can't agree with reports published back home that the Japanese are giving MacArthur the runaround or that he's giving them a soft occupation. Everyone is scared stiff of the general. We notice it indirectly because they seem to look upon each of us, at first, as his personal representative, with considerable awe and some fear. It is only when we display a certain humanity toward them that this extreme deference gives way to normal politeness. The military government itself could hardly be more tough and autocratic than it is; not one will make a move in business or politics without its approval.

What worries me, rather than the softness of our policy, is the possibility that the Japanese may go from one authoritarian regime to another without being freed from their dependence on direction from above. As long as nothing can be done except by allied decree, little progress will be made toward setting the people on their own feet politically.

I hope there will be a letter from you when I finally reach Sasebo.

Ted

◆ ◆ ◆

FROM DAVE OSBORN IN KWAJALEIN
TO TED DE BARY IN TOKYO

(The following is a letter from David Osborn, who was at Kwajalein in the Marshall Islands at the time. He went down there with two prisoners from Pearl Harbor in his custody. They were to testify in the Wake and Mille war crimes trials. His idea in volunteering for the assignment was to get involved in the occupation of Ponape and learn the language of that island.)

September 25, 1945

Dear Ted,

It looks as though my wildest dreams are on the verge of coming true, once I can crawl out from under this war crimes business.

Things looked pretty black at first, though. My plane brought me to Majuro from Johnston, instead of to Kwajalein, and Majuro's commander is something of a Captain Bligh. Fortunately, however, only the Mille [atoll] investigation was being held there; Wake was to be investigated at Marshalls and Gilberts Command, which is on Ebeye in the Kwajalein group. So I left one of the prisoners in the clutches of the Majuro people and brought the other along to Ebeye.

When I arrived, there was already a language man here, but he was about to go to Wake with a Nisei on this same deal, so I was snagged to take my prisoner's testimony. That was no trick at all; I simply acted as interpreter for the officer in charge of war crimes. It was tedious, though. First we got his story in the rough; then question and answer style under oath; finally I had to read the transcript back to the prisoner and get his signature on each page.

Before we got around to the last page of this procedure, a dispatch was received here to the effect that a "Jap" hospital ship, *Tachibana Maru*, was about to make port at Eniwetok and an interpreter was needed. I got up to Eniwetok the next day to find that my services were not required. A commander in the island command office spoke a little Japanese, and the purser of the "Jap" ship spoke a corresponding amount of English.

I was not particularly put out by this, since travel is broadening, and it gave me a chance to go aboard the hospital ship with no responsibilities attached. Conversation with her skipper was one long stream of gripes, in that inimitable Japanese way: "Hiss, haha. It doesn't really matter of course, but if we don't get more rice tomorrow, we will all starve. Haha, hiss."

Actually he had plenty of legitimate gripes. The ship had been in Subic Bay for a couple of weeks, and during that time a souvenir hunter or two seem to have gotten aboard her. Such things as compasses, charts, engine room clocks, nameplates, china, cooking utensils, navigation instruments, floor mats and so forth were naturally taken. Even less portable articles—beds, wardroom chairs and tables, mirrors, toilet seats—had somehow disappeared. It didn't surprise me, but the skipper was a little dazed.

Back at Ebeye, I read the prisoner's testimony back to him and got his signature on each page. On thus reviewing the case, it became painfully apparent that his story was composed entirely of hearsay, with a little conjecture thrown in. It offered no clear evidence to refute the story told with striking unanimity by the present garrison of Wake: during an American carrier raid against the island, the air raid shelter in which half of the Americans were quartered was hit and its occupants killed; the rest of the Americans in another shelter, believing an American landing was imminent, killed their guards, took their weapons, and escaped into the brush. They showed fight when a "Jap" platoon was sent out to round them up, and were killed. This story certainly sounds fishy at one or two points, but my prisoner's testimony certainly can't shake it.

The question of why he was sent for at all, when we have on Wake people who took part in the shooting of the Americans, was answered last night. The legal officer went over the whole affair with me, expressing considerable disappointment and even some suspicion of our prisoner. He produced the latter's original story as told to Otis, where the flat statement is made that

"Captain Sakaibara wrote an order for the execution of the remaining Americans." The prisoner now claims he never made a formal statement to Otis, just told him the outline of what he thought had happened.

The legal officer was hot for Otis' blood for a while. I tried to soothe him somewhat by pointing out that the Japanese language is not very precise in any case, and that a protest would accomplish nothing now. This succeeded, at least, in bringing down his wrath in some measure on my own head, which made me feel a little better, since Otis' mistake is one of those "for whom the bell tolls" things. In this case, the bell tolls for all of us who have at any time reported a prisoner's story as a definite statement.

About getting down to Ponape or Kusaie, there seems to be a pretty good possibility of working it on some deal or other. Not for a while, however; tomorrow I go to Wake for more of the same business.

Dave

◆ ◆ ◆

FROM SHERRY MORAN IN TOKYO
TO DON KEENE IN GUAM

September 26, 1945

Dear Don,

Otis walked over to me while I was eating steak at the "Electric Building" (the Tokyo Electric Company's offices have been converted into a junior officers' barracks and mess) and we just grinned at each other for a few seconds. We didn't know what to say, or how to begin—and it is just the same now. I am over my head in thoughts and impressions of really being out here with you fellows, of seeing Japan after ten years, of seeing it as a countryside devastated by a terrific storm and the people coming out to look at the damage, like farmers at their wheat knocked down, only their looking continues longer. I guess it will take more than a year for a new crop this time. And that first, shocked silence with which people view calamity, eventually to continue about their business, seems here to be a perpetual state of shock and silence.

Tokyo, the first war casualty I've seen, is a devastated, immodest mess, but the silence is what gets me most; no honks, yells, clangs—none of the stuff you hate in a town but come to expect. For Tokyo, for all Japan I suppose, the calamity is past, but everybody is still staring in that god-awful silence.

You'll hear more when I recover my own equilibrium. Bataan!

Moraan!

◆ ◆ ◆

FROM TED DE BARY IN TOKYO
TO DON KEENE APPROACHING TSINGTAO

September 29, 1945

Dear Don,

Tonight I am aboard a seaplane tender in Tokyo Bay, waiting for a plane ride to Nagasaki. However, there is a typhoon sweeping up the islands from south of Okinawa and all flights in that direction have been canceled. This means several more days of waiting, which would be enjoyable enough in the city but is a nuisance here. My quarters are below decks, hot and stuffy as only a ship can be, whereas Tokyo was refreshingly cool. I sit naked at the supply officer's typewriter, but there seems to be nothing I can do to strip my brain down for work.

You are certainly familiar with the name of Kawasaki; the prominent family whose interests, I believe, include shipbuilding and aircraft production, and of whom we may hear when the warguilt of Japanese capitalists is discussed. When I left Hawaii, Mutsuo Hamada asked me to deliver a box of cigars to a friend of his in Tokyo, an insurance man who once visited Honolulu on business. The name was Kawasaki, but it didn't strike me as particularly significant, because there are about as many Kawasakis in Japan as Fords in America. So it wasn't until I looked him up the other day, first at his office on the Ginza and then at his home, that I realized he must be related in some way to the well-known family.

The office building wasn't easy to find. City directories are no help, since most addresses today represent a pile of bricks and beat-up concrete or else a usable building now taken over by the occupation forces. The Nippon Fire and Marine Insurance Company was more fortunate than most, however; it was burned badly enough to avoid appropriation by the Allies, but two floors were still in fairly good shape. I stumbled around in the darkness of the fire-blackened ground floor until I could feel the first step and railing of an unlighted stairway. At almost the same instant I collided with someone coming down, a girl whose eyes were more used to the darkness and could distinguish me as an American. Her embarrassed giggles were swallowed up in the cavelike atmosphere as I climbed on up to the second floor. It, too, was gloomy, but for a different reason: Japanese business places do not seem so well-lighted as ours, and this, together with vitamin deficiency, may account for their poor eyesight.

Mr. Kawasaki was not in. He spent little time in the office, I was told, and could most often be found at his home. His nephew, a young man dressed in the very best Western style (which was pleasant for me after seeing everyone else in a patriotic uniform), took me to a nicely furnished conference room and wrote out the directions to his uncle's residence. It was up on a little knoll called Fujimi-cho ("the section from which Fuji may be seen"). Fire had leveled everything around it, but the knoll itself was protected by a firebreak from which all inflammable houses and material had been removed before our fire bomb raids. There were also high stone walls around the principal homes, as is customary in Japan, where privacy is so hard to get that frequently a fine view will be blocked off to prevent outsiders from looking in. In this somewhat exclusive section only the French Embassy had been damaged. Its two main buildings were completely wrecked inside, while nothing else in the vicinity was touched. It seemed impossible to me, on carefully examining the ruins, that two such direct hits could have been scored against such an unlikely target, exactly in the center of each building. Incredibly precise and definitely suspicious. Someone who didn't like the French or their representatives must have planted those bombs during an air raid. But who in Japan was that mad at the French?

Both the embassy and Mr. Kawasaki's home were designed by an architect who came to Japan with Frank Lloyd Wright. The home is more Western than Japanese in style, but the main principles of Japanese construction are not abandoned. The house is supported by a group of interior pillars so as to be earthquake-proof and still allow for the wide use of sliding glass doors in place of outside walls. To provide still more light and air there is a central courtyard, glass-enclosed, where a pair of ducks played around a bubbling pool. A separate wing is done in strict Japanese fashion, both inside and out, but an abrupt contrast in styles is avoided, for someone approaching from inside the main building goes through a long connecting corridor which arouses the expectation of something new beyond.

It was in this wing that I ate my first Japanese supper in Japan, squatting on legs bent awkwardly before a low table for two. Mr. Kawasaki sat opposite, while a serving girl knelt quietly at one side, watching carefully to see that we had everything at precisely the right time, but without making us feel that we were being watched or even that a third person was in the room. The master of the house seemed no more a Japanese in this setting than he did at the dining table in the Western wing; if anything, he seemed less, speaking English without effort, with assurance that both his ideas and vocabulary were understood. Even relaxed as he was, but as few Japanese are in Western company, his mannerisms were those of any tired American businessman enjoying a quiet supper at home. His wife and two children, I had been told, were sent away to the mountains when our bombings started, and without much business to attend to, though with many more worries on his mind, he had plenty of time to be lonely in such a large house. He invited me to live there while I was in Tokyo; a car would be put at my disposal, geisha girls, movie actresses and so on. But Japanese hospitality is apt to be oppressive; before long one is swallowed up in it, and to save my soul I had to decline.

Fortunately the ordinary amusements of Tokyo had been destroyed with everything else, and there was no choice but to do what I wanted most—talk together. Kawasaki had been educated in both England and the United States, spoke English with a slight public school flavor, and was proud of being a Psi

U. His father was one of the first Japanese to go abroad for schooling, and an older cousin, whom I met later in his villa at Hayama, had wound up similar training by taking a Scottish wife. They were a family closely bound together by common education, political outlook and business interests. Everything I saw of them indicated wealth, not just the remnants of prewar wealth such as their villas, Western furnishings and clothes and automobiles, but a current buying power which could provide me, for instance, with black market steak three times a day during my brief visit. And yet in our conversations I could establish no direct or indirect connection between these people and Japanese war industries. My presumption was that there must have been some such connection in the family, but Kawasaki repeated many times that his own interests were limited to insurance and banking except for one sulfur mine in Hokkaido. I was skeptical, but had no reason to doubt his word when he described for me how unprofitable war industries were as an investment, even if Japan had not lost the war. The military, with whom one had always to deal, were very unreasonable, "tied up in red tape, slow, fickle and dictatorial." For a while it had been the fashion among prominent concerns to appoint admirals and generals to their boards of directors as a means of obtaining big war contracts. Some of them, the Mitsuis especially, made big money in this way. But Kawasaki was soured by his experience with the sulfur mines in Hokkaido. In the middle of the war a government directive closed the mines down; sulfur supplies were adequate for the moment and the labor was needed elsewhere. Then six months later he was ordered to reopen them and go into operation immediately. The military thought such mines could be opened as quickly as they were closed, but actually it took over a year to get them operating again, and by that time the war was almost over.

At this point in our conversation, I thought of telling Kawasaki about a prisoner I had known on Okinawa who called himself a Marxist. He was a frail intellectual from Tokyo Imperial University, not the kind of recruit Marx really wanted, or the Japanese army for that matter (he was a private). Several times we talked together about *zaibatsu* [leading industrial and financial family combines which dominated Japan's prewar economy] and I told him of America's intention to punish them for their part in starting the war. Surprisingly enough, my socialist was not pleased by the idea.

"It's true that the great families owned industries which profited from the war. But this doesn't mean that they necessarily supported it; in fact, some of the biggest *zaibatsu* opposed the war as long as they dared, favoring a peaceful penetration of world markets with cheap goods produced by cheap labor. At this game they were already winning. Why risk war, a good chance of defeat, and the certainty of subjection to the military?

"Rather than the industrialists, it was the landlords who contributed most heavily to pro-war political movements. Population pressure in the thirties threatened to break down the high-rent system, and in the midst of worldwide depression, industry could no longer absorb surplus rural population. In the provinces there were more and more frequent rice riots, demonstrations against the high-rent system, and talk of revolution. To divert this pressure and save themselves, the landlords turned to a policy of aggressive expansion on the continent of Asia. It is a fact that the Japanese army drew most heavily on rural areas for its manpower; as fighting men the city workers were considered low-grade, since their health was generally poorer and they were apt to be a little more sophisticated. It is also a fact that the political spokesmen for the military were men with an agrarian background and following, reactionary with respect to agricultural problems but revolutionary with respect to industrial ones. On the one hand, they spoke of farmers as the backbone of the nation, the defenders of ancient Japanese virtue against unhealthy foreign influences; on the other, they advocated nationalization of industry and campaigned against city capitalists as the demons of Western corruption.

"But it was not so much this political attack as it was terrorism which brought the military clique to power and the capitalists into submissive alliance. More and more of the latter signed up with, or gave money to, the right-wing extremists, thinking fascism the only alternative to communism. Naturally they were well-off as things stood, and wanted no political change of any kind; but if there were to be a revolution, the *zaibatsu* wanted it to go right. Some of them, including a few of the most powerful, still held out against the militarist trend until their leaders were assassinated in the February revolt of 1936. Thereafter the *gumbatsu* [military clique] had things pretty much their own way, enough, at least, to prevent political interference with their aggressive moves on the continent. If a capitalist got out of line, he was arrested by the military police and released only upon making a large contribution to a 'worthy' militarist cause.

"As far as the war and aggression are concerned, all big decisions were made, or won, by the military. The *zaibatsu* were their tools, not the masterminds behind a great plan of conquest. Of course, you will not mistake what I say for an apology for monopoly capitalism, as if it didn't have something to do with bringing on the war. We are talking now about the war guilt of individuals."

I replied, "Yes, I understand that point. Yours is not exactly a new interpretation of the politics which lead to war, but I am a little surprised to hear it from a Marxist."

He answered slowly, a little tired after making such a long speech in the heat of Okinawa's summer sun. "I have been thinking a lot about it since I became a prisoner of war and met you Americans. The average Japanese knows little about America and nothing at all about democracy. Look at these prisoners around us—hardly a political thought in their heads. All they know is obedience, and perhaps that Americans are surprisingly kind people. So I have been wondering what will happen after the war when you try to reorganize Japan along Western lines. Who is there to help in the job but those educated in the West and exposed in some way to democratic ideas, who but the somewhat Westernized capitalists and a few intellectuals with almost as little courage as the *zaibatsu*?

"I am afraid the problem is more complicated than you Americans think. Unless you run the country from top to bottom for a generation, which is not exactly democratic either, you will have to take what cooperation you can find and not be too particular about it."

As I told this story to Kawasaki, he listened quietly and nodded assent to most of what the prisoner had told me. About the landlords, however, he disagreed. "They were hardly more anxious for war than the industrialists. Like everyone else, the landlords supported the *uyoku* [right wing] for fear of communism, without knowing quite what the rightists were headed for or what the consequences would be. When they found out, it was too late, or at least too difficult for them to change."

This was a vital point of disagreement, for if Kawasaki were right, one was left wondering what sort of financial support the militarists had, or whether they had any at all aside from that extorted by threats of violence. When I pressed him about this, his answer only partly satisfied me. "Money was not so important at the beginning as you may think. To start with, the militarist ideology (this is the only English word which I can remember Kawasaki fumbling for) was nothing more than a feeling that the military class was not receiving its share of power, prestige and compensation in the new society which grew out of the Meiji Restoration. This feeling grew especially strong after the turn of the century, after the Russo-Japanese war, when Japan's tremendous commercial and industrial expansion left the once-dominant military class with a comparatively minor role to play. Their pay, for instance, was nothing compared to the salaries and profits in civilian enterprise, and their political influence declined as feudal concepts gradually gave way to Western ideas. Consequently, they were waiting for any breakdown in the new system, any pretext to reassert their old authority. Bad times in the late twenties gave them their chance."

He stopped there and I pushed it no further. We were getting away from the point, it seemed to me, for all this could be true and still not absolve either the financiers or landlords from responsibility, if they had any, for what happened in the thirties. I would have to wait with the questions still unanswered: were the landlords more or less a separate group in their political interests, and if they were not, along what lines did Japanese capital split in support of or opposition to the militarists? We know that there was a split somewhere, that there was considerable opposition prior to February 1936, for most of the men murdered in the February revolt were capitalists or their political representatives. On one side there was money to get and keep the *gumbatsu* going; on the other side was enough opposition to attract the bullets of young military fanatics.

In writing this I wonder if I have not stated the problem too simply. As it is here, the thing may seem much more complicated than most Americans realize, but perhaps a well-informed Japanese would think my distinctions—capitalist, landlord, militarist, etc.—far too general, would say that the personalities involved, their loyalties, motives and actions are far more complex than my explanation allows.

There will be more about Kawasaki soon.

Ted

◆ ◆ ◆

FROM SHERRY MORAN IN TOKYO
TO DON KEENE APPROACHING TSINGTAO

September 30, 1945

Dear Don,

Even after four days I find that my feelings have undergone a change. I have become somewhat hardened to the wreckage around me, and the sight of little above ground except chimneys and heavy office safes does not seem as strange to me as it did at first. I feel like a tramp who has become used to sleeping in a graveyard. Tokyo's gravestones—the chimneys and safes—no longer provoke my imagination. I have ceased to speculate on the homes, the lives, the hopes that went into this vast cremation.

A continual downpour of rain was partly responsible for my depression when I last wrote. It was cold and damp to walk in, and made the city even more dreary to look at. Since then the weather has cleared, the days are warmer, the nights brighter, and many more people are out on the streets. I realize now that a great many of the buildings are actually untouched. The greater part of Tokyo was not hit by demolition bombs, but by incendiaries. For this reason it was possible, with luck and constant watchfulness, to keep buildings of reinforced concrete from being seriously damaged. Quite a few of the business buildings in the Marunouchi district are unhurt, although wooden houses adjoining them are burned to the ground. It is in the business buildings that we live and have our offices.

I guess you have some idea what my job is—making a study of Japanese war industries. Recently a group of us visited a small firm which manufactured personnel parachutes, and which had pioneered in the design of chutes used by both the Japanese army and navy. It had survived the war undamaged. I acted as interpreter for the interview which took place in the director's office. We had them bring in samples of their chutes, sprung the container bags, and opened the chutes up to examine their construction. We must have had six or seven of the things spread over the desks and chairs, clear across the room in all directions. With all that silk billowing about and hundreds of colored cords tangled up in each other, the place looked like a remnant counter at Macy's.

You may wonder what sort of reception we get when we barge into one of these factories. First of all, there is a guard who salutes us at the gate. (Japan is salute crazy; even two-year-old kids salute us on the street.) We return the guard's salute, tell him who we are and what we have come for. All the talking is left to me, of course, and I make a point of being polite about it: "Would it be convenient for us to inspect the plant and ask a few questions?" There is only one answer, as both parties are well aware, and if anything is gained by being polite, it is that the Japanese will not become frightened and flustered to the point where intelligible conversation is impossible. There is less strain on both sides when they feel that we understand the rudiments of everyday courtesy, to which the Japanese, by nature, are much more sensitive than most people.

We are immediately ushered to the main reception room or the Board of Directors' conference room. There is a few minutes' wait while an appropriate official is called and tea is served. People keep shuffling in and out and sometimes it is hard to tell whether the man standing in the doorway, bowing, is a top official or just another company flunky who has been sent in to see that we are properly provided for. In these factories there are no well-dressed, well-fed executives who can be easily distinguished from less prosperous hirelings. Dress hardly varies from the highest to the lowest; all wear worn-out clothing or standardized uniforms. Almost everyone looks underfed. In one case there was a very awkward moment when we noticed a uniformed young man bowing repeatedly at the door to attract our attention. He was tall, thin and looked like an adolescent schoolboy. We assumed that he was just an office boy, who would go on about his business without disturbing us, but his embarrassment was so noticeable that I could not help asking what it was he wanted. To our surprise we learned that he was the man we had come to see, the chief engineer and designer for one of Japan's biggest manufacturers of precision instruments.

But such embarrassments are usually smoothed over during the first few minutes of the interview, while we drink tea, pass around American cigarettes and get better acquainted. Most of us were unprepared, when we started our investigations, for the cooperation and cordiality with which we were shown through the plants. Our every question was answered. We are still somewhat amazed by these people's frankness; we have not yet run into a single instance of equivocation or evasiveness about information which was highly secret just six weeks ago.

Take the case of an engine plant we visited. When we asked about bomb damage, the officials brought out a blueprint of the plant indicating when and where each bomb had fallen, what type of bomb it was—high explosive, incendiary or dud—and the extent of the damage done by each. We asked for a guide to show us through the plant. The production manager, construction engineer, and maintenance supervisor all accompanied us. We stopped by an obliterated machine shop. "You did a pretty good job on this one," they told us. "Would you like to see what it was like before?" And before we could even answer their question, they broke out blueprints of the shop drawn from all angles. They told us we could have copies of the blueprints in a few days; their own blueprint machine was blasted on February 27, but an outfit on the other side of town could turn them out in four days. They expected to serve us lunch, but I don't think they were offended by the excuses we made to get away somewhere with our K-rations. After lunch we tried to hurry our inspection of the remaining buildings, and once when we showed too great haste in going from one shop to the next, they said, "Don't you want to see the underground passageways between heat-treating and machining?"—something our information on the place didn't even suggest.

It is a Japanese custom to give guests presents when they depart, and at these factories we are given souvenirs of the articles manufactured there. The parachute makers gave me a couple of heavy silk handkerchiefs, which are much too fine for anyone to blow his nose into. How do you think blue silk would look in the lapel pocket of my uniform?

Sherry

◆ ◆ ◆

FROM TED DE BARY IN TOKYO
TO DON KEENE APPROACHING TSINGTAO

October 2, 1945

Dear Don,

In my talks with Kawasaki it seemed that he did not speak with equal frankness about all aspects of the political situation in Japan. On such short acquaintance one could hardly expect to be taken into complete confidence, but since he was very open on some points, I could not help wondering why he should be reserved on others. Was he being elusive in a Japanese way, or was his the wariness of businessmen wherever you find them? Or was it, as I began more and more to think, a habit of mind to be expected of people whose thoughts have been closely watched for years? He had told me, for instance, of the trouble he and his friends had with the domestic spy system. One man, imprisoned during the war, found that all the evidence against him had come from his cook, an agent of the military police.

Kawasaki remarked on the new free speech which came with

American occupation: "To most Japanese, freedom of speech does not mean very much, because most Japanese are not inclined to be outspoken. But I like to be frank when I talk and it will mean something to me.

"Still, you know, it isn't enough just to issue an order declaring freedom of speech, the press and so forth. People will not speak their minds until you have eliminated the old military gang they still fear, and you haven't even started to do that. So far you have only arrested the figureheads, who rarely held real power. It's a good idea, of course, to punish the men who took nominal responsibility, but if you really want to eliminate the military curse from Japan, you will have to do more than disband the army and tell everyone to go home. You will have to seek out the younger officers, the ones who wanted and planned the war, who terrorized all others into supporting it. You must destroy them."

Several times I had heard this opinion expressed by prisoners of war—that a group of field officers in army headquarters, together with a smaller and less powerful group in the navy, had been the *gumbatsu*'s brain trust. In few instances did they take important commands (Tōjō and Doihara are two who did), preferring to keep a stranglehold on the key bureaus at headquarters. Thus, they could not be eliminated by simply placing well-known military figures on the war criminal list. It would require considerable detective work by men thoroughly familiar with the Japanese military.

Kawasaki thought they could be rooted out by either of two means: get friendly Japanese to put the finger on key men, or just ship all graduates of the military and naval academies to the South Seas for a lifetime of hard labor. The latter method he thought best. "It's very unlikely that any officer will abandon the code and philosophy with which he has been indoctrinated. You can do nothing with them, and eventually they will cause trouble, even as civilians."

Turning from this subject, I pressed Kawasaki for the names of financial houses most closely associated with the military. He started, "Mitsui, deeply mixed up in it; Mitsubishi (the firm now controlled by the Iwasaki family)," and then, whether by design or not I don't know, he somehow turned the conversation away.

We soon got talking about prominent politicians. Prince Konoye had a great responsibility for the war, not so much as a man who wanted it, for he did not, but as one who sought power and still lacked the courage to prevent war. I asked Kawasaki about a prisoner's story that Konoye had taken Kagawa, the Japanese Christian, into his house and protected him when the war broke out. "Nothing of the sort," he answered. "He had a notoriously jingoistic Buddhist priest living with him." (Incidentally the same prisoner had told me that Kagawa was less well known in Japan as a Christian than he was as a popular novelist and publicist. The prisoner also believed Kagawa something of an opportunist, by no means an outspoken opponent of the war.)

Kawasaki did not have much to say for the present government of Prince Higashikuni. It had been necessary, just after the surrender, to have as premier a man who could command the disarming of the country and prevent bloodshed. The prince was an old army man; if that were not enough to assure the success of his mission, his royal blood would be. But having Higashikuni as premier meant having a lot of the old military and bureaucratic crowd in the cabinet. To reorganize the government along Western, democratic lines, this cabinet would soon have to give way to a more liberal one.

Already there was talk of a new government. I heard some of it when we visited Kawasaki's cousin, Jimmy, at Hayama, where the emperor has a villa and marine laboratory. Jimmy is the one with a Scottish wife, a young woman with a gypsy's spirit and energy. Jimmy himself was a likeable old man who dressed in magnificent, but well-worn, English tweeds, had the look of an English gentleman—ruddy face, white mustache, blurred eyes—and the heart of a boy. That night he had just returned from Tokyo, where he talked with Konoye and I think Hatoyama. They wanted him to join the cabinet (I suppose it was a proposed new cabinet that he meant) and they apparently wanted money, too. But Jimmy put them off. "No, no, not now. It's too early. There is nothing we can accomplish. We'd be caught between the old guard, which has not been liquidated yet, and Mac-Arthur, who would not give us enough power to act. Besides, I can't afford it. I'm broke.''

His conversation was a little incoherent, or at least it seemed so to me, because he spoke more to his cousin Mori (the original Kawasaki in this story) than to anyone else, and I could not fill in the gaps for myself. Then, too, he had just come in out of the rain after a long walk from the railroad station, was wet, somewhat winded, and worried about a sick relative with a high fever, who could not get into any of the few remaining, badly crowded hospitals. Maybe it was just his age, but Jimmy looked rather haggard. The war years had been quite a strain on a man with a Scottish wife. In Japan it would have been simple for him to get rid of her; instead, he stuck by her and they both went to prison for a while. How they got out I was not told, but the military police probably did not consider him a truly dangerous character and he came from a powerful family, able to pay a ransom.

"You know, Mori," he explained to his cousin for Otis' and my benefit, "the reason we can do nothing now is that America does not want a friendly government in Japan. She is just sore as hell at us and wants to go on being sore at us. These people in the government ask America to understand us and the terrible situation here, but that only gets the Americans angrier. Why should they understand us? How can we ask it of them after our people have committed so many outrages against theirs, after so many American boys were killed in the war?"

He turned to me: "I know how American mothers and fathers must feel toward us if they lost a son in the Pacific. I would feel the same way, too. And the other day I saw Wainright's picture in the paper. It was terrible, terrible. What they did to him was inexcusable. I tell you, lieutenant, I cannot face you or any other American to ask for understanding. I am too ashamed of myself and my people for that."

By this time he seemed about to lose control of himself, switching back and forth from Japanese to English as if no language, no words were adequate for what he wanted to say. His eyes, already misty, might have been moist with tears without one's knowing it. "During the battle for Guadalcanal I told Konoye we must stop the war somehow. Defeat was just a matter of time; further bloodshed would embitter the world against us forever." But Konoye, he said, thought peace impossible at the time. When all but Japan and Formosa were lost, peace might be possible.

The story fascinated me. I wanted to know how he had happened to approach Konoye about making peace. Was his suggestion a casual one, made when they happened to meet at dinner or tea? Did Konoye have any influence then in court or wherever a decision might be made to end the war? Was he regarded as the spokesman for an opposition minority? I tried like the devil to get something more from Jimmy, but he could not understand what I was driving at.

"Things are very bad now, you know. We are happy that the war is over and you Americans are here, but the future is black. You perhaps cannot tell because things seem so quiet, there are no disturbances. But a great deal is going on underneath—as you say, "Still waters run deep" (he had his sayings mixed, but I saw his meaning). There may be some shooting soon, especially if the cabinet is changed when we try to evict the old guard. Some of the new cabinet men may lose their lives. There may even be an attempt on MacArthur."

"Good, let them try it. Then we'd catch those bums and really clean the place up." I was annoyed to hear again the old bogey of militarist reprisals. Were Japanese politics, even now, to be dominated by threats of terrorism? But Jimmy was a little wiser than that: "No, you might catch the assassins, but would you catch the ringleaders? I think the occupation authorities would simply lose patience and crack the whip over the whole country. Then everyone would suffer, the innocent more than the guilty. If you want to clean the militarists out, you only need to make an intelligent search. Certainly you don't need any more evidence of their guilt.

"Anyhow, you can see what we're up against, the people who are friendly toward you. We can do nothing now, maybe not for two years. The road is blocked at one end by America's bitterness and at the other by the viciousness of the old guard. I don't like to stand by and do nothing, when so much needs to be done. It is my duty to do what I can, and I offered to help if things get better. But right now it seems useless to try."

How are politics in China?

Ted

◆ ◆ ◆

FROM DON KEENE APPROACHING TSINGTAO
TO TED DE BARY IN TOKYO

October 3, 1945
(Aboard ship)

Dear Ted,

A certain tenderness sweeps over me this evening for people I have loved, for sounds and perfumes caught before they dissolved into the commonplace. The sea presents a gray worried face with a white tooth here and there fanging its surface. Ships with their lights on parallel our movements. Men stand about the deck talking, a loud laugh or a curse occasionally breaking the low conversations which take the form of a kind of unlistening stichomythy.

"This ship is like the one in which we went to Guadalcanal."

"Or the old freighter that took us to Bougainville."

"A New Zealand ship with six-inch guns, fore and aft."

"A Dutch captain with a 'Dutch wife' he slept with."

This will be the last operation for us, not in any melodramatic sense, but the end of days on transports cursing the navy crews, the last time down the cargo nets. The stupid staring lights of the file of transports reflected in the water reminds us that the war is over. A marine tosses a cigarette overboard. "Over."

"These things I have loved." I catch myself, saying, "You have forgotten the drab frame, the days of boredom," but the excuse falls into mere logic. Do you remember how, when our ship approached Oahu on our return from the Aleutians, we could smell the fragrance of the island? Or the paper-pink of the hibiscus on the tree in front of our house in Honolulu? Or the pleasure of listening to music together again after one of us had returned from an operation—the Beethoven quartets, *Figaro*, the Mozart quintet, all in a circle of those friends with whom our work provided us? Is this not what the war has meant for us, as much as cold noses on Attu, or the sign warning of the black plague on Kiska, or the heat of the Philippines, or the child with a mutilated arm on Okinawa?

The experiences, the real things, I sought so long have passed, blurred clouds losing shape over the sky. The horror of the dead and wounded was for me no more than words once read had taught me. When I was a boy I could never bear to look at the description of the World War in the encyclopedia. I was afraid even to take the volume off the shelf to look up "whale" or "Wallenstein" for fear that it might open to the war, the dead young man under a flag. Now I have seen war, on Attu, like Fabrizio in Stendhal's novel, uncertainly wandering on the battlefield looking for the action; on Okinawa as a guest, objective. Impressions filtered through my senses, leaving only what I have been schooled to expect.

How amazing it is that the nameless terror of war, which I have felt since my earliest days so strongly that I could curse the fact that, having been born a man, I should be forced to go to war, has given place to the real emotion I feel, say, when "From the Halls of Montezuma" is played. This may merely be an artificial sentimentalism, closing its eyes on the many stupidities that surround the deeds, and on the countless appalling sights of war in an effort to simulate the emotions which must be popularly felt. I think, however, that it is rather the recognition scene of the tragedy evoked by the only channel open. I mean that we have been so close to the reality of war that we see it too much in terms of details of maladministration and inefficiency. As a result, we are unable to be aroused, usually, by fairly accurate accounts of fighting, let alone by the hysterical or sentimental ones. When I hear the Marine Hymn, however, I find the logical objections dissolved and I feel imprecisely the heroism of Tarawa or Peleliu. It is horrible for young men to be killed and for their bodies to be torn apart, but that is not all. It is glorious, if that word has any meaning.

Glorious to charge into death? Yes, because life means so much to the man who is throwing it away. For a Japanese drunk with suicidal intent dying would mean much less. If we had a great poet he might tell us why or how our dead have been glorious, but until then it will only be through such emotion as would be engendered by the playing of "From the Halls of Montezuma" that we can divine the word.

This evening I feel for the first time that the war is over. I feel the end of a period which began one night when I arrived in Berkeley to start work at the Language School. The image just returned of my first Chinese lesson, sitting on a bench in Central Park while a Chinese friend drew the numbers on the ground with a stick: "One stroke for one, two strokes for two, three strokes for three, and a box with a mustache in it for four." I turned to Chinese as a kind of escape for all that dissatisfied me in our own civilization. I read Lao-tzu and Chuang-tzu and as many of the poets as I could find in translation. I ate Chinese food every day.

Japanese was just something that happened along. I now feel rather ashamed that I should have to search for Chinese words across the Japanese, or that I should catch myself so often preferring this or that aspect of Japanese civilization to its corresponding number in China. Stirred a little also by the nonsense of our propagandists, "In her four thousand years of history China has never started an aggressive war," I am often moved to view with cynicism China's boasted record. Certainly China's relatively poor status as compared with Japan's (until recently at least) was as much a result of disunity and corruption as of a democratic or antimilitaristic tradition. If a powerful dynasty had been in control in China in the nineteenth century, no pacifist or democratic sentiments "inborn in the people" would have stopped a vigorous reaction to Western encroachments. (If the Dowager hadn't used the money given her for a navy to build a stone boat . . . But these are reactions to our propaganda rather than to the Chinese, about whom I feel the same since my first lesson, and before.

The news of Chinese communist activity in the area into which we are about to move is naturally disquieting, for I have no desire to chase possible "Reds" around the country or to act as a spy for liberal, democratic old Chiang. An attempt is being made to sell us on him, but without notable success. I am reminded again of Malraux's *La Condition Humaine* with its remarkable parallels. I wonder if a communist defeat this time (abetted by Russian higher politics) will not succeed in again prolonging China's reign of ignorance.

I think that our entrance into China strikes a strangely untimely note. An ex-missionary confided to us that abolition of extraterritoriality is "not an unmixed blessing," meaning that the Westerner in China is now doomed to what he believes to be the caprices of Chinese justice, with the persistent undertone of "getting even." If this is the case, there will be no further need of Americans to guard and guide. I wonder if the Chinese who celebrated the 1st Division's arrival at Tientsin knew just what they were so loudly welcoming.

Life aboard ship is tiresome as usual, but uncomfortable here beyond all expectations. It is so hot at night that sleeping is a real effort and weary wakefulness the rule. The one cheering note is the news that I am to be transferred to a destroyer in mid-sea and sent ahead to Tsingtao in an advance party. A few days more, then China!

Don

◆ ◆ ◆

FROM HISASHI KUBOTA IN SASEBO TO DON KEENE IN TSINGTAO

October 3, 1945

Dear Don,

We are now quartered in what was formerly the dormitory for men and women workers at the Naval Technical Depot. I seem doomed to stay in Sasebo for some time, and am pleased to find that a few improvements can be expected in the dismal chaos we first stepped into. We now have a *furo* [Japanese bath] going full blast, and can soak ourselves to our hearts' content each evening. This takes the place of my daily beer in helping to dispel the day's disappointments. The galley is being set up and it should not be too long before we start eating from plates instead of from cans. And there is ample room for everyone, especially the enlisted men. But there is one great defect which cannot be ignored—the Japanese toilets. No one can face the filth and smell long enough to do anything about it.

So far the greater part of our rations have been going to the kids in this neighborhood. This is one way of utilizing considerable amounts of food which would otherwise end up in the slop can. The Japanese government has put out a non-fraternizing order, which is supposed to keep anyone from accepting such gifts, but the people around here just ignore it. The police cannot prevent children from accepting our food, because there are so few policemen and so many children and marines. Furthermore, the police hesitate to be tough before us, since the occupation forces represent a higher law than theirs. I may be giving ourselves a little more credit than we are due, but I believe our presence here is rapidly undermining the faith these people once had in their leaders. The amazing array of equipment we bring ashore, the nonchalance and easy ways of our men, and most of all the American soldier's generosity are winning the people to new ways of thinking. If it is possible to sway such a stubborn and provincial section of the country as this, the rest of Japan ought to be a pushover. Anyway, it gives our morale a boost to play such a benevolent role around here.

And then the thought comes to me that these people were until a few weeks ago our mortal enemies. Who really knows what goes on behind that poverty-stricken and submissive exterior? Even though I have lived my whole life among people descended from the same stock, I am at a loss even to approximate their true sentiments. Is their pride only limited to the extent that survival comes first? Are *bushidō* [warrior code] and similar concepts shared by many but practiced by just a few? Until I am more sure of these things and can speak with greater conviction, please take my opinions as simply reflections of the moment, tentative conclusions from my observations of Japan.

Schools will reopen tomorrow with an entirely new curriculum. All day today kids have been running up and down the hallways of our dormitory, and it will be a relief to be spared the incessant clatter of clogs on the resounding floors. Physically, it is a sorry crop of kids with which Japan must face the future, but, ragged and undernourished as they are, this bunch should be an improvement over their elders, for they are given the opportunity, early enough to benefit by it, of seeing what life can be like if lived properly. Still, I should not give you the impression that the older generation is totally without redeeming features as far as we are concerned. In gratitude for our generosity to their children, a number of men and women from this neighborhood came on their own initiative to clean out the buildings and grounds we occupy.

One of the first things I noticed in the everyday behavior of these people was the attitude of Japanese men toward their women. Here man is the absolute ruler and hardly a moment of the day goes by without his imposing his will over the weaker sex. This is evident even among the children, for at play boys will not mingle with girls, but drive them away from any spot which the boys choose for their own activities. I have also seen a man leisurely resting in the sun while his wife washed nearby, elbow-deep in suds and laundry. When the master decided to smoke, his slave was summoned to get the tobacco, which lay two feet beyond his reach. A few minutes later she again had to wash the soapsuds from her arms to get him an ashtray, then a glass of water, and so on. And on a rainy day I saw a cart being moved by two women; pushing from behind was a lady about fifty or sixty years old; ahead was a frail but pretty woman of about twenty-five. As I watched, it began to rain quite hard, and so a husky brute, evidently the young woman's husband, gallantly condescended to walk beside her and hold an umbrella above her head. No, chivalry isn't quite dead in Japan—just saving itself for the right moment.

Hisashi

◆ ◆ ◆

FROM TED DE BARY IN TOKYO
TO DON KEENE IN TSINGTAO

October 5, 1945

Dear Don,

I took a great liking to old Jimmy and so did Otis, who went with us to Hayama that night. In manners and dress Jimmy was a cosmopolitan; he must also have been something of a playboy. I remember the bad impression we first had of his house, when, coming in from the beach through a veranda door, we saw Petty and Vargas girls pasted around his bar. Now these seemed an innocent display of bad taste in one who so closely resembled an *Esquire* sugar daddy. Still, Jimmy affected no detachment from the affairs of his country, as phony sophisticates of the "international set" might do. Japan's sins, her shame and misery were as much his as anyone else's, though he had tried harder than most to avoid them. "All Japanese are damn fools," he said, "and that includes me."

Perhaps his responsibility was actually greater than I supposed, and he was thinking of his own mistakes in saying that. Despite his opposition to the war, he may have become heavily involved in it financially. Like Konoye in politics, he may have had more power than he could handle, more money than he could hold onto without compromising himself. Certainly I could not tell how progressive a capitalist he was, or how conservative. He was Westernized, to be sure, but practically every businessman in England or America, whether reactionary or progressive, isolationist or interventionist, had been involved in our war effort, and we should expect the same to be true in Japan.

The business of fixing war responsibility gets very complicated this far from the point where actual decisions are made, and in any case, it was not exactly my business that night. Whatever else Jimmy might be, I was happy to have found a man who was ashamed himself of what had happened, who made no pretense at being a citizen of the world because it was too tough at the moment being a citizen of Japan. The pretense is common enough among all kinds of people, not just in Japan and not just among international financiers. Sometimes it passes for cosmopolitan sophistication, sometimes for intellectual objectivity, but usually it is a case of some parasite trying to disentangle himself from a sick body.

In Japan, family interests are closely tied together and the various members generally consult one another about the big problems facing them. Our visit in Hayama seemed in part to be such a consultation between the two Kawasakis. Otis was the one who sensed this particularly. He got the impression that Mori had come to get "the word" from Jimmy, his elder.

These cousins were hardly two of a kind, however. Mori always spoke of the Japanese as if he were not quite one of them, and of course his speech, his habits, his home and everything else about him were such as to make you unconscious of race or nationality. But I wondered whether or not his Westernization was all to the good; what he did not owe Japan in the way of allegiance may simply have been switched to the international business world. Like Jimmy, Mori had been asked to participate in the new government. He refused, not just because things are so tough now, but because politics generally is a game involving greater risks than he wants to take. He talked as if he were full of ideas about what needed to be done in Japan, but in the final analysis he was unwilling to dirty his hands with the job (though under present conditions, I must admit, getting one's hands dirty might amount to losing one's life).

"I have always been a business man and I will stick to business. If I can't make a decent living here, I'll go to China when things settle down, to Shanghai. The Chinese don't care who you are—that is, what your nationality may be—as long as they like and trust you. Personal loyalty is the important thing to them, and I have many friends there. Shanghai is where the big fortunes are made; it was that way before the war and will be afterwards.

"No one can make any money in Japan now, unless it is the Americans. Lots of people are asking why the U.S. does not add another star to the flag and make Japan the forty-ninth state. We'd by very happy if you did; just take Japan from us as a Christmas present."

At first I thought he meant this as an ironical reflection on

Japan's prostration under our rule, but then I began to see how much real sense it made to a man like Mori Kawasaki, who cares less about national integrity than he does about preserving a society in which he can make a good living. Whenever he talked like this, which was most of the time, I kidded him for being so much of a "Chinese Taoist." Strictly speaking the term would not apply, because a Taoist should sit in the mud of a lazy river rather than in the comfort of a modern Tokyo home; but many Chinese are Taoists in the same inconsistent way and Mori knew what I meant.

So much for the man whose hospitality brightened my first few days in Japan.

My last afternoon in Tokyo I decided to have a look at the Diet Building. Ordinarily it would not be very high on my list of sights to see; now that the garish Tokyo Station is largely a ruin, the parliament building is probably foremost among the monstrosities which the Japanese have built for themselves in Western style, and even in the ruins of Naha I had seen enough of such perversions to sicken me. Still, I was beginning to wonder if my judgment had not been too naively exacting. Modern society seemed to require big office buildings, and once the Japanese had swallowed so much else from the West, it was too much to ask them immediately for a native architecture with which to coat the ugly pill. Besides, I had forgotten that the Diet was not in session yet, and expected that some politicians would be available for my instruction, someone in a threadbare morning coat who might describe the function of legislators in a military dictatorship.

My route took me through a cemetery of government office buildings. Every third or fourth block held intact a ministry into which several others had been jammed. Its entrance would be littered with signs; first, a metal plate saying "The Finance Ministry" in Japanese, then a wooden shingle with its English translation written in longhand (printed letters would have been easier both to write and to read, but the Japanese apparently feel that longhand, being more difficult, involves a greater display of virtuosity). Another set of shingles indicated that the Home

Ministry was making itself at home with the Finance people, and still more signs belonged to an agency whose title was so ambiguous that I can remember neither the characters nor their supposed meaning.

The vehicles in Tokyo were limited generally to two standard types: brown trucks of military design such as we found all over the Pacific, and the incredible Datsun, a midget car even by comparison to our jeeps and so frail that cranking almost shook it apart. All cars and trucks carried identification posters. A Datsun in front of one ministry was marked: "The Navy Department." The use of "The," not just "Navy Department" in the American fashion, somehow suggested to me that this flimsy contraption was all that remained of the department itself, an idea not now so far from being true. Every sight of the Japanese government struck one as ridiculous and pitiful in the same way: the rattletrap official cars which carried charcoal burners— clumsy, rusty, smoky devices—where the rear trunk once was, or, if not, which smelled of the alcohol used in place of gasoline; slender, harrassed-looking officials running their legs off for MacArthur and jumping out of their skins every time he said boo to them, while at the same time trying to preserve some authority among their own people, enough respect to command obedience to the orders they carried. I was thinking of MacArthur's directive in the morning's paper, which asked the Japanese government to present a mass of production statistics covering all goods made in the empire for the past ten years or so. The statistics were to be prepared in English, typewritten on a certain kind and size of paper, and to be handed in a few days hence. I could imagine these frenzied little bureaucrats sending out a call for all usable English typewriters in the metropolitan area, searching through battered supply shacks for the right-sized paper, climbing all over one another in those crowded offices to dig up something in place of the statistics lost when such and such a ministry burned down or in place of the statistics which were never kept because the national research bureau was closed for want of clerical help before the war.

The Imperial Japanese Government was certainly a sorry

sight, even if its predicament was a necessary one. MacArthur was not abusing these people—just doing what a businesslike occupation required. But I thought of the things being said in the American newspapers and over the radio before I left Hawaii: talk about the sly Japanese having everything under control, but pretending otherwise in order to evade Allied instructions; a great conspiracy, they said, waiting to trap MacArthur the minute he weakened or showed any inclination to "compromise" (the word as it is used these days seems to include any attempt by occupation authorities to inform themselves of the situation before issuing a directive).

I remember what Colonel O'Sullivan of the 184th Infantry told his officers before they went ashore at Kiska. The band had just finished "California Here I Come," when he called the men together on the bow of our LST for final instructions: "No matter how much we plan or how hard we try, you can expect a hell of a mess when we get ashore. But however tough things are, remember this: it's sure to be two or three times as tough for the 'Japs.' Try not to let the confusion get you down."

With no Japanese on Kiska, it turned out that the confusion there was one hundred percent American, but his advice applied to every other operation in the Pacific and to the occupation of Japan as well. Americans were caught unprepared for Japan's surrender and, lacking a considered policy or the information to implement it with, they immediately tend to despair of the occupation and to damn all Japanese for it. When, to start with, Americans were kept waiting so long for the final surrender announcement, they accused the Japanese of haggling, delaying and trying to embarrass us. Actually those were much more hectic days for the Japanese than they were for us. Until the emperor finally read the surrender rescript, no one knew what might happen. Suzuki and the peace group were trying desperately to prepare the people for what was certain to be shocking news to them, while a group of mad young army men tried to assassinate the premier and kidnap the emperor before the announcement could be made. In fact, if it hadn't been for an army general named Tanaka, who suppressed the insurgents with loyal troops from Manchuria, we would never have got the surrender and everyone would have said, "It was a hoax from the start. You just can't trust those 'Japs' in anything."

I don't know how much you have heard about this version of the pre-surrender days. *The Nippon Times* had it buried on page 3 about a month and a half after the events took place, and their story was not complete. Mori Kawasaki added a few details as follows: when peace negotiations were first undertaken, it was decided to disperse the fanatical Imperial Guards throughout the Tokyo area and to replace them at the palace with more reliable troops, veterans from Manchuria and China. The pretext for this dispersal was the danger that the whole Guards Division might be wiped out in one air raid, if their barracks were hit. On the eve of surrender, some of the Guards started to act up as feared; they gathered a mob, half military and half civilian, and headed for trouble. You know what suckers the Japanese are for mob violence. Anyone with a half-brained idea and some determination can get a crowd to follow him, which means that this disturbance need not have been planned much in advance. After machine-gunning and firing the prime minister's official residence and private home, the mob abandoned their search for Suzuki and blustered off for the Imperial Palace. However, Kawasaki said, the new palace guard was well-set for the insurgents, who dispersed as quickly as they had gathered upon seeing their bluff called by well-armed loyal troops. Another report describes it differently: the insurgents had actually broken into a part of the Imperial Household and were looking for the emperor's recorded speech, when General Tanaka arrived to quell the disturbance. He persuaded its leaders to give up their plan and leave the palace grounds, whereupon both the leaders and General Tanaka committed suicide.

The Diet building is really not worth telling you about, pretty much what I expected to find except for the two fancy house chambers, which looked even less worn and used than a Japanese doll in a glass case. The best part of my visit was the official guide, a starved little man who got his job because he had learned English while working at a Yokohama tourist hotel many years ago. Several of his sons were in the army. Two were in the Philippines, one in Manchuria, another in China, and there was still another who had just been demobilized in Japan. I told him not to give up hope for his sons in the Philippines; there was some chance of their being prisoners, regardless of what the government might have said. The rest of his family were lost in the fire-bombing of Yokohama, so he lived by himself under the Diet building somewhere.

It happened that my Japanese was a little better than his English, and we conversed in either language depending upon the complexity of our ideas, the emotion involved and the necessity which he sometimes felt in the presence of other Japanese for confiding to me in English. As we wandered around the building without paying much attention to it, I helped him with a few problems he had on his mind: how to express in English the idea of a resting house in a park; what American soldiers meant when they asked for "geesha girls"; what the English word was for it—whore, oh yes, he scribbled it down in a beat-up notebook. He had no ambition to be a pimp, this simple old man. To him American boys were the salt of the earth, and as an interpreter he wanted to serve them in any way he could.

The high point of my tour was a little speech he made under the dome of the central hall. Around us were three statues of great Restoration statesmen, and a fourth pedestal, empty. Jokingly, I suggested that General MacArthur would soon stand on the empty one, but he took me seriously and agreed that it should be done, not because he thought MacArthur a great man—that was beyond his own ability to judge—but because, as the Allied commander, the general was doing more good for Japan than any of her own statesmen had done for years. We stood under each of the three giant figures, while he explained to me what each man had done to establish constitutional government in Japan.

"This is Itagaki. Like Ito Hirobumi, he work to make Japan a democracy during the time of Meiji. He want strong constitutional government and Itagaki was a very courageous man. When he die—he was killed by his enemies—he said, 'Itagaki die, but liberty never die.' "

His talk was slow and tortured. At almost every verb he halted for correction. He thought hard for words in English, said them in Japanese and asked for the equivalent expression. But each delay only built up the suspense more.

"Since that time it has not gone so well. Now there are many clever men, but few have the courage of Itagaki and only the fools seem to be brave. The work must be started all over again. Then someday we may have great men for this hall again."

Ted

◆ ◆ ◆

FROM FRANK TURNER IN TOKYO
TO DON KEENE IN TSINGTAO

October 7, 1945

Dear Don,

Last night I had dinner with one of Japan's most influential investment bankers. His name is Miho, president of Nissan enterprises and of several large holding companies. "Miki," as he likes to have his American friends call him, went to school in the States and looks like a college politician in his natty tweeds. Before the war he did business all over the world, and it wasn't long before he showed us his interest in resuming that trade as soon as possible. When he learned that a friend of his from Dillon Reed, the Wall Street firm, was in Japan on a survey mission, Miki immediately tried to capitalize on the acquaintance by a series of elaborate entertainments, usually geisha parties, and frequently dinners at his home where he could display his attractive and talented family. He has showered expensive Japanese gifts on his guests and serves them the best prewar Scotch and gin. No American seems too high in rank to escape Miki's invitations, and from what he told me I would not be surprised if MacArthur himself had been approached. "If you aim high," he demonstrated by stretching a hand up over his head, "you will at least hit here," and he brought his hand down to the level of his eyes.

A remarkable thing about Miho is his knowledge of American politics and especially of American politicians. He knew in detail the careers of men like Forrestal, Byrnes, Sumner Welles and other figures of such recent prominence as to be generally unknown in Japan, where wartime censorship made it difficult to follow foreign developments. He must stay up nights memorizing the overseas editions of *Time* and *Newsweek*.

I will try to reconstruct some of the things he said as we drove out to his residence in the once-fashionable Omori district.

"The Scientific and Economic Section of MacArthur's head-quarters is trying to do away with the *zaibatsu* [giant financial combines]. I wonder what they will wind up doing? All day long I have been in conference with a major on this matter, and it certainly is a hell of a mess."

I remarked, "From what I know of it, our economic experts have a good idea of what should be done with the *zaibatsu*, but they aren't sure how to go about it. You know how complicated the organization of these holding companies can be. It will take a lot of study and research before they can act."

"I doubt if they will do anything serious to us," he said. "They will find that few of the big fellows really made much money. The inordinate profits were made by smaller business men. What worries me now is that the men who determine economic policy are amateurs at it- -all military men. What's more, none of them stays long enough to fix a given policy. No sooner do I make connections with some officer than he tells me he is going back home for a discharge. There should be some permanent body of civilian experts in charge of financial and economic policy."

I suggested that the State Department was the logical place to look for such a policy-making group. "Yes, the State Department would be an improvement, but it would be best to have a special agency comparable to the Export-Import Bank, which would be specifically designed to handle this sort of problem."

Miho gave me the impression that he did not take too seriously MacArthur's intentions in the economic realm. Not that he didn't expect a lot of changes to be made, but he seemed to think that the U.S. and England, being capitalistic countries, would sooner or later send over businessmen to handle this side of things. It was simply a question of absorbing Japanese business into ours. Plainly he did not realize how closely related American business and government had become in the last twelve years, or else he would not have said, as he did, that, "MacArthur has no real purpose in controlling financial affairs."

I pointed out that more and more civilians were coming into the Economic and Scientific Section, some of them doing a particularly important job in the Foreign Trade Division. This led Miho to ask why there were so many Germans and White Russians, formerly interned by the Japanese, holding important jobs in that division. I was in no position to answer that one, but suggested that a shortage of American personnel made it necessary to hire foreigners who had lived in Japan and were acquainted with its foreign trade problems. That didn't satisfy Miho. He wanted to deal with persons who had some influence in America, and could facilitate the investment of American capital in Japan. He wanted to talk to someone who spoke the language of business. However much he knew about political trends in the U.S. (and he was probably aware in some sense of the increasing government control over American economic life), Miki was disposed by nature to hope that he could talk business with businessmen, not, as in Japan, with bureaucrats and army officers.

When we reached his home, Miho showed me around the yard which had saved his house from fires that swept the neighborhood last May. He pointed out a small crater in the lawn, at the bottom of which still lay an incendiary pellet. Next, I was introduced to his family. They are all attractive, especially his eleven-year-old son, who has a frank manner of expression and keen perception. When we came in, he was busily repairing the electric phonograph. With his passion for mechanical things, the youngster immediately engaged me in a discussion of American planes and jeeps, but it developed later that his greatest achievement was in piano playing. He happily sat down and rattled off by heart pieces from Beethoven, Bach and Brahms with an amazing vigor and agility, considering that his tiny hands could hardly reach an octave and his feet barely touched the pedals.

During cocktails and dinner, our conversation turned to the latest list of war criminals. I brought up the name of Mr. Aikawa, who was associated with Miho in Nissan industries and was president of the Manchurian Development Company. Aikawa will probably be accused of instigating the outbreak of the China Incident, but Miho thought him innocent of any warmongering. He claimed that Aikawa had been named as a war criminal because of Chinese pressure (I couldn't quite see what was wrong with that), and because of a certain Diet member who had entertained a long-standing grudge against Aikawa. This Diet member has a glib command of English and tried to ingratiate himself with MacArthur's headquarters by presenting it with many misinterpretations of Aikawa's complicity in the China War. Miho was confident Aikawa would be acquitted, and repeatedly asked me to speak to Americans about his innocence and sincerity.

From what little I knew of Aikawa, however, he did not seem to be doing his own cause much good with the occupation authorities. Friends of mine spoke of him as cocky and uncooperative during interrogation, said he refused information and statistics to a survey mission—the first time in their experience that a Japanese had given so much trouble. A few days later, Aikawa was named a war criminal.

Miho obviously felt that the war crimes program was ridiculous. Even in the case of Tōjō he said, "I think Tōjō made a bad mistake, but no one can deny that he was sincere. He honestly believed that he was doing what was best for Japan. To indict him is not going to prevent another war or discredit the principles for which he stood. There will always be men who consider their objective so noble that the possibility of becoming a war criminal would never affect their resolution."

Another thing Miki tried to impress me with was Japan's potential part in postwar trade. He showed me a Japanese-made record player and other mechanical contrivances, which, to me at least, seemed the equal of similar products made in America. He described a deal whereby he was allowed to use the Columbia trademark and sell his record players in all countries except the United States. The Columbia people got 20 per cent of the profit, retailers in South Africa and Europe got about 10 per cent and the Nissan people got 10 per cent. Everyone was satisfied including the ultimate consumer who got excellent merchandise at a reasonable cost.

I should have asked him whether or not his workers were satisfied with the deal, but I knew more or less what his answer would be. He did not hesitate to say that Japan's main trade asset was Japanese labor, "conscientious, diligent, clever, and normally well-disciplined." He had no sympathy with the current strikes, but stressed that labor unions would eventually become a stable part of Japan's overall industrial organization.

"Japan is a nation of organizations. Every phase of her economic life is regulated by close-knit groups, and nothing is done except by working through the established channels, through the control associations for industry, labor associations for hiring and managing workers, neighborhood associations for rice distribution, and so on. This characteristic group system makes Japan a more efficient and reliable business partner than, say, China, where expediency rather than a fixed process is followed in business."

After this little sales talk, Mr. Miho had his daughter address a number of letters to American friends and asked me to deliver them in person when I arrived in the U.S. I couldn't promise anything, but said I'd do my best. Guess I'll need a new calling card: "Frank L. Turner, New York Representative of the Japanese *zaibatsu*!" Will you still be willing to talk to me?

Frank

◆ ◆ ◆

FROM DON KEENE IN TSINGTAO TO OTIS CARY IN TOKYO

October 13, 1945

Dear Otis,

Today the troops are beginning to land. Each moment's developments make it clear that my hour of glory in China has ended. No longer will there be a gaping, close-packed crowd pressing against the entrance to the International Club, hoping to get a glimpse of the Americans, nor will I draw a host of people to the entrance of every store I visit; nor will children come running after me laughing, applauding and giving the "up" sign with their thumbs. With so many Americans in Tsingtao, the Chinese will cease to marvel or to acclaim. Even the sailors are coming ashore now. Today a sergeant in our office was hit by a half-dollar thrown at the mob by one of our boys in blue. How long now before largess assumes the familiar pattern of Africa or Italy?

The night before I landed the destroyer was caught in a great storm, waves that smote the ship with iron fury and the clang of metal on metal. It was impossible to sleep, and the thought that I would be in China the next morning scarcely consoled me. When my watch at last showed that it was almost seven, I arose, put on my clothing, and felt my way through the darkness out onto the deck. There the air was cool in the pale light of the early morning. The sea had died down so much that the destroyer barely rocked. Against the horizon I could see the black shape of mountains—China. What China has represented in my dreams I think you know. China was always the unattainable, the wish that could not be fulfilled because too much desired. I stared unbelievingly at the shore until Tsingtao appeared in the distance, white and towery, something like San Francisco from out at sea.

When I finally was in the ship's boat, dressed in fatigues with a helmet on my head, I felt for a moment the sudden fear I had known before other landings, as when, off Attu, our landing barge pushed through the dark fog to an invisible island. The fear vanished with the next instant when a junk flew by and we caught a glimpse of smiling, waving Chinese. In a few minutes we were at the pier and disembarking while a small crowd of Chinese applauded briefly. The colonel turned to me and said, "Ask if there is any official representative of the Chungking Government here." I started to ask the question and then stopped, in the face of the blank passivity of the crowd. I asked instead if there was anyone who spoke English, to which I received the reply that there were some who did to be found at the end of the pier. We walked the length of the pier self-consciously, our helmets rattling on our heads, a very incongruous note among the many dark-clad Chinese passing silently before us.

My first feeling was how unstrange it was to be here in China. The small pieces I had known before were at last in a whole, a whole with which I felt only little less familiar than with the sum of its parts. Thus, when I saw death and mutilation on Okinawa, my horror was insulated from me by the horror of the past, the books I had read, the pictures I had seen, the hospital I visited after Pearl Harbor. Now in China, I had multiple component experiences on which to draw, and I was not surprised.

When we reached the end of the pier we found a group of young Chinese officers. I addressed one in hesitant Chinese, only to be anwered in much better English, "Captain, could you tell us where the International Club is?" I was a little taken aback by this request so soon after my landing, but managed to help the officers to find the Club by picking it out on a large map of the city with which I was provided. At the Club I staked myself out a cot and changed at once into less formidable attire, feeling ridiculous in my warlike get-up in this peaceful city.

I went out into the street and climbed into one of the rickshaws which gathered about me. All the prejudices and convictions of many years made it almost impossible for me to sit still in a rickshaw, to keep from digging my nails into the wood of the armrests as the coolie pulled me up a hill. A fellow human being, after all, I thought, a little self-consciously. As we went through the streets we passed staring children and bicyclists who almost fell from their bicycles in an effort to get a better look at me. A working party of Japanese soldiers under a sergeant saluted as I was drawn by.

Later I met up with a Chinese officer named Louis Chang, an interpreter, who volunteered to take me on a shopping tour. As we pushed through the crowded streets, I felt a marvelous exhilaration. On either side were fresh shrimp, live fish, candy, cookies, dried fish, meat on a block being cut, books, children staring, cigarettes, brushes, and the medium was the swirling Chinese crowd. The word "China" echoed from each thing I saw so that there could be no possible doubt but that my dream had been realized. We went into silk stores filled with great bolts of silk, a jade store where I bought a gold and jade ring. "How much?" "30,000 dollars! Not bad at 1800 to 1!" Louis was so proud of his ability to beat down the price. Then a pair of Chinese shoes and a Chinese gown amid much laughter—"just like a Chinese now except for the face!"

I started to return to the Club with my packages. The wide-eyed wonder of my walking through the street was a reflection of the naive blue of the sky and the sunlight on the preposterous German Gothic buildings which ring the hills. On the way back, I heard the noise of Chinese music and laughter down the street. Louis and I pushed our way through to the curb and saw a procession on stilts, characters from the Chinese opera. Some wore the conventional rice-powder masks, others the ferocious plumes and mustaches of a Tartar chieftain. One with a pig's head moved about in solemn gyrations. Another with a blind man's disguise peered through his black glasses at me. He lowered the glasses to the end of his nose and then saluted comically. When I reached the Club and made my way through the audience pressing at the entrance, I felt that this had certainly been the happiest day of my life.

The Club itself was a monstrosity of German days, with stained glass windows portraying the apotheosis of Bismarck as well as the coats of arms of Lübeck, Bremen, Hamburg and other famous merchant cities. The manager, an Australian lately released from the internment camp that the Japanese ran at Wei-hsien, greeted me between rapid bursts of pidgin English in which he threatened to kick the houseboys down the stairs if they failed to provide what he wanted. After speaking briefly with him I went to the room where all American officers in town appeared to be staying. As I reached the top of the stairs I could hear certain of them, aviators, arguing about the price of their laundry, claiming that the rate of 50 dollars (or 2½ cents) an article was robbery of an unspeakable nature. "I never used to care about the price of laundry," one was saying, "but would just throw things in a bag and wait for them to come back. Here I won't let them get away with anything. I'd argue with a rickshaw coolie for 10 dollars. Never give them what they ask. I can't stand that shit-eating grin of theirs." Another picked up the argument. "They're all beggars and bandits, every one of them."

The joy of a moment ago vanished entirely. When I attempted to answer their accusations, they turned on me in surprise and anger. "What the hell do you know about it? We've been in China a long time." Or, "Then how do you account for the fact that they're always standing around with nothing to do? Just wait until you've been here as long as we have, then you'll see what we mean."

I was too disgusted to answer. I have been so intent on defending Japanese from the charge that all of them are fiends, monsters of treachery and degenerates, that I forgot that there were some people who feel much the same way toward the Chinese. It's all one, of course. The exception we have been making with respect to the Chinese is in the same category as the one the Germans made to the "Aryan" Japanese. It is, of course, more shocking to hear talk like that of the aviators at the Club, but the faint, "Chinamen are all right, I guess," is scarcely less offensive. You must surely remember the same attitude on Okinawa toward the "gooks" at whom the marines would shout "habba-habba." If permissible toward the enemy, it is hard to understand in China, as it was on Guam, or even in Hawaii. The superiority complex of the Americans which catalogues the rest of the world, the non-Coca-Cola drinking world, as barbarian, will certainly prove one of the greatest obstacles to any real union of nations.

That evening, though, I saw numerous evidences of the potency of the American claim. I walked through the deserted streets, my revolver bouncing on my hip. The walls of the buildings lining the main street, lately renamed Chung-shan Road in honor of Sun Chung-shan (or, more commonly, Sun Yat-sen), were covered with posters. "The U.S. Navy is the model for the world." "Welcome the American Navy." "The cooperation of the United States and China is ernest [sic]." "The Allies are the angeles [sic] of peace and the sign of night." Others showed a Korean flag borne aloft by arms swathed in the flags of the United States, China, Russia and England, the poster bearing the single stark word, "Gratitude." I walked into a bar which I guessed from the outside to be White Russian. One or two men with pale thin faces were drinking beer, but the atmosphere inside was one of utter loneliness. I ordered a curaçao and drank it slowly while the owner and his wife engaged in a long, low conversation in Russian. I noticed on the wall an enormous "Ice-Cold Coca-Cola" sign, the replica of thousands throughout America, with its inevitable bottle-swigging girl. While I was smiling a little at the incongruity, the bartender left his conversation and went to change the record on the phonograph. He searched through the pile of records and then put one on, in my honor I suppose. It was "My Heart Belongs to Daddy." When I left the bar I noticed that Chinese workmen were stringing tiny flags across the streets, Chinese flags of two kinds, American, Korean, Russian, French and British flags. I remembered that the next day was Double Ten Day, the anniversary of the Chinese Republic.

Double Ten Day I first heard from my window overlooking the bay and Pacific Road when a parade marched down the street to the music of tuneless bands. Louis called on me and suggested that we take a trip to the stadium where there was to be a celebration in honor of the occasion. We were driven there in a dilapidated right-hand-drive Chrysler, the driver honking the horn all the way at the crowds of schoolchildren in uniform who thronged the streets. We passed through the entrance in arrogant splendor, Louis waving his gloves at the guards. Chinese soldiers dressed in nondescript uniforms surrounded the car, their potato-masher grenades scraping against the fenders. I looked down the barrel of one of the rifles. It was filled with dirt. As each successive group of soldiers passed through the gate they broke into a marching song. We left our car and followed some soldiers into the stadium. Inside, I wished to take an inconspicuous seat in the middle of the stands, but Louis insisted on our going all the way across the field to the reviewing platform. I felt acutely embarrassed as we passed through the crowd of soldiers waiting to fall into formation and the students tentatively waving their banners. We finally sat down on a bench in front of which there was a table covered with bunting. No sooner had we done so than a Chinese official arrived to shoo off almost all the Chinese on or near the bench "to make way for the foreign guests." As it turned out, I was the only foreigner in the stadium, and I felt miserable that I had even unwittingly been responsible for causing the Chinese to be chased away.

There were some twenty thousand people in the stands while on the field there were soldiers in khaki, students in black or gray (girl students in blue), sailors, and a large miscellaneous crowd off to the right carrying brilliant banners. The students waved green and pink flags. A phonograph started to play the third movement of the Chorale Symphony through the amplifiers. More and more people arrived, including army officers wearing collar devices of solid gold and a rear admiral resplendent in blues who was escorted up to the reviewing platform by a number of other naval officers. The chief of police, a tall handsome man wearing a black uniform and white gloves and missing only a cape, strode somberly through the dignitaries. Then, just as the loudspeakers started to scream "*Oh, Freunde!*" Mayor Li, attired in morning clothes, made his entrance. The Chinese national anthem was then sung by the entire gathering, a little disjointedly, but very movingly. I watched Louis, carefully saluting when he did, and hoping only that it would .not be thought that my mistakes were those of an official representative of the American forces. As a matter of fact, though, there was less attention paid to me than I would have expected. Although there was much exchanging of cards and introducing, I was far from the center of curiosity that I would have imagined any foreigner alone in so large a crowd of Chinese would appear. This was a good sign I believe; the Chinese seemed to realize that this was their day, one without any tiresome burden of thanks to America.

Later in the day, as I roamed about the city looking for a place to eat, staring in restaurant windows and attempting to read the menus scrawled outside the door, a fellow jumped out of one of the restaurants, took me by the arm and asked in English if I would like some Chinese food. No sooner had I answered than I was seated at a table with his non-English-speaking brother, eating what was left of their dinner. Mr. Yuan, my new friend, ordered some Chinese wine, a clear liquid called *pai kan* (or *bei gerh*, as he said it), which I am told resembles vodka in its effects.

He was soon calling me "younger brother" and swearing eternal vows of friendship. Moved by the drink, I started writing Chinese characters on the table. People flocked from all parts of the restaurant to witness this, pressing calling cards into my hands and making exclamations about the quality of my handwriting. Yuan then gave me his own card, which was really the card of a restaurant. On one side was the Chinese and on the other, "Laoshan Café. Bar et Restaurant Francais. Open All Night. Cold Drinks and Any Thing Special You Like." Yuan insisted on taking me at once to the restaurant, which was only a block or two away. In front of it were two flags, Chinese and American. Yuan, leaning heavily on me, cried in English, "No British, no Russian, no goddam Japanese. America and China, like brothers."

Inside the Laoshan Café were four tables and a tiny bar. About six or seven Chinese girls, one in Western dress and made up like a Japanese actress, sat waiting with their hands folded in their laps. Yuan and I sat at an empty table and drank Asahi beer while he showed me off and introduced me to a number of people all of whom he referred to as brothers. As I rose to depart, pleading important business, Yuan handed me a number of cards to distribute to American sailors "who like Chinese girls instead of White Russian girls." I promised to come back at noon the next day for a big dinner and a Chinese lesson.

When I returned to Yuan's café the next day at noon he greeted me with the cry, "Ah, my brother! You came here night before last and I had a Chinese dinner ready for you yesterday because I know you like Chinese food. But today, nothing." I started to correct him on the day, but stopped halfway, knowing that he was as aware as I of the facts. He encouraged me to talk Chinese. In the middle of one sentence in which I was saying very slowly, "I came here to . . .," Yuan interrupted with, "*Kan-i-kan*" ["Take a look"]. So saying, he took me by the arm and showed me the back part of the restaurant. There were four cubicles, each large enough for its bed and no more. Yuan apologized for the disorder, remarking that the girls were busy until late the night before and would not return until one o'clock. I imagine this was the "any thing special" I might like.

Yesterday was also memorable for my first visit to Japanese headquarters. I confess that I was a trifle apprehensive when ordered to pay a call on the Japanese chief of staff for some information. Although I could reason that the war was over and the Japanese were under our control, I couldn't help feeling rather like the little brat in one of Chaucer's tales who sang about the Virgin Mary while walking through the ghetto and wound up in a privy for his efforts. My own glib explanations of the Japanese psyche which I had furnished to countless ill-informed naval and marine personnel afforded me no comfort as I walked into what was for me a novel experience, a visit to enemy headquarters. When I walked into the building I was initially terrified speechless when the corporal of the guard screamed "Saa-lute!" to his retinue of three privates. When I had recovered sufficiently to permit controlled utterance, I asked in Japanese to see the chief of staff. The corporal smiled politely with a look of, "I'm sorry, but I don't understand a word of English." He pointed to a sign which requested me to wait until an interpreter arrived. At that moment the interpreter did appear. I was furious at my lack of success with the corporal and informed the interpreter that I had no need of his services, answering all of his English remarks in Japanese. He was not at all discouraged, but ushered me gravely through the barren corridors which smelled faintly of urine, refusing to acknowledge my command of Japanese. We entered a waiting room where he asked me to have a seat. The room was in Western style with heavy, uncomfortable chairs in a tight circle about a table. It was virtually impossible for me to sit in the oppressive constraint of the room so I walked over to the open window. Below, in a courtyard, a number of Japanese officers were exercising. One stood on his hands. At that moment an enlisted man walked by and saluted. The officer, still on his hands, gravely responded with a little nod.

The first Japanese officer I met was a rosy-cheeked major who answered all of my questions politely, but without any particular cordiality. My dealings with Japanese up to this time having been exclusively with prisoners whose situation was clearly defined, it was more than a little difficult to determine the correct method of approach to the new conditions. Here the Japanese have not formally surrendered, nor have their arms been turned over. They are in possession of their headquarters and staff while their troops are still out in the hills on guard. When I left the major's office and went back through the corridors and down the broken marble stairs, I had the strange feeling of having fallen into a Japanese headquarters, not a captured one but one that differed very little from what it had been like during the war. The smell in the halls reminded me again of the figure in Chaucer and his fate. If the Japanese were to drop me in one of their bottomless privies, I would certainly never be found.

This morning I met some of the Japanese naval officers and found them much more agreeable than the little I saw of the army yesterday. Although I started out with a formal interview of two of the intelligence officers, I was soon chatting with them as with old friends. One, named Shimagawa, is particularly likeable. He has irregular, very Western features, and even freckles which he combines with a kind of American frankness which I find very pleasant. We talked a little about modern Japanese literature. I was interested in knowing what kind of books were turned out during the war, but Shimagawa was not very helpful, remarking that almost everything was "propaganda first and literature second." He promised to get me copies of the best war literature and whatever classics are available in Tsingtao. As I started to leave, he nudged me and asked with a grin, "How about getting together and having a drink, now that the war's over?"

These, then, are my first impressions. As I write, I can see trucks going by loaded with marines in battle dress. Someone said that they made an assault landing this morning, climbing down nets and storming ashore in landing craft while the band played on the dock. That would not surprise me too much. It must almost seem the easiest way now.

Don

◆ ◆ ◆

FROM TED DE BARY IN SASEBO
TO DON KEENE IN TSINGTAO

October 15, 1945

Dear Don,

Sasebo is a dim, dirty town. It never was more than a naval base—Nagasaki and Fukuoka handled the commercial traffic for this area and Sasebo has no civilian industry to speak of—so today it is a weird collection of abandoned workshops, cranes, dry docks and flimsy warehouses. Like most other Japanese cities, its residential areas and a good part of the business district were burned up by fire bombs. But the city's emptiness would not be so depressing if it were not for the derelict state of the people here. They are almost as lifeless as the abandoned navy yard. Their attitude toward us seems not necessarily hostile, but cautious and reserved. None of the openness, curiosity, and even gaiety with which Tokyo met American troops or which I found when we stopped on the way down at Wakanoura.

It may be that occupation by marines has something to do with the dampness of Japanese spirits here. Fifth 'Phib Corps takes non-fraternization seriously; there is a six P.M. curfew and other restrictions which keep the troops and citizenry from enjoying each other's company in the holiday fashion of Tokyo. Then, too, Sasebo is a small place and our servicemen cannot lose themselves as they would in a great metropolis. There are fewer opportunities to display their natural friendliness and curiosity, to be themselves. I suppose Sasebo's unattractiveness also has something to do with it, and the dismal weather. No one is in a party mood.

But anyone who has not visited the gayer spots in Japan will tell you that the occupation of Sasebo is almost corrupt with fraternization. The other day I saw Sherry's father [Lt. Col. Sherwood Moran], who has been here from the start. He thought my impression far from the truth: "Fraternization itself has been a problem. The MPs, in fact, had to forbid any more congregating on the large bridge by our headquarters, so congested had it become with eager marines talking and using sign language to grinning and friendly Japanese. It has been that way from the first."

Nevertheless, there is a definite non-fraternization policy here, and it has its disadvantages for people who are genuinely interested in learning what they can about Japan. One day, for instance, some language officers discovered a country village where fine pottery was made by descendants of Kakiemon. Returning from a field trip, they stopped off to price the pottery and place an order for some. Just then a general drove by. He noticed the men there and decided that they were "fraternizing," since there could have been no military pretext for such a visit. I don't think anyone was disciplined for it, but that night the general raised hell at our headquarters and for the time being anyone must be cautious who is looking for pottery.

Still there are a few advantages in non-fraternization. There have been few drunken incidents, and from what I hear the Japanese are favorably impressed by the sober conduct of our men on liberty. People here make a practice of telling me, at the outset of any conversation, that "all American servicemen are gentlemen." This is partly their way of putting all conversation with Americans on a polite and gentlemanly basis, but there is some significance in the fact that most of them choose the same way of doing it.

My work here has been for a navy captain whom I knew back in Hawaii. More as a matter of personal curiosity than anything else, he is making an informal investigation of the recently disbanded Reservists' Association. Nothing startling has come out of our interviews with navy and civilian officials on the subject; indeed, if there were anything startling to be learned, we could not have obtained it by this means. The Reservists' Association seems to have been a group much like our American Legion which got together several times a year for military training with ancient firearms, wooden spears and other obsolete weapons. Their influence on the community was felt most in educational matters, where they played a big part in preparing children for a military life.

As so often happens in these interviews, the Japanese learned as much from us as we did from them. In an earlier conversation at naval headquarters, my captain had told about one of our highest-ranking prisoners of war, a meteorologist whom he had seen in Hawaii a few months ago. The subject came up again when I was there, because the officer being questioned had been a classmate of the prisoner's at the naval academy. He pointed casually to a letter lying on his desk: "That letter is to the navy personnel bureau. I am passing on to them the information that Captain Yamaga did not die as it was announced, but became a prisoner of war."

This show of alertness and efficiency impressed me. I don't know whether Yamaga's case interested this officer as a choice bit of professional gossip or, more seriously, as a matter involving treason; but the dispatch with which he handled it made me wonder if the captain had not been indiscreet to give such news to a Japanese navy man.

We also visited the municipal building, and in its black, ruined offices talked to the mayor, a kindly, dignified gentleman who had just turned in his resignation because of pressure against him from many sides. According to Griff Way, who was working across the hall with military government, the mayor had been a favorite of the Japanese navy and was regarded as too conservative to meet the changed situation. But replacing him was a difficult job. The choice of a successor was up to a council of thirty elders and three candidates were being spoken of, one the president of the chamber of commerce, head of a bank, professed Christian and all-around opportunist, who had been in the thick of war activities and now was just as active on our side; another an old liberal, head of an agricultural station or college, but a quiet man without too much aptitude for politics; and a third candidate who did not seem to count from any standpoint.

Griff was worried about the prospects. Even though most Japanese knew the businessman as an untrustworthy character, he had ingratiated himself with the American command by a lot of fancy talk and entertaining, and the council, anxious to please our military government, would probably choose whomever they believed to be the American favorite. Griff had talked with the old agriculturist and thought him a fine, unpretentious person with an understanding for what had to be done. But his chances of winning the election were poor, unless a few people like Griff could correct the widespread impression that the military government wanted the businessman for mayor.

The captain had rather liked the retiring mayor, who seemed to be a person of integrity, forthright and dignified in answering our questions. And I, too, felt a certain respect for this man who made no attempt to ingratiate himself with us or, on the other hand, to play a clever game of wits with his interrogators. He seemed a little weary of the position which our occupation had put him in, but apparently felt no shame or embarrassment over his record.

The captain, when he heard Griff's election forecast, thought it a mistake to remove the old mayor so quickly. "After all it is not so great a sin for a man to be patriotic. I'd expect any man of character to assist his country's war effort, and I'd be damn suspicious of the people who flock around us now professing to be pacifist and pro-American. If the liberal loses to the opportunist, we'll be worse off than before."

It is certainly not an easy job to start a political revolution from the top down, as we are doing in places like Sasebo, and the difficulties increase when there is so little popular support to work down to. The politicians, almost all of them, were associated with the old regime in some way or other. How else could they keep their influence or power in a community whose function in national society was completely military? The few untainted individuals are like the agriculturist, politically inept and unknown. And they are old men, which is something people in America may not take into account if they expect the present bureaucracy to be replaced by young progressives.

A few days later we went by train to Fukuoka to interview some scientists at Kyushu Imperial University. They were not, it turned out, scientists who had collaborated on technical projects for the military. That sort of thing was handled in Tokyo or in areas easily accessible to Tokyo, for the centralization of Japan's war effort was extreme, mainly because of transportation and communication difficulties (anyone who has traveled far on Japanese roads or crowded trains will understand this). The professors were extremely hospitable, glad to show us whatever they had to offer. It was Saturday afternoon, their afternoon off, but they took pleasure in guiding us through a long itinerary of laboratories, libraries and lecture rooms which quickly outran our time and curiosity. The university being closed, I was disappointed to find no students around; nothing but decrepit watchmen and a few truck drivers who were bringing in laboratory equipment from storage places in the country where it had been sent after the first air raids. None of the buildings were damaged, but all looked dilapidated or showed signs of the university's painful struggle to get back into business again. Very noticeable, because the Japanese are usually so sensitive to the condition of their natural surroundings, was the tall grass of the lawns and the untidiness of the shrubbery. The professors apologized for it, but their own shabbiness was apology enough. Even in their best clothes, collars were frayed, shoes completely broken down and out, and suits about to fall apart from sheer exhaustion. To make up for not wearing the patriotic khaki uniform, each had a little military cap, which alone of the items in their dress appeared to have been little worn.

The war had certainly not been a good thing for them. Despite their being scientists, no particular favors had been shown them by the military, as one would expect in a war which placed a premium on scientific skill. Indeed, things seemed to have worked the other way around; scholarly gentlemen, living on a fixed income, were not in a good position to provide for themselves against inflation and a rampant black market. But they showed no special bitterness toward the government or the military. Whatever they may have felt they kept to themselves, even before us. In an imperial university, faculty members are regarded as government officials, and they have cultivated great restraint in political discussions, lest they lose their jobs for "dangerous thinking." The Japanese passion for order, their susceptibility to control, has left no institution free from the bureaucratic blight. Even when freedom of thought is guaranteed by our occupation, there are few to take advantage of it, few in the habit of thinking freely.

We were only in Fukuoka twenty-four hours and there was no

time to see those parts of the university which might have meant more to me than the laboratories—the library in particular. We did spend a few minutes in a Shingon temple near our hotel, which featured relics of the famous courtesan Meigetsu. Upon visiting this temple hundreds of years ago, Meigetsu had decided to abandon her prostitute's profession for a life of prayer. From that time until her death she was known throughout the city as a woman of great virtue and piety, and a few days after her burial in the temple grounds, a lotus is said to have grown from her mouth and bloomed above her grave. The chief priest told me this flower was still preserved; he even had a picture postcard of it, though the relic itself, like everything else of consequence in the city, had been sent to the country for safekeeping.

A short distance away was a Zen temple, which the Shingon priest described as the oldest of Fukuoka's many temples and shrines. I soon learned, however, that the common Japanese method of reckoning a temple's age did not actually pertain to the age of the temple buildings but to that of its oldest relics. In this case, it was an image of the temple's founder, carved by himself, which gave the place a claim to being six hundred years old; otherwise it seemed quite new and clean. We were shown about by a priest who typified the monks seen in Japanese painting—bony, shaven head, distended ears, piercing brown eyes and a rosy, clear complexion. He was surprised by our visit and highly agitated, not knowing what to do with such strange visitors to his secluded retreat. I tried to explain that my friends had just a few minutes to spend before train time and would like to look around quickly. But my Japanese, which had been adequate with the Shingon priest, produced only nervous bewilderment in our Zen host. He answered in Japanese, with a look of almost fanatic anxiety: "Oh, is there no one among you who understands Japanese? It will not be possible to make you understand all these things."

I apologized for my shortcomings with the language and offered to do my best as an interpreter, trying to ignore this lack of tact, unprecedented in my experience among the overpolite Japanese. But my offer seemed to give little comfort. He shuffled about the main hall, excitedly pointing out relics, images, prayer tablets and inscriptions, starting to explain one and then breaking off to take up another. It became apparent that he could not bear to tell us anything, unless he could tell all. We could not be permitted a superficial acquaintance with the externals of Zen art and philosophy; the calligraphy of each poem must be appreciated in full, every implication of every character must be pointed out to us. And when we pressed a small sum into his hand he seemed to understand that we were sincere in our curiosity. I'd like to pay a similar visit to a Chinese temple soon.

Ted

♦ ♦ ♦

FROM TED DE BARY IN TOKYO
TO DON KEENE IN TSINGTAO

October 25, 1945

Dear Don,

Tokyo has changed during my absence of a few weeks in Sasebo. When I first reached here, a good start had been made toward removing the public traces of Japan's wartime propaganda. All one could find on telephone poles, billboards or buildings were a few remaining characters from posters that had been hastily torn down; maybe just the word "Enemy" would be left, or the old motto "Certain Victory." As yet no new propaganda had appeared in place of the old.

Now, only a short time later, everything that stands has a new poster pasted to it announcing the formation of some new political party, youth movement or conference along with the slogan by which each group wants to be known: "Throw Out the Old Gang!"; "New Japan Needs New Leaders!" Even businessmen are cashing in on the attempt at national resurrection. One promoter has a giant sign in a burned-out lot on the Ginza, telling Allied sightseers about a big dance palace to open soon on the premises with a modern "swing" band and two thousand dancing partners. In one corner of the same billboard is a smaller sign in Japanese: "Patriotic Girls! Assist the Reconstruction of Japan by Serving as Dance Partners!"

Almost every day some political group has had an organization rally at the Public Hall in Hibiya Park, and I have watched the notices for a meeting that would be scheduled for a time when I was free to go. With me it was a case of hit or miss, since none of the parties prominently advertised could be identified in Western terms by their names or slogans. None claimed to be democrats, socialists, communists or any combination of the three. Most names suggested that their appeal was to patriotism and mass action, as for instance the Japanese Working Masses Party, to the foundation of which I was soon to be the only American witness.

A woman at the door gave me a handbill as I came into the hall, and I did my best to read the party's platform in the dim light of the auditorium, which, incidentally, was noticeably smaller than public halls in America, as if it did not have a real place in Japanese political tradition. I sat in a row of folding seats which were far from steady and had come loose from the floor, so that I had to balance myself delicately to stay upright. A young fellow next to me was reading a magazine called "Mountain Skiing." While we waited for the speakers to come out on the stage, I asked him what sort of political party was being organized here. "Is it like the socialists or the communists?" Without too much assurance he answered, "It is something like the Social Democrats."

The hall was filled, but I got an impression that most of the spectators were park bums, unemployed factory workers (the number of these is tremendous because few are particularly concerned about finding a job while they have war savings and fire-insurance payments to live on), or schoolboys like my skiing enthusiast who no longer had a school to go to. A scattered number in the audience took the meeting seriously enough to shout, when it was slow to start, "Let's get going here!" and "What are we waiting for?"

When the proceedings finally got underway, a stuffy little man came out as master of ceremonies to go through all the formalities which Japanese tradition requires on such occasions. Then he introduced another functionary of the same fussy, deep-bowing type, who read from a scroll almost as big as himself the platform contained in the handbill. I don't know whether it is customary or not, but this gentleman and the one who followed with the party constitution delivered their speeches at the highest possible pitch. It was as hard on my ears as on their throats. Ordinary Japanese is difficult enough for me, and I barely made sense out of this. What I could understand, however, convinced me that they were adding little of significance to the printed program, especially since the rest of the audience seemed as unimpressed by all the shrieking as I was. A small claque spread thinly through the hall was all that responded to the speakers' most urgent appeals, and when a voice vote was called to elect a party chairman, it was accomplished by the acclamation of perhaps ten voices.

Since the meeting was obviously well staged, if not well received, I was curious about the promoters behind it, particularly the party chairman, Seiji Mikami, who marched around the stage in a brown leather jacket. He was plainly not the intellectual type of radical, nor did he seem a weather-beaten old labor leader. Young, erect and well-fed, he affected the role of "a man of action, not words." If he had any appeal at all, it must have been personal rather than ideological.

The party platform started off with the following provisions:

1. To demand the suicide of all elder statesmen and military leaders and the resignation of all bureaucrats.
2. Confiscation of the industries and wealth of the *zaibatsu*.
3. Immediate abolition of noble titles.
4. Cancellation of pensions to high-ranking military men and officials.
5. Investigation of the finances of war leaders and confiscation of funds illegally obtained.
6. Resignation of both houses of the Diet.
7. Publication of the true record of the war and of campaigns which led to Japan's defeat.

The remaining items were exclusively concerned with economic or financial measures: inquiries into military expenditures; the disposition of surplus military goods, food and clothing; the rationing systems and black markets. Every attempt was made to capitalize on the acute food shortage and the recent scandals involving the disappearance of marketable military supplies and the profits made from their sale by army officers now discharged.

On first reading the platform, I did not take great pains to analyze it, and failed to notice two things which strike me as significant now. One is the surprising omission of any talk about the extreme need for housing in all cities, certainly as urgent a problem for the bombed-out masses as food. How could a party, which otherwise affects such great concern for the physical welfare of the masses, have overlooked so big an issue? The second omission is perhaps less striking but just as big in the eyes of an American—the absence of any proposals for democratic political reform. There is nothing about revision of the constitution, limitation of imperial powers, creation of a responsible cabinet system or of a representative Diet; nothing about basic political freedoms, extension of the franchise or reorganization of the police system. Apparently these people want to change the government without changing the system. They are not against giving a few men great power with little responsibility— they simply want that power for themselves.

I might not have stopped to notice all this, had it not been for an acquaintance I made that night after the meeting. I went with Sherry Moran to the home of a new friend of his, Mr. Miyauchi, in the suburbs of Tokyo. Miyauchi is a small-time publisher of what the Japanese call "cultural" books and magazines (meaning the intellectual side of culture—philosophy, politics and economics—rather than the artistic). He had been a prisoner of the "thought police" from 1938 to 1940. I don't know what he had published to get himself thrown in prison; even knowing the charges one could not be sure, for the charges were often so vague and ridiculous as to indicate little about the supposed criminal. The interesting thing was that his wife had spent at least part of the term in jail with him, extraordinary for any Japanese woman. Even if her ideas were not strictly her own, they must have been remarkably intense to persist against not only the traditional subjection of women's minds but the general subjection of all minds to the military will. I wondered if this imprisonment did not follow from loyalty to her husband, rather than from independence of mind, but the evening's conversation proved that it must have been from both. Ordinarily a Japanese woman takes very little part in dinner talk. Usually there is not even a place for her at the table and she acts only as a maid, except at the end of the dinner when she becomes a hostess just long enough to apologize for the poor hospitality. But Mr. Miyauchi's wife spent as much time as possible at the dinner table, and was assisted in the cooking and serving by her husband's beautiful secretary, who was apparently invited to keep us company but hardly said a word. Our conversation with the publisher was so lively that his wife had little chance to speak for herself, but she did follow carefully everything that was said. Occasionally when we got stuck for a word in Japanese, or when Mr. Miyauchi had similar trouble trying to speak English, she would supply the right word for us, quickly and accurately. It was amazing.

Our friend called himself a socialist and a democrat. Most of the socialists I have known in America felt no necessity for emphasizing that they were also democrats, but elsewhere in the world it has long been necessary to specify what kind of socialist one is—National Socialist, Christian Socialist, Social Democrat, etc. Also in contrast to the socialists I had known at home, Mr. Miyauchi was not primarily an intellectual, a laborer or a member of any low-income group. He was a businessman and apparently successful; he owned property in Tokyo (all bombed out) and in the country, and was living in a rented house that seemed fairly good for Tokyo these days. Indeed, he was a radical in much the same way as a French bourgeois might have been during the French Revolution.

Before we had gone very far into the political situation, I asked him if he knew anything about Seiji Mikami and the Japanese Working Masses Party.

"Yes, we know him well. Before the war he was a professional leader of rightist youth movements and other fascist activities. His elder brother was one of the army officers involved in the assassinations of the May 15 incident. Today Mikami talks like a leftist, but whatever he says, he is still just an unemployed politician trying to put over his old act with different lines.

"You should not be misled by any of the parties that are coming out these days. As far as I know, none of them is genuine. Each is led by a spurious politican like Mikami, who somehow makes his living that way. If he gets enough supporters, I suppose party contributions alone would provide a living, but it is more likely that a few wealthy individuals finance the party. The real leftists and democrats are waiting. Most of them are too timid; they have been browbeaten so long that they hardly know what to do in a situation like this. Those who are not timid have been in prison for many years, and they hardly know what Japan is like today. It will take time before they get used to it."

Hoping to learn something more definite about capitalist support of rightist movements, I asked Mr. Miyauchi if he could name any of the persons who contributed to Mikami's group. He could not. Then Sherry and I questioned him about the money behind the prewar fascists, especially about the role of the *zaibatsu* in politics. His answers agreed with those we had been given by many others in Japan: the *zaibatsu* hardly counted for anything with the *gumbatsu*. A few big capitalists did actively support the militarists, especially a new class of industrialists which grew up within the *zaibatsu* empire but who did not actually belong to the "big four" families. The "big four" themselves were roped into the war like everyone else in Japan. Some resisted the military with whatever political influence they had; the rest accepted the new order passively or submerged their better judgment in the rush for war contracts and profits. Again and again he said, "They were weak, the *zaibatsu* were weak," and I have heard this said so often that I wonder if it is not the sign of common indoctrination. The army, during the thirties, must have propagated the idea first and then have proved its truth by buying out or intimidating the *zaibatsu*.

We explained to Mr. Miyauchi that most Americans thought of the *zaibatsu* as equal to the *gumbatsu* in their responsibility for the war—in fact, most people thought them the real heart of

Japanese fascism. I further explained some of the things which you have already heard in my letters about Kawasaki, and brought up the questions which remained unanswered in my earlier conversations. Was it correct, I asked, that the landed aristocracy was distinct from the capitalist class and that it was one of the original promoters of Japanese fascism? Generally speaking, he said, it was correct.

"It is an interesting point, because most Westerners do not seem to understand that Japan is still a semifeudal country. That is to say, they talk about the feudal system here as if it had been completely consumed by capitalism in the last century, at the time of the Restoration. In other words they think it is all one unified system now—feudal capitalism. Actually the Meiji Restoration hardly touched the feudal system, and the feudal families retained much of their old power, though a few did add capitalist enterprises to their other interests. Capitalism grew up under the hard crust of feudalism, and was constantly trying to break through it. The movement made great progress during the period just before and after the First World War, stressing the Western concepts of big business, internationalism and modernism. It was in answer to all this that the extreme reaction developed which eventually brought the military back into full power, supported by feudal elements in open opposition to the capitalists. Of course, I am only giving you a rough idea of what happened. Many capitalists saw that they could make a profitable compromise with the "new order," which is actually a very old order in Japan. To some enterprising industrialists, the conquered territories offered great opportunities. The conquest of Manchuria, for instance, converted many of them to aggressive imperialism; they saw that the Western powers were not going to contest Japan's seizure of this rich territory, and it was too good a thing to be passed up. Nevertheless, it remains true that the fascist political campaign was anticapitalist, that the most ardent militarists regarded themselves as revolutionists, like the Nazis, as crusaders against plutocracy.

"To understand recent Japanese history, you must realize that Japan, for all her modernization, has not undergone the same stages of development as the Western nations. Only now, by the grace of MacArthur, is she getting the democracy which you people won ages ago, and since we did not win it for ourselves, one can hardly say that we have progressed from the feudal stage yet. Agriculturally we are still deeply sunk in feudalism, and the occupation has barely touched this—politics and the *zaibatsu* seem to hold your attention exclusively. But we cannot ask you to do everything for us. It will be better if we can do this job for ourselves."

At this point I suggested that the large landholders would probably increase their power during an inflationary period like the present. They are the only people who have real wealth untouched by the war. Whatever happens to the yen, they would still have their land and the food it produces. But Mr. Miyauchi said it was too soon to say exactly what would happen. The rent system was being changed by the Diet so that rent would be paid in yen rather than in rice. This would favor the tenants during an inflationary period, since they could sell their rice on the black market at an enomous profit and would have an easy time paying their rents, which are fixed and not as susceptible to inflationary pressure. And yet the landowners, with a view to the future, were apparently in favor of the change. Present rents might only be a fraction of the return rice brings on the black market, but if the food situation returns to normal and the price of rice goes down, those fixed rents would be highly favorable to the landowners. Only time could tell who would benefit most by the change.

Apparently Miyauchi was not so concerned about the wealth of the landowners as he was about the hold of feudal tradition over the peasant mind, a hold which is almost as strong today as it was hundreds of years ago. He spoke, for instance, of the largest country estates, where it is still customary, whenever the lord drives in, for his tenants to kneel in reverence along the route—a route which is never used for any purpose but the lord's coming and going.

Economic independence, he said, is only the first step toward liberating the peasantry. Liberating their minds will take much longer and will require an atmosphere which Japan is not likely to have in the next few years. Despite the temporary advantage held by tenant rice-growers—the selling or trading value of rice today—Japan's overall destitution is such that violent revolution seems almost a certainty. In the larger cities which have been badly bombed, or in the smaller cities swollen with refugees, the masses may turn to any leader who promises food and shelter, whether he is fascist or communist, pro-American, pro-British or pro-Russian, and whether or not he is actually in a position to fulfill his promise, since in any case a solution to the problem will be hard to find.

Mr. Miyauchi guessed that the crisis would come in March or April, when present food stocks will run out. The elections for the Diet are scheduled for early spring, and he hoped that the violent surge of discontent would wash Japan clean without overflowing orderly processes of government. But those processes are working so slowly now, partly because of the occupation paralysis, that an orderly solution seems unlikely unless American troops enforce it.

What would we do, Mr. Miyauchi asked me, if violence broke out? Would our troops try to prevent it, or just stand by on the sidelines and let opposing forces fight it out? I answered that the question was being much discussed in America, especially by persons who feared that American troops would be used to defend the status quo. This struck my socialist friend as a rather strange attitude under the present circumstances, since the actual status quo is what our occupation makes it and there should be no need for violence as long as we guarantee political democracy. Indeed, it was difficult for him to see how we could both guarantee political liberties and condone violent revolution which frustrated or prohibited the exercise of those liberties. We must inevitably make a choice between the two courses, and if we chose the latter, we would also have to choose what sort of revolution we wanted, what groups we would support and how far we would let the violence go. At the moment, it seemed to him, violence was much more likely to come from the right than from the left. The true leftists, after all, appreciated America's gift of political freedom and intended to use it to good purpose. Unless we withdrew the gift, or failed to accept its harvest, revolution would do more harm than good.

Later in our conversation it developed that Miyauchi is busy getting out a translation of Edgar Snow's books about the China war and Chinese communists. Publication of such books was forbidden, of course, during the years of military dominance, but an associate of Miyauchi's had kept a secret library of them. Right now they are working on *The Battle for Asia*. The project is not moving very swiftly, however, for paper is scarce and Tokyo's printing establishments have been hard hit by the bombings. Miyauchi had lost his original place of business, found temporary space elsewhere, and lost that when Allied headquarters seized the building because its principal tenant (or owner I'm not sure) was the Manchurian Development Company, an outlawed firm. Now his business is conducted at home.

I could not help but realize from his story how close the Japanese are to starting their general education all over again. I am not thinking of the school reforms which have already been directed by MacArthur's headquarters, since these affect only those who go to school. I mean the reeducation of the people as a whole, which is dependent on existing news services, printing the information we supply, and on a small number of publishers like Miyauchi, who must work against terrible odds to meet the demand for good, new literature. It is even possible, when the present crisis in Japan reaches full intensity, that the job of reeducation will be stopped short rather than given new impetus. Perhaps the Japanese reading public will never have a chance to learn what Edgar Snow reported about the China war. Perhaps there will be no paper to print it on, and the printers, instead of working at their presses, will have to spend their days in search of food. And even if the book is finally published, who knows whether anyone will read it. The country might be too far gone for such reasonable pursuits. At best, the book might have a limited audience; at worst, it might have none, since the problems of food, shelter and self-defense always take precedence over this sort of education.

Nevertheless, it does not seem to me that the outcome must necessarily be so dismal. There is certain to be great suffering, but there need not be violence or national paralysis if the occupying authority commands that everything possible be done to relieve suffering, and if it stands firm for an orderly solution of the political crisis. From everything I have seen, the Japanese people have great respect for our power and will be highly sensitive to our wishes as long as that power is not seriously weakened.

Before closing this letter, I should not forget to tell you of a few significant words which Miyauchi spoke at the start of our evening together, while we sat drinking tea in a little reception room and waiting for dinner to be announced. After Sherry and I had told him something of our personal histories, Miyauchi, by way of introducing himself, told us about his arrest and imprisonment by the *kempeitai* [military police]. We were naturally struck by the fact that he had finally been released from prison just before the war began and was not again arrested when thought control became even more oppressive during the war years. Had he, we asked, changed his opinions or softened them while in jail? Had he just decided to be more prudent in the future?

"I suppose," he replied, "those years in prison taught me to be more circumspect in the things I wrote and published. But the war itself was what affected me most. Japan did so well at the beginning. It looked as if we might win, and no matter how much I disliked war, it was difficult not to feel a certain national or racial pride in the first great victories. Like most other men who share my political opinions, I began to wonder if my people might not be able to turn final victory into something great and good, to show a hostile world what the yellow men of Japan could accomplish."

Miyauchi said this with penitent frankness, but his confession implied more than a lesson for the disillusioned Japanese. It meant that we could spend a lifetime trying to educate the Japanese for peace and democracy, and the attempt might still fail if they felt themselves separated by a color line from the other peoples of the world. There might then be a showdown on the fashionable interpretation of Japan's race fanaticism—that it simply grew out of the masses' frustration under native tyranny. When that tyranny was ended and Japan lived in the light of native freedom, war might still breed in the shadow of white contempt.

Ted

◆ ◆ ◆

FROM FRANK TURNER IN TOKYO TO DON KEENE IN TSINGTAO

October 25, 1945

Dear Don,

Recently I met an Indian named Raj who lived in Tokyo throughout the war. His father had been an exporter of semi-finished products from Japan, and left Raj here to carry on the business when hostilities appeared imminent. When the export business stopped, Raj switched to selling machine tools. He claimed to have made more money than ever before through the sale and resale of machine tools to war industries. Apparently the venture was a highly speculative one which operated on the principle of buying the tools cheap and holding them until they could be sold at high prices. It was a little hard for me to understand how this sort of speculation could be attempted with something so vital to war production as machine tools. How could production be maintained when essential tools were passing around from factory to factory, or factory to warehouse and back again? Raj explained that the resale of tools did not cause inefficiency in production, but was instead the result of it. The tools would originally belong to some producer of peacetime goods. When the war started they would be converted to military production and sold to a war plant, but through material shortages or some other failure in the military's planning, the plant would have to close down. Raj would then buy the tools back and sell them to another war plant.

The trade ceased to be profitable when our bombing raids last spring put machine tool users out of business. Things finally became so disorganized that little attempt was made to rebuild and reequip the blasted factories. Consequently Raj took off to the mountains in Nagano, living off his earlier profits. Since then his funds have dwindled while prices have steadily risen. Raj is not too well off now, but he still managed to entertain five of us at a Japanese feast which must have cost him over a thousand yen.

Though Raj has a Japanese wife, he is a British national and all was not so easy for him during the war years as his business success would make it seem. He spoke with special bitterness about the close scrutiny to which the *kempeitai* had subjected him—the annoying visits at all hours of the night, the embarrassing questions. He was the first to admit that he had a comparatively easy time of it, however. A White Russian friend had been beaten on the chest until one of his lungs was punctured. Raj's funds were frozen at first and he suffered minor personal indignities, but later his way was smoothed by the arrival in Japan of the Indian Nationalist leader, Chandra Bose. Bose was the man Tōjō hoped might rally Indian support for a projected Japanese drive into India. After a puppet Indian government had been organized in Singapore, there was a certain advantage in being able to say, as Japanese propagandists did, that Free India was a supporter of the Greater East Asia Co-prosperity Sphere. Bose was in a position to ask favors for his countrymen in Japan. Raj, faced with the necessity of earning a living in Japan, could not overlook the possibility of getting Bose's protection. When the puppet leader came to Tokyo, Raj went down to a big reception in Bose's honor. What further steps he may have taken in support of the leader Raj did not suggest to me, but from then on his funds were unfrozen and he was able to carry on his business as usual.

I do not doubt that Raj did whatever was necessary to identify himself with Japanese aspirations in India and to free himself from suspicion as an alien. Like many other foreigners living abroad in the Far East—I have known many of them in China—Raj felt no compelling allegiance to any nation or cause. Aside from his desire to eat and stay alive, his feelings and opinions on political matters were largely negative. He knew what he didn't like. From the way he spoke, Raj hated the Japanese military intensely. Alternately he told of his delight at seeing the military suffer for their misdeeds, and warned us that the military were not yet dead in Japan by any means. "You should have seen the cocky fellow I saw this afternoon, swaggering along the street in a *hakama* [skirtlike outer garment] just the way soldiers did before the end of the war."

Raj was also critical of Japanese military equipment, their feeble air raid defense and ineffective interception of approaching bombers. He had always regarded military press reports with extreme skepticism, and was surprised to learn that the Japanese had indeed been effective in many combat operations. He was surprised at the respect we, as naval officers, showed for the Kamikaze attacks at Okinawa, the protracted land campaign conducted by the Japanese there, the beach defenses at Iwo and for Japanese aerial torpedo tactics. The fact that we had actually been slowed down by Japanese defensive measures seemed to amaze him. He had prided himself on being an intelligent skeptic, but now began to wonder if he had not discounted Japanese bravado a bit too much.

Raj reported that most Japanese regarded our mass incendiary raids as an inevitable part of the war. In Japan a lot of publicity was given the fire-bombing of London, and very early in the war repeated warnings were given the Japanese people that the same thing would happen to Tokyo unless everyone did his utmost to crush the Allied offensive. Thus our bombing of urban areas had a precedent in Japanese minds; it was not unexpected. The people were angered, however, by the action of our fighter planes. Apparently the fighters encountered so little air opposition during the final stages of the war that they had to seek out ground targets. Of these, trains were special favorites for strafing attacks. Everyone travels by train in Japan, as you know, and the interurban electric trains were particularly conspicuous from the air as they crawled slowly along in all directions. Fighters frequently strafed them from low altitude and the helpless passengers were unable to take cover. The attacks came so suddenly and cars were so tightly packed that indescribable terror panicked the passengers, adding to the high casualties from incendiary bullets. The Japanese classed such attacks as atrocities, because the passenger trains were not thought to be military targets.

For the immediate future Raj hopes to get a job with the occupation forces, perhaps as an interpreter. Later he hopes to leave Japan for good and start again in the export business in India. He feels that the economic future of Japan is hopeless, unless American capital is brought in quickly to get production going again, control inflation and prevent complete collapse. This is hardly an attitude peculiar to Raj; all Japanese business people seem to share it. They have thrown up their hands over the postwar situation, and wait for Americans to take the first steps toward Japan's reconstruction.

How is the fall weather in China?

Frank

◆ ◆ ◆

FROM SHERRY MORAN IN TOKYO
TO MRS. FRANCES MORAN IN OHIO

October 28, 1945

Dear Fritz,

It is probably too soon after the war for people in America to realize what an amazing course the occupation has taken in its first eight weeks. Even I, who expected the Japanese to surprise us by their adaptability, who always thought it a mistake to hold that the Germans were simply misguided human beings, susceptible of re-education, while the Japanese were animals to whom decent behavior could not be taught—even I find the Japanese reception of us heartening beyond all previous expectation. And I cannot help but wish that there were some adequate way to convey my feeling to you at home, to make you sense what it is like for us living and working among the Japanese.

I was going to tell you about the flood of letters which Japanese have been sending General MacArthur, who is now regarded by many as a savior, in approval of his policies. Some of the letters have been translated and their general contents published in the *Nippon Times*; twenty-four letters in favor of prosecuting Japanese war criminals, sixteen in criticism of the Japanese government, and so forth. But a sample of this kind is not very convincing evidence of the Japanese state of mind. It has no statistical validity, unless perhaps one considered how unlikely it was that even this many letters were sent by Germans to their Allied masters. And it will not impress you with the genuineness and human appeal which the same sentiments convey when presented, as they are to us, in the context of personal relationships in the course of everyday life.

One day recently I had to visit someone who lived outside of Tokyo. When my party reached the town, we stopped to inquire the way at the local police station, and, as always seems to happen, we were furnished with a policeman for a guide. I had hoped this could be avoided, since the man we were calling on might be frightened when he saw us approaching with a police escort. It proved unavoidable, however; the policeman insisted on coming along for what I later learned was his first ride in a jeep. The ride was a bumpy one, of course, and conversation was difficult above the thump and rattle which marked our passage over each hole in the road. But the policeman kept looking at me as if he had something important to say, and when we ran into a short stretch of fairly smooth road, he finally came out with it.

"I am truly grateful to America for bringing us peace. Before, it seemed as if hardship and suffering would never end, and now suddenly it is gone."

"Do you think that everyone looks at it the same way?" I asked.

"Oh yes, almost everyone."

"How about the police?"

"I think most of the police feel as I do. I realize that we have a reputation for oppressing the people and preventing criticism of the war, but what else could you expect the police to do in wartime?"

"Well, the bad reputation of the police did not start with the war. Their tyranny has been well known for years."

He was stopped for a few seconds, then remarked that he had not joined the police until a few years ago and could not speak about their earlier conduct. But he was sure that even the police were struck by the fine behavior of the American troops. "They are," he said, "an inspiration to us; as representatives of democracy they are winning many Japanese over to your way of doing things."

"How long do you think we will have to stay in Japan to get the country started on the right road?"

"Sah . . . (the Japanese equivalent of "You've got me there"). It is hard to say how long it might be, but I think you should stay until the job is done."

I do not think the policeman told me these things just to please me. He was under no obligation to say anything more than "Right," "Left," or "Straight ahead," when we came to crossroads along the way. He may not, it is true, have been speaking for the majority of the police in Japan, but his sentiments must be those of many Japanese, for otherwise Americans would not find it so safe and pleasant as they do to travel around the countryside. These trips frequently take us far from the protection of any occupying force, and it would be an easy thing for hostile elements to do away with us, leaving no trace or clue to our disappearance. On dark nights I have traveled alone in a jeep, unarmed, in wild country far from an occupation outpost. A well-placed boulder in the road, at the end of a sharp curve, might have thrown the jeep and myself into a deep canyon, where the wreckage would not be found until the next day, too late to start a search for saboteurs.

Almost every day I meet people who speak as the policeman did. Only once so far have I run into a person whose feelings toward Americans did not quite fall into the common pattern. In our barracks building there was a girl named Aiko, who served in the mess upstairs. When our medical facilities were well-enough equipped, it was decided to test the waitresses and kitchen help for venereal disease and tuberculosis. Aiko was declared tubercular and had to stop waiting on tables, but apparently she was not anxious to look for a job elsewhere. Her home was in northern Japan and she had no desire to go back there; so, I learned on speaking to her in the hallway one day that an arrangement had been made for her to stay on doing maid's work while the medical people continued to treat her for tuberculosis.

"I never expected them to be so kind," she said, "I hoped they would let me stay on, but it did not occur to me that I would also be given medical treatment. The kindness of Americans amazes me. Your arrival here has meant just the reverse of what we were told it would mean. It actually seems better that Japan did lose the war."

A few days later I heard that Aiko was acting as an assistant to the army doctor who treated the Japanese personnel working in the building. He had established a dispensary on our floor, and I began to notice that Aiko seemed to have a lot of spare time on her hands, for she would hang around the officers' quarters and occasionally offer to darn someone's socks. I also noticed that she gradually adopted the un-Japanese habits of chewing gum and smoking cigarettes, and that she attempted to enhance her natural attractiveness by an increasing use of make-up, which must, I thought, have been received from an American admirer.

One night after supper I was standing in the hall, eating an apple and thinking over what I would say in a letter I was about to write you. Aiko came down the hall and sat down at a desk near me. She seemed less gay than usual, avoided my gaze, and hardly answered my "Good evening." When I asked if anything was the matter she was slow to speak, covering her mouth with her hands so that I could barely understand her request for me to sit down at the table and talk awhile.

"You know about my tuberculosis, don't you, and the work I am supposed to be doing for the doctor in his dispensary."

"Yes, I know. Have they told you to leave?"

"Oh no, it is not that. I am not really consumptive. I am sure the doctor just said that to make me work for him; he knows that I can't get a job anywhere else after being declared consumptive. You see, there is really no dispensary here at all and the doctor does not even intend to establish one. I have tried to ask him for work, but he doesn't understand my poor English.

Won't you please speak to him about it? Ask him to get me some work and a girl to keep me company at night."

I did not like the idea of prying into matters that did not concern me, and since Aiko seemed to be accusing the doctor of some vague foul play, I hesitated to approach him without a much better case to present. At the same time, I have run into many misunderstandings which arose simply from language difficulties, and felt obliged to offer myself as an interpreter in getting the matter straightened out. I indicated to Aiko that her story was a little hard to believe. Trying to get at the heart of things, I asked what reason the doctor had for keeping her on.

She started to cry. "The doctor forces me to sleep with him."

"Forces you to sleep with him?"

"Yes," she sobbed.

I wondered what could be done or said about such a delicate problem. Aiko thought my puzzled look meant that I did not believe her. She pulled me up by the sleeve.

"Come with me."

I followed uneasily. Through my mind ran a suspicion that the girl's distress might be faked, a device to get me alone with her in the dispensary.

We entered a little suite of rooms, over the door to which was painted, in English and Japanese, the word "Dispensary." Inside I found a scene which quickly dispelled my doubts—a little love nest of makeshift but adequate couches, a whiskey closet fairly well stocked with "Suntory" Scotch and some American liquors, a few novels and miscellaneous furniture which could hardly have been put to any medical use. The doctor had apparently been drinking and playing solitaire. Dirty glasses and cards were strewn about the table. Most convincing of all was a .45 pistol lying among the cards. I stared at it. Aiko murmured, "He threatened me with that pistol."

Plainly Aiko was not deceiving me, but those sordid surroundings made me very uneasy and I left quickly, pausing outside the door just long enough to make sure of the sign above it: "Dispensary." As we hastened back down the hallway, she begged me to write a note to the doctor in English. She did not wish to sleep with him that night because she was menstruating. I had a little difficulty over the Japanese word *mensu*, which I realized later was borrowed from the West, and my difficulty was heightened by her female embarrassment in explaining what she meant. After the note was written (it said that she "would appreciate waiting a few days before going further with the doctor"), I agreed to meet her again in the morning and promised that I would bring enough yen for her to buy a ticket to her home in the north.

Aiko must have left very early the next morning because she did not meet me as we had planned and I have not seen her since.

The whole experience shook me pretty hard at first, but I guess nothing can be done about it now. Americans have an awful lot of power over people here, and those who want to misuse it can do our cause plenty of damage without getting caught.

All my love,
Sherry

◆ ◆ ◆

FROM FRANK TURNER IN TOKYO
TO DON KEENE IN TSINGTAO

October 29, 1945

Dear Don,

Last night near Hibiya Corner I noticed a Japanese fellow walking briskly with a bottle of sake under his arm. Catching up with him, I asked if he would be willing to sell me the sake, but he replied with an amused smile that he wanted to drink it himself. I walked along beside him in silence, hoping he might relent. Finally he broke the silence by inviting me up to his room in a nearby office building. After climbing three flights of stairs, I entered a dimly lit office which seemed to serve him as living quarters despite its bareness and chilly atmosphere. My sake-bearing host offered me a chair and proceeded to explain that he was the caretaker for the building, which belonged to the "International Transportation Company." This concern had operated a trucking business in Manchuria before the surrender.

My host introduced himself as Mr. Takebe, opened the bottle

of sake and poured some drinks. He told me that he had been discharged from the army and rehired by his former employers, the trucking company. Takebe had worked in Manchuria for many years, driving trucks between Harbin, Chahar, Manchuli, Tsitsihar and Tientsin. He asked me if I had heard about the treatment which Japanese in Manchuria were receiving from the Russians. I had heard a few rumors on the subject, but answered in the negative, not wanting to give my support to a campaign of gossip, when the actual facts were so obscure. Takebe informed me that his wife and two children were in the Russian-occupied sector of Korea, and proceeded to describe the Russian policy of deliberately starving the Japanese and driving them from their homes. Men were allegedly fed two, and women one, *nigirimeshi* a day [a *nigirimeshi* is a handful of cooked rice packed together in the form of a ball]. All Japanese were assigned to hard labor, like common prisoners. I interjected that, even supposing these things to be true, there was no reason to believe that the Koreans themselves, rather than the Russians, might not be responsible for such a policy.

But as I said this, our conversation was broken up by a group of women who assembled in the room. One of them, very outspoken, remarked that I talked Japanese like a young soldier. "Of course," I replied, "Japanese soldiers, prisoners of war, taught me how to speak your language." Whenever anyone asks how I have learned Japanese, I make a point of mentioning prisoners, in order to impress upon people that many Japanese were actually taken prisoner during the war. Generally my listeners are surprised to learn about it, but that night my remark provoked no particular reaction. Instead, a thin, old woman, who was warming her hands over a scanty pile of charcoal in the brazier, complained about the weather and the chilliness of the room. Takebe looked over at a young girl in the group and casually suggested that they keep warm by sleeping together that night. She brushed off the suggestion with no visible embarrassment. In fact, her nonchalance made me laugh, and soon the whole group joined in, probably laughing at me more than at what had been said.

By this time the warm sake was beginning to soak into our chilled bodies, and I thought perhaps the party's growing gaiety might justify my inquiring into a delicate question—what did they think of the increasingly common fraternization between Japanese girls and American servicemen? Takebe did not hesitate to denounce it emphatically. Americans could not be truly interested in Japanese girls, considering the barriers of language, race and war prejudice which prevented such friendships from developing into something permanent. It seemed to him that Americans sought the company of Japanese girls for only one reason, which would become sufficiently apparent, if it were not already, next June when a prodigious crop of "occupation babies" was brought into the world. For many, many years, these babies would be a constant reminder of American excess and Japanese folly. The men and women in the room all solemnly nodded their assent.

Just then a rather prepossessing, middle-aged gentleman joined the group. When we were introduced, he gave me a card which showed that he was vice president of the International Transportation Company. I asked when he expected to start business again, and he answered that MacArthur could answer the question better than he. His overseas business was gone for good, unless the Chinese took over Manchuria and wanted Japanese firms to remain, and anyway he doubted that there would be anything left of his business by the time Japanese assets abroad were unfrozen. Any remaining capital in Japan would lie idle until some statement of policy was issued by MacArthur. The vice president claimed that his business was typical of many Japanese concerns which did not dare to take a step until it has official sanction. I asked what sort of sanction he hoped to get, but he could not be specific. He just assumed that all economic activity would sooner or later be prescribed by Allied headquarters as it had been earlier by the Japanese military. I tried to explain that Mac-Arthur would probably never concern himself with such details, that the American way was to direct things at a few strategic points in the economy and otherwise to let business take its natural course. But it was unthinkable to him that so much anarchy should be permitted. No one could possibly take any initiative until his course was well laid out in advance. I could not help but be amused at the way this Japanese attitude contrasted with that of American businessmen toward economic controls. In Japan, free enterprise was out of the question. If the authorities imposed no controls, businessmen would be lost until perhaps they got together and devised some controls for themselves.

From this subject, the vice president went on to make another complaint against our occupation. He thought our campaign to spread democracy in Japan was the worst sort of hypocrisy. America always talked about equality of opportunity, but in Japan's case that equality had been denied. Proof of it came from the fact that even now, with famine threatening, Japan was still denied access to food materials. "If you are going to preach democracy, you will have to feed the people before they will listen to you."

I tried to explain that Americans did not feel responsible for Japan's present plight, and would be reluctant to send food to their enemies when people were starving in friendly countries. But I realized, as I spoke, that this was no answer to his argument, even though it was true in its own way. To convert the Japanese to democracy, we would simply have to stop thinking of them as enemies. Consequently, I attempted to reach some common ground by suggesting that when Americans and Japanese got to know each other better, this feeling of hostility might diminish. The presence of so many American troops might build friendship on both sides.

The vice president proved unwilling to accept even this. He argued that the Japanese is too accommodating and servile, and that any friendship he might show for Americans would soon be exploited. He mentioned many instances in which American troops had been invited to the homes of Japanese acquaintances, only to eat their ration-bound hosts out of house and home. Also, GIs had embarrassed well-meaning families by making dates with their daughters and then staying overnight in houses already badly overcrowded with bombed-out relatives. He argued that this sort of thing was inevitable because Americans are so aggressive and make no attempt to understand Japanese etiquette or social customs. The Japanese are thus at a loss as how to handle the Americans properly, being unable to adapt themselves to a situation wherein traditional rules do not apply. Added to this difficulty is the people's engrained fear of their own military, which is now transferred to the occupation forces. When an overly sociable GI wants to stay overnight, his Japanese host cannot suggest that he leave, since sign language or the host's poor English is inadequate for that purpose. And, of course, his fear of military men (especially when they are so much bigger than he is) prevents him from resorting to any direct means of eviction.

I concluded from all this that the Japanese will have to develop a certain resiliency before mutually satisfactory relations can exist with the GI. If enough Japanese can acquire this resiliency, this hearty ability to give and take, it may lessen the national tendency to compensate for a sense of inferiority by bullying and deceiving the white man.

I did not take these remarks as a hint that I myself should make a move to leave the little gathering, but it was getting late, and I remembered some things which had to be done before I turned in for the night. When Takebe offered me some sliced sweet potato, however, I felt obliged to refuse this final gesture of hospitality, saying that we Americans were very well fed at our quarters. I left soon afterward, pleasantly warmed by the sake and grateful for an evening of informative conversation.

Frank

◆ ◆ ◆

FROM DON KEENE IN TSINGTAO TO TED DE BARY IN TOKYO

October 30, 1945

Dear Ted,

It is now almost a month since I came to Tsingtao. What was then unusual is now part of the routine, and it is with difficulty that I attempt to bring into focus those peculiar qualities of China which once I sought. The chief obstacle is the black haze of marines and sailors which obscures every natural quality of the city. The streets that once were filled with cheering and applauding children are now crowded with servicemen who stride from money-exchange shop to souvenir shop, and back again, attended by a fringe of beggars and peddlars crying, "Very good, Joe!" or "Cumshaw, Joe!" depending on whether they do or do not have anything to sell. The wares are usually offensive to the senses—magenta and yellow-green kimonos of indeterminate material or use, and the like—but they are sold without effort, no price too high. The restaurants also bear witness to the subtle metamorphosis that has taken place: the Chinese restaurants which once served sharks' fins or the "eight precious grains" now offer steak with or without eggs. Chinese food may be obtained on occasion, but it is a rare serviceman who would demand anything more esoteric than steak without eggs.

Amazingly enough the very servicemen who first upset the economic system here by pressing dollar bills into the palms of rickshawmen or giving quarters to the kids (or even tossing hand-fuls of peanuts on the sidewalk for the kids to scramble for) are now protesting the most vigorously about the high prices. American generosity always seems cursed with the need for gratitude, not gratitude in the heart, but gratitude over the counter. It is hard for the American to remember also that the Chinese are not a conquered people, nor, strictly speaking, have we liberated them. As a result, it is with profound indignation that Americans slowly discover that there are two prices, one for Chinese and one for Americans. If the propaganda movies we were shown before coming to China had emphasized the fact that the Chinese are not bound by quite the same code of business ethics that we are (even though they have a tradition of four thousand years of democracy), it would have been with somewhat less indignant horror that the marines and sailors learned about the way that prices may vary. This argument is a little too objective, as a matter of fact, for I am guilty of most of the sins I have deplored in others. It is irritating, regardless of reasons, when a paper-bound little volume is quoted at ten times its real value and the store-owner refuses to discuss the price. It is even more irritating if, when one returns with a Chinese friend, the price goes down substantially. Although I can tell myself that this is all a part of traditional methods and that the Chinese here have no particular debt to us, I still find myself wishing that there was a little more of the spontaneous generosity of which I have heard so much.

My circle of acquaintances among the local population is still very limited. After a week here, Dick Beardsley and I decided to take Chinese lessons. We had just passed a newspaper office and I suggested that we go in and place an advertisement for a teacher. Inside we were greeted with much enthusiasm, and while I was painfully framing the words of the proposed advertisement, the editor came in with Mr. Lin Chien-sui. The latter greeted us in good English and announced that he would be willing to become our teacher. Mr. Lin and some of his associates at the newspaper are almost the only Chinese I have been able to meet in Tsingtao, although I have tried in every way I know to be introduced to some people with my interests. My impression of the local population is surely distorted by my inadequate number of friends, but I can sense something fishy in the atmosphere. One of our officers, a man who was formerly the American consul at Tsinan, told me that the Chinese in Tsingtao are the "worst bunch of bastards I have ever met," and he is a person who has many Chinese friends and who loves certain other Chinese cities. One wonders to how great a degree the Chinese here have been corrupted by almost eight years of Japanese occupation. In the building in which Lin's newspaper is published, for example, the furniture, the pictures on the wall, the scrap paper he uses in giving a lesson—almost everything one sees—bears a Japanese imprint. One is led to the conclusion also that the people have not remained unaffected. Lin was denounced to me the other day by a former company associate of his as "notoriously pro-Japanese." I can hardly believe this to be true, but the fact remains that it was felt possible to make such an accusation.

There is something uneasy and mysterious about the atmosphere that I don't like. One evening when we came for our lesson we were told in rapid succession by various people that Mr. Lin was not able to meet us because "he was taking dinner," "he was busy," and "he was ill," the last from his brother who tapped his head in such a way as to suggest that Lin had gone insane. On the way back, Dick and I noticed a group of Chinese soldiers who were remarkable for the smart tailoring of their uniforms standing in front of what might properly be called a sleek, black limousine. One of the soldiers, almost unmistakably an officer, stood apart from the others. He made a gesture with his hands just then which reminded me sharply of a Prussian officer pulling off his gloves. He turned around as we approached him. Dick and I had the same thought, "Alas, poor Mr. Lin." Lin showed up a few days later to belie our anxiety, but the mystery remains about him.

The charge of collaborationist is no less pervasive than the generally suspicious character of the city itself. A few days ago a Chinese came to our office to report that his apartment had been burglarized by some American sailors acting with the connivance of his landlord. We rushed off to investigate. The landlord, a Hungarian Jew with an attractive Czech wife, was furious at the charge and at first denied everything. When the Chinese's radio was found in the landlord's apartment, he then admitted much of the Chinese's accusation, but countercharged by asserting that the Chinese had not paid any rent in six months and that he had been protected by the Japanese from eviction because he was working for them. "I can prove that he's pro-Japanese," the landlord cried. Perhaps he was, as indicated by the facts that he ate Japanese food on occasion and was able to read Japanese. I was inclined to sympathize with the Chinese until he produced a bullet which he said "dropped" from an American's gun. The bullet proved to be of a type not used since before the last war. Other little inconsistencies in his story soon had me doubting him, too. The spirit of intrigue was in every corner of the house. I noticed a postcard that had been mailed to the landlord. I picked it up and glanced at it surreptitiously, hoping illogically to gain from it some piece of information that would declare him villain and end the case, but the card was written in Hungarian and incomprehensible to me. When later I heard from the Japanese that the landlord was on their list of suspects, I was no longer capable of feeling sympathy for either side. The charge of collaborationist loses its meaning in a city where for eight years everyone has had to comply, while being suspected by the Japanese might mean only that one had a dog that barked after curfew.

Most of the people in the city government are those who were there when the Japanese were still in power. Some of these undoubtedly will be replaced, but there is only a limited number of persons who are trained in governmental work. The mayor was put in office with Japanese connivance. His secretary (and second most important person in town) was formerly the president of the Japanese-sponsored Anti-Opium League, an association which had a monopoly on the sale of opium in the city. One would scarcely suspect fragile, scholarly Mr. Lee of such a career, but the longer I stay in China the less paradoxical such a contrast appears. The mayor's chief of staff, a quiet little Chinese with a face which is almost caricature Japanese, has distinguished himself by having confiscated for his own purposes most of the Japanese stores in town. I hear that he suffered somewhat of a check when he attempted to declare confiscations effected by other parties illegal and was thereupon rebuked by the mayor. The vice mayor is the one person in the municipal government from Chungking, but aside from the excessively harsh, anticommunist editorials which appear in his newspaper, one would be hard put to see the influence of the superior Central Government in his doings.

As a natural result of my work and my relative degree of proficiency in spoken Japanese and Chinese, I have met many more Japanese here than Chinese. This is a shame, I know, but I seem unable to meet any Chinese other than those at the newspaper and the merchants and officials with whom I have daily contact. On the other hand, I am forced to see a large number of Japanese army and navy officers every day, some of whom are interesting in themselves and all of whom have a peculiar value for me in the contrast they afford with the prisoners I have known. In addition to the military personnel, I have met some Japanese civilians, one of whom is a most fortunate acquaintance.

The circumstances of my meeting Mr. Masakatsu Yokoyama are unusual in that the meeting was entirely unpremeditated and fortuitous in this town of calculation and intrigue. One day when I was in a Japanese bookstore talking to the owner about some literary matter, a Japanese I had noticed to be listening to our conversation turned around to me and asked if I was interested in Japanese art. When I replied that I was, he said, "Why don't you come over to visit me some day when you are not busy? I have just a few books, but you might be interested in them. Come any time at all." We exchanged cards and separated, each secretly confident that he would never see the other again. Invitations of so vague a nature, as you know, seldom bear fruit, but for some obscure reason I did telephone Mr. Yokoyama one afternoon and went to his house.

It took only a very short time for us to be on the most informal and even intimate terms. I could see that, as he said, he had been unable to talk about those things which interested him most for a long time. Our conversation leapt from one peak to another, from Minoan art to Mozart concerti, from the temples at Kyoto to the comparative merits of modern English and American literature. If it had been a long time for Yokoyama since the last such discussion, it seemed almost as long for myself. He had prepared a little package of books which he intended to send me, certain that I would never come to visit him. Other books of his I saw in a bookcase included James Truslow Adams's *America*, several by Van Loon, something by Coomaraswamy, *Werke* by Schiller and other German masters, and a number of books on Japanese and Chinese art. "I have really nothing to show you here," he apologized, "most of my books are in Tientsin." I learned from him that he had come to China about eight years before as a representative of one of Japan's largest department stores. It struck me as rather unusual that Yokoyama, a man of wide cultural knowledge, should have been so proud of his concern, so anxious to associate himself with it. I can scarcely imagine a young American college graduate of similar talents boasting about his connections with one of our department stores.

Mr. Yokoyama introduced me to his family—an extraordinarily beautiful wife and three little girls. I was surprised, again, to see how typically Japanese Yokoyama's treatment of his wife was. It is true that he did not use derogatory personal pronouns in addressing her, but she sat on a chair in the next room near the door when Yokoyama and I conversed, and she did not join in any discussion. The next time I visited Yokoyama's house and we had dinner together, Mrs. Yokoyama did not eat with us, but disappeared into the kitchen after serving our meal. I wonder if this is a conscious attitude on Yokoyama's part, or if all that he assuredly has read in Western books about our treatment of women has struck him as irrelevant in a Japanese home? Or if it is Mrs. Yokoyama who insists on behaving in the manner of the traditional Japanese housewife? In other respects, if this is to be taken as an exception, Yokoyama is a democratic and courteous man, as is witnessed by the large number of Chinese and Korean friends who have chosen to stand by him now, when it is relatively dangerous to have Japanese acquaintances. The last time Dick and I visited Yokoyama he had arranged to have all of his neighbors lend him their books on art and their phonograph records so that we might be better entertained. Just that afternoon some of his simple Korean friends visited, listening uncertainly when Yokoyama played Bach on the violin or when we spoke about art. One of them opened a book which contained some fanciful Chinese paintings of mythological men and animals. "Were there really people like this once upon a time?" he asked.

I realized then that undoubtedly Yokoyama had kept secret all of his interests until then for fear of overwhelming his friends. It may have been more than that, for I could gather that his violin-playing had not only met with the uncomprehending boredom of people like his Korean friends, but had also been objected to as a Western affectation or as an unsuitable pastime in wartime. Considering the propensity of Japanese for informing on other people, it might have been at some risk that Yokoyama continued to enjoy his violin, or, for that matter, the company of his Chinese and Korean friends.

Inevitably, Mr. Yokoyama showed me the family photograph

album. At a picture taken of him wearing the "people's patriotic uniform" I was momentarily taken aback. I realized that had I seen the picture before I knew Yokoyama, it would have appeared to me the likeness of a typical, painfully typical, Japanese. His hair was closely cropped as was expected of him as a member of the Home Defense Guard (to which all Japanese must belong). On his head he wore an adaptation of the ridiculous Japanese army cap which I have seen transform dignified Japanese officers into jokes. Horn-rimmed spectacles and a frozen expression completed what was almost an inevitable picture. Looking up at Yokoyama from his picture, I could scarcely reconcile the wonderful person, who even then was preparing to show me sketches he had drawn of Peking, with the stranger, many times removed, in the photograph. Yokoyama is, I believe, one of that small class of Japanese men of goodwill which it will be most difficult to uncover—the intellectuals who are not to be found in universities or other likely places, but rather in private industry. I am convinced that he must have been horrified by the attack on Pearl Harbor, although, as a Japanese, he must have felt some sort of gratification at its success. Powerless to protest, he lived during the war in the gradual realization that a Japanese defeat was necessary. The actual defeat, however, came as a sudden great shock which could be resolved into acceptance only after many of his basic patriotic sentiments had been reasoned away.

Yokoyama is one of two Japanese civilians I have met socially. The other is Dr. Kibata, a graduate of Columbia a long time ago, who was introduced to me for that reason. My first impressions of any individual are almost always entirely wrong, but the initial dislike I felt for Kibata I have been unable to find cause to change. Of course, as a Japanese language officer, there is always a certain amount of resentment on my part toward Japanese who speak English better than I do Japanese, but there was nothing in Kibata which attracted me over this initial and formidable barrier. The first time I met him was when I was invited to dinner at his house. Twice before, the dinner had been cancelled, and this time I was in my room at the hotel faintly recovering from an attack of diarrhea, unable to bear the thought of more food and suffering, when one of the other officers came to my room to say that Captain Tabuchi, the Japanese army intelligence officer with whom I had been working, wanted me to attend the dinner even if I couldn't eat anything. Considering the previous two cancellations on their part, I thought this quite unreasonable, but my better nature prevailed and I giddily made the trip to headquarters where I was to be picked up.

Four of us left together for Dr. Kibata's house: Tabuchi, a Captain Nagasawa, a Chinese named Chang, who was described to me smilingly by Tabuchi as "my last remaining agent," and myself. Kibata's house was, as I had heard, "very Western," which meant cold rooms with stiff-backed chairs and bookcases filled with unread classics bound in maroon or brown. On the walls were Japanese and Western paintings. I think I first disliked Kibata after a conversation about one of his paintings.

"Yes, it is a very fine one, painted for me by a Japanese artist who studied in Paris."

"Foujita?" I inquired, mentioning the only such artist I knew of.

"No, someone much better."

This American liberation from Japanese modesty offended me somehow, particularly in the superior, intimate way in which he spoke, as if entitled by his stay in America to dispense with the usual politeness. Again, after Tabuchi told us that it was Dr. Kibata who had assured the local Japanese that the Americans who landed would be gentlemanly, Kibata felt enough a part of America to do what no other Japanese had dared do in my presence, criticize the Americans. On this occasion Kibata was speaking about Japanese swords and what a shame it was that American servicemen who know nothing about their history or beauty were carrying them off to America to rust and be covered by dust. I was irritated at his words, although not entirely disagreeing with them, and answered with some anger, "I think it is far better for Japanese swords to rust over some American mantlepiece than for them to remain in Japanese hands, the perpetual symbol of militarism."

Kibata answered, a little surprised, "But you do not understand.

The sword is not a weapon like a gun or a bayonet. It is an object of art, a wonderful piece of the finest craftsmanship."

"Regardless of its value as a work of art, its feudal significance makes it dangerous." Nagasawa agreed with me while Tabuchi, ever politic, giggled and called for a song. They sang a few pieces, Tabuchi claiming the right to sing last "as the best."

Kibata started then to speak again, this time with a list of his firsts. "I was the first Japanese to ride on the *Empress of Britain*." "I was the first Japanese to cross the George Washington Bridge." "I was the first Japanese to dance with Mary Pickford." Everything he said managed to annoy me, and finally, when he declared in the middle of a conversation I had politely started about his books, "All Western philosophy is embraced in Buddhism and there is much in Buddhism of such profundity that the West has never remotely approached it," I stopped talking to him entirely. I concentrated instead on Nagasawa who appeared to be distinctly liberal and who was unusual in that he would talk about his opinions in front of other Japanese.

As we talked, I heard again the familiar, "The defeat of Japan was unexpectedly a great blessing," a statement which I hesitate usually to accept at face value. As Nagasawa and I became more absorbed in our talk, Kibata and Chang could be heard exchanging biographical data, while Tabuchi, growing more and more restless, again called for music. Tabuchi was very jolly, but always one could sense the careful limits which his training at the military academy and as an intelligence officer had set for him. I could hear Chang telling of having studied in Japan and of his elder brother who had married a Japanese woman. Considering the fact that pro-Japanese sympathies nowadays can lead even to execution, Chang's attempt to associate himself and his family with the Japanese was surprising to me.

A short while later a Chinese naval officer, Ensign Jen, whom I had met once before at Chinese naval headquarters, was ushered in. He seemed on terms of great familiarity with Kibata and Tabuchi. When last I had seen Jen we had spoken in Chinese, to the limit of my abilities, for he spoke almost no English. Although at the same time I had reasoned that almost all of the young Chinese naval officers had probably been trained by the Japanese, I had not wished to offend him by speaking Japanese. Now Jen deplored the fact that I had had to speak with his superior officer, Captain Wan, in my halting Chinese when he could have interpreted for me in Japanese. Jen announced that he would probably soon be going to Annapolis. This was greeted with enthusiasm by all. Someone whispered in my ear that Ensign Jen was "an extremely nice person," a statement that seemed a trifle suspect coming from a Japanese.

Throughout all the above, the others had been eating and drinking while I contented myself with an occasional sip of tea in deference to my diarrhea. Nagasawa was by now very drunk and was imitating all of my gestures from across the table. Tabuchi was singing to himself and joking in a knowing way with Kibata's niece. I felt very tired and we soon left. Ensign Jen remained behind to safeguard the house. On the way in the car, Nagasawa was speaking so wildly that the old woman with us had to caution him about what he said when drunk.

The more I have to do with people like Dr. Kibata among the local Japanese civilians, the easier I can see what they must have been like before surrender compelled them to be courteous even to the Chinese they used to despise. In addition to the few Japanese with whom I have had social relations, I have met a number of civilians in connection with my work. One who came to my office wearing plus fours and who asked reproachfully, "How can you think that a man of my position would stoop to petty spying?" turned out to have done exactly that. This individual had started life as a guide to American tourists in Yokohama and had come to Tsingtao in the early thirties to make the fortune that it was generally believed was awaiting any Japanese in China. He failed to achieve any success and returned to Japan, coming to Tsingtao again in January 1938, aboard a warship in the fleet which staged the Japanese landing there. Presumably as a reward for the information he supplied, the navy allowed him to confiscate Chinese properties, ostensibly in the name of the Japanese navy, but actually for his own use. In that way he became wealthy, influential and tweedy. He joined the International

Club and became great friends with foreigners who liked him for his ability with English, the one crucial test in the relations of Americans and English with foreigners. He formally broke his connections with Japanese naval intelligence, but continued to be known as an ever-ready source of inside information on activities within the city.

Now this pillar of the community is shocked at the Chinese who have confiscated his place of business, so shocked indeed that he wants to give his possessions away to the Americans "so the Chinese can't have them." He is typical of a large percentage of the Japanese community here, except that most have not achieved the aura of respectability with which he clothes himself. Others attempt to ingratiate themselves, one by offering to supply (in conjunction with Dr. Kibata) a list of undesirable Japanese. This person, incidentally, was dismissed from Japanese naval intelligence for having stolen money orders out of letters he had censored.

I am afraid that such men are almost typical of the civilian Japanese here. There are, of course, others like the bookseller or the poor fellow who visits me every morning to leave his treasures, in anticipation of return to Japan, a return he believes to a liberal country of free speech and thought. But it is not such people, whatever their percentage, who give the tone to Japanese society in China. Rather it is the failures, the men who have lost in many places and who finally saw a chance here, who make for the bad reputation shared by all. There is no occupation, however reprehensible, in which they have not engaged in their search for riches, but they have used Koreans and Chinese to absorb the shame of engaging in the most odious employments, opium-selling and the like.

Behind the civilians, it goes without saying, stood the military who were the force backing every civilian move. There was always the threat of action on the part of the *kempeitai* or naval intelligence to enforce any demand, however unreasonable. This is true to the extent that Chinese agents of Japanese naval intelligence would have this fact printed on their calling cards. When such a card was shown to the proprietor of a restaurant, store or brothel, it would generally assure the agent of free service. Similarly, agents would threaten to turn merchants over to the Japanese navy if they failed to grant the agents' demands. In such a case, the agents would report that the merchants in question had engaged in anti-Japanese talk. The situation became so bad that twice, once in 1943, and for a final time in November 1944, lists were published in the Chinese newspapers of agents employed by the Japanese navy who were being dismissed for their illegal activities, and warning civilians not to be coerced by them.

The officer who decided last November to end once and for all the skullduggery of the Chinese agents is Captain Okabe of Tsingtao Base Force Headquarters. Okabe is one of those persons whom one thinks of in terms of "an officer and a gentleman" as soon as one has met him, almost the only Japanese officer I know of whom this can be said without reservations. One always risks being very much disappointed when one decides that any given Japanese officer is not a monster, or, at best, a will-less tool of his superiors, but I will take this chance with Okabe. He has always thought of himself as being above the battle, perhaps because he saw no action during the war. When officers of our 7th Fleet first came to Tsingtao to make arrangements for the surrender of local Japanese naval units, Okabe was surprised when they refused to shake hands and chat in gentlemanly fashion about old times and the things of interest to all men of the sea. He was further shocked when they refused to take his word that there were no mines in local waters, insisting on proof. Okabe's word has apparently come to be more respected by the Americans, for he is now regarded by them, and by the Chinese as well, as the brainiest and most important of the Japanese military here.

The difference between the Japanese army and navy here is surprisingly great, and more surprisingly, like the difference between similar American organizations, there seems to be a higher percentage of regular army officers than navy, perhaps because regular navy officers are usually sent to sea. The navy officers are young college graduates, most of whom entered the service in 1942 or 1943. They are very proud that they are in the navy and of the gentlemanly traditions of the navy, which they contrast at every turn with the crudities of the army. Captain Okabe told me, "I have stated my conviction over and over to the army that they cannot hope to continue with impunity their policies. I have let them know how horrified I have been at various actions of theirs. They, unfortunately, have not seen fit to pay any attention to my words. I am proud to think that the navy has never been guilty of any crimes such as those that may be charged to the army in China. We have always sought to maintain the traditions of the naval service, not only of Japan, but of the entire world."

One of the officers in particular, Lieutenant Ishihara, is always going out of his way to show how American the navy really is. "We 'young officers' (in English) have a kind of code we use that the army wouldn't understand at all. We say 'res' for a 'restaurant,' 'white' for a person with no experience, and 'black' for a person who knows the world. We say 'gunroom officer' for wild young fellows like some of your marine officers here. Oh, there are many words that are the same."

This seems to be the general navy attitude: "We are the gentlemen who have not been so blinded by the war as to forget our cosmopolitanism. The army is all right for fighting, but it is composed of hopelessly crude people." And yet, an officer like Lieutenant Shimagawa, who seems so bright and worldy wise, could use the expression "when Japan was still winning the war" for an event that took place in May 1945.

The army's attitude is not very different from that of our own on occasion. "We were never beaten here in China; our troops are still strong and capable of fighting indefinitely. Of course the navy has been wiped out, but that was only to be expected, considering the methods employed by the navy. We wonder if the results wouldn't have been somewhat different if the army had been in control of those islands in the South Seas or Saipan. We don't think it would have been so easy for you to have occupied them. By the time the fighting reached the Philippines it was too late for us to show our capabilities, for all our supplies had been sunk en route, thanks to the navy."

The navy and army are each very curious to know my attitude

about the other. It is incidentally assumed that Dick and I (as American navy) are as unwilling to associate with the few American army people here as our Japanese counterparts would be, and care is taken to invite us to different parties.

The Japanese admiral in command here, Vice Admiral Kaneko, is mentally deranged, as appears to be recognized tacitly by all hands. Once when I visited the coke factory where the navy is being quartered, I was amazed to see the admiral walking through crowds of sailors with no one paying any attention to him. The commanding general, on the other hand, is still very active. General Nagano invited Dick and myself to a dinner the other night. The dinner was given at the home of a retired general. The house was a trifle less gloomily Western than most Japanese efforts along those lines, but the contrast with the beautiful, spacious Japanese-style rooms was as great as usual. At dinner, the Japanese officers present discussed what they would do when they were demobilized. General Nagano smiled and said, "All I have ever done is to be a soldier. I don't know any useful trade. I guess I'll have to be a dish-washer." "But," someone objected, "even dish-washing requires a certain amount of skill." General Nagano laughed. "Perhaps I can't even do that then."

After dinner the general presented Dick and myself with a fine sword each, as well as a piece of pottery. With each sword came a letter describing it. I read my letter through hastily and was amused to discover that the general had written that he was giving me the sword because I stood as a representative of the highest ideals of *bushidō*. That indeed was a novel role for me to be playing. Can the general really have been so deceived as to think that I possess the military virtues that are generally associated with *bushidō*? Or does he mean merely that I have been considerate to him, a great simplification of the term.

The retired general, our host, was full of praise for the marines. "When the marines first landed, we heard many dreadful stories of what we could expect from them. One day my daughter was forced to go by a marine post on the way to the hospital. She could scarcely sleep the night before, worrying about that dreadful moment when she would have to pass the sentry, of the possible indignities she might suffer. When she came home that evening I was surprised to see that she looked quite calm. I asked her, 'What happened today? Did you have any trouble?' 'Oh no,' she replied, 'quite the contrary. Just as I was passing the sentry, an old Japanese man, equally frightened at the prospect, was hurrying so fast that the cord of his right clog was broken. He looked around for a piece of string or something with which to fasten the clog to his foot. The American sentry saw this, reached down and took out his own shoelace and gave it to the old man. I have never been more moved.' That is only one case of many kindnesses of the Americans." Even as our host spoke, I could see tears in his eyes. It was impossible for me to believe the story, and yet Americans are capable of such kindness, I know. I hope that this is the type of *bushidō* for which the general was complimenting me.

So far all the persons I have described I have met because of my duties or as a result of my special effort. I thought surely there would be more people who would be actively interested in meeting a young American officer. I did indeed find one note under my door, not necessarily addressed to me.

We-Wel-Come the Great U.S.A. Friend
To Establish the Eternal Peace of the World
ELISHA YOUNG
(Regeneration 18th March 1933)
The Prime Minister of
the International Christian Association
The President of
the Tsingtao Christian College
The Master of
the Chinese Light Association.

I wish he had left his address.

Don

◆ ◆ ◆

FROM OTIS CARY IN TOKYO
TO DON KEENE IN TSINGTAO

November 5, 1945

Dear Don,

The other day I finally got the full story on the Wake trials.

As you know, the people down on Kwajalein quickly found out that Dave's prisoner had been misquoted. His testimony was honest, and he had told me before that it rested simply on hearsay. The mistake belonged to those who exaggerated his claims in reporting them.

That part of it was straightened out when I went down to Kwajalein. But I was not satisfied to throw the prisoner's testimony out just because it was hearsay. I had known the prisoner for some time and thought him a reasonably intelligent person. It was hard for me to see how he could be taken in by such a rumor, on a small island where it could be checked immediately, unless there was some fact behind it. The unanimous testimony of the Wake garrison, contradicting the prisoner, did not impress me too much. They had had plenty of time to rehearse it.

I left Kwajalein before anything more was learned, but the investigation was continued on the assumption that there must have been some truth in the prisoner's story. More than a dozen key men from the Japanese garrison were detained after the others were repatriated to Japan. Most of them were staff officers. Dave had a big hand in selecting three or four of them who were segregated from the rest and placed on a separate island. With them were the two prisoners from Pearl Harbor, and a Nisei who had been discovered among the Japanese on Wake and put to good use by our forces as an interpreter. A special attempt was made to treat the three or four men squarely and well, so as to gain their confidence. They had some work to do around an admiral's quarters, polishing floors, cutting the grass, and doing other easy jobs, but they also had considerable time to themselves, had good food, and were taken to the movies frequently. The two friendly prisoners and the Nisei were with them constantly, and gradually sounded them out on the truth about Wake. They were made to understand that there was nothing to fear from the Americans, as long as they told the truth, which would in any case come out eventually. That was enough. They broke down and substantiated the original prisoner's story.

Meanwhile Admiral Sakaibara, the Wake commander, had been worked on without success over at Kwajalein Island. When he was confronted with the others' confessions, however, he gave in and confessed himself. He wrote out a detailed account of the crime, which was given to a language officer named Gardiner. The hundred Americans, he said, had been shot by the headquarters company at his command when an American landing was thought imminent.

At the trial, Sakaibara made a last attempt to exonerate himself by repudiating the confession, but there was already enough evidence from other sources to convict him. He and nine others were sentenced to hang; five more got life imprisonment. Just before the sentence was read, Sakaibara made his final stand against the court and American justice. "As we are about to receive the decision of an American court, I would like to request that the people who planned and carried out the dropping of atomic bombs on Japan should be regarded in the same light as we."

When I was there at Kwajalein, I had occasion to discuss the case with an American admiral whose command was roughly analogous to that of Sakaibara at Wake. I described the circumstances of the crime, as originally told to me by the prisoner. The Japanese garrison had been given an extra ration of grog, in expectation of an American landing the next morning. They girded up their loins to die for the emperor and killed the Americans as a precautionary measure. The American admiral imagined himself in a similar position and admitted that he would have done the same thing Sakaibara did, if he had had a hundred Japanese prisoners on his hands. Atoll fighting is such that it would be hopeless to keep the prisoners alive, without ruining his own defense or surrendering early in the fight.

Lastly, I should mention that, except for a very lucky accident, the true fate of the Americans on Wake might never have become known. The prisoner who gave us the story was the only man ever to "escape" from that island. In the fall of 1944, starvation was already threatening the Japanese garrison, and the men apparently took turns fishing just outside the reef. One day when the future prisoner and a comrade were out there in a small boat, a storm came up and drove them out to sea. They drifted for thirty-odd days and the other fellow died. An American destroyer finally picked the prisoner up when he weighed less than fifty pounds.

Otis

♦ ♦ ♦

FROM TED DE BARY IN TOKYO AND OSAKA TO DON KEENE IN TSINGTAO

November 12, 1945

Dear Don,

During the past two weeks I have been traveling around the countryside a good deal, part of the time by jeep, but mostly by train. It has made me realize how few Americans in the occupation force could say that they had actually been living among the Japanese for the past two months. Those who are stationed in smaller towns and cities could, perhaps, say it with more justice than those in the metropolitan atmosphere of Tokyo, but it has been impossible for anyone to live here as the Japanese do, and few would want to if they could. An American necessarily lives the life of a colonial, in the sense that he obviously does not intend to become a part of native society, but continues to be a foreign observer, living on the fringe of that society in the manner to which he has always been accustomed.

Americans come to Japan, or to any country in the Far East, with what they like to think is a charitable attitude toward other human beings. This is probably even more true of the tourists, businessmen, and diplomats, who lived here before the war, than it is of the GIs, whose kindness and generosity are given so much publicity these days. I don't mean that the average GI is less well-intentioned than prewar visitors, but he is naturally inclined to think of the Japanese as enemies, and any little act of charity toward them seems, with that in mind, like a big one. To the Japanese also, expecting to be treated as they would treat enemies, it seems like great charity.

It is often said that this characteristic American attitude is something deeper than simple magnanimity, that it is fundamentally a sense of respect for the personal dignity of every human being. Perhaps this is true of the best among us, but I am not sure that it is true of the majority. Only when you have placed yourself on a level with the Japanese, and have given up, in some situation common to them, the privileges which an American usually enjoys, do you realize how much the attitude derives from our privileged position among other peoples. Our generosity seems hardly to be more than would be expected of persons who have been given, or are owed, everything. We are top dog, we have almost everything we could want for ourselves, and it is easy to be generous with what is left over. To take care of ourselves, we generally do not have to push other people around.

It is not so easy, however, to preserve that same generous, respectful attitude when the privileges are gone. It is not so easy, for instance, when one faces the comparatively simple problem of riding for a long distance in a third-class coach on a Japanese train. Ordinarily, American servicemen have second-class coaches provided for them. If the second-class seats are filled when an American gets on a train, the stationmaster frequently clears out enough of the Japanese occupants so that he does not have to stand. This sort of service is new to most Americans, but it is also very convenient, and we quickly come to accept it, even to expect it.

But occasionally it happens that one of us will have to take a train which has no second-class coaches, or will board a train when no stationmaster is available to clear the conqueror's way. Then travel becomes for the American exactly what it is for the Japanese these days—a long, painful struggle to keep on his feet, with others pressing in upon him from all sides, lurching with the train, sticking their snot-filled noses under his (malnutrition has brought colds to everyone, and handkerchiefs are almost unknown) and gaping at him with their stinking mouths open. To the foul odors of breath and body are added those which arise from the ubiquitous packs and bundles, full of pungent vegetables, that Japanese carry from farm to city on passenger trains because the system of food distribution has broken down. There is, I find, an advantage in having one's feet pinned to the floor by a sack of sweet potatoes; I lurch as crazily as before, but at least I am anchored to one spot. There is no compensation, however, for the radishes which scrape back and forth across my cheek. With the train already so crowded, I wonder to myself, my irritation mounting with each prickly caress, why these crazy people could not make some other arrangement for their vegetables and their bulky packs of household effects. Reasoning that they have no immediate alternative does no good. In my furious annoyance at such prolonged discomfort, any sympathetic reasoning is shortly disposed of; I curse the Japanese as a nation for not having taken care of the problem on a national scale the way we Americans would have done. Lashing out against a whole mass of people, even more sluggish and immovable than this train crowd, I am, of course, just doubly frustrated.

My self-control did not return, no matter what efforts I made, until the ride was ended. In the meantime my silent agony continued. Even innocent babes, suffering on their weary mothers' backs and buffeted mercilessly by the jolting crowd, did not move me to sympathy. On other occasions when I was riding comfortably in a second-class coach, I can remember eagerly seeking the company of mothers with tiny live bundles fastened to their backs. I would talk with them when I could, and I was always delighted when the infant was given a ball of rice, because it amused me to watch him clutch it with his small hands and smear his face trying to eat it. Actually I would save the sugar and candy from my K-ration just for an opportunity to watch some baby suck blissfully on it. But here in this third-class car both my heart and my humor were frozen within an hour. I talked to no one and smiled at no one. The babies became almost repulsive, sucking into their mouths the mucus that streamed out of their noses, emitting from their other ends an odor of excrement that smothered me. Japanese infants must relieve themselves like any others, I suppose, even if the primitive train toilet is inaccessible to mothers so caught in the mob they cannot make one step in its direction. At one station I saw a mother, lucky enough to sit by a window, hold her child on the sill with its bottom in the open air. When the excrement had been safely deposited on the station platform, at or on the feet of those pressing to get inside, the baby was brought in and matter-of-factly rearranged to nurse at its mother's breast.

It is common for passengers to board the train through windows as well as through doors. Persons sitting next to windows generally help others to climb in and out. Indeed, the Japanese seem quite used to the problems which arise from having far more people than facilities to provide for them. They are both good-natured and very unreasonable about it. Few ever get angry about the confusion or discomfort, but at the same time few try to minimize it by acting sensibly. At each stop the crowd trying to get aboard will press into the entrance before anyone can get off, and the result is a long deadlock of opposing forces, shoving, burrowing, charging and shouting at each other. At such critical moments there is no gallantry toward women or kindness to babies and small children. Only occasionally, when once inside the train, some traveler will offer to help an old lady remove the pack from her back.

Even to an old New York subway rider, this sort of melee has little resemblance to rush hour at Times Square. On one of my trips, having finally reached my stop, I walked away from the station and wondered what in my experience could approximate the scene I had just left. My memory brought forth a curious parallel—the sight of ants on Okinawa pulling a captured worm to their hole under my cot. The worm got caught on a little twig sticking out of the ground, caught like a horseshoe ringing the stake. The ants pulled for hours on both ends until finally, by accident I think, they managed to pull both ends of the worm around the same side of the twig. Their irrational behavior was certainly close to that of the mob struggling to get on and off these trains.

I realize now how dangerous it is to be reminded of ants in such a situation. The next step is to think of all fellow passengers as more animal or insect than human. All considerations apart from my own personal wants are then too quickly tossed aside. It becomes easy to wish, for example, that the price of a train ticket might be raised to keep so many people from traveling—not a generous idea for an American who rides, however he rides, at the expense of the very people he wishes to keep off the train.

I remember, Don, what you said in an earlier letter about the great gap which separates Western morality from that of the Far East. But despite this, it is an easy thing, when you are devastated by discomforts of all sorts, to fall into a brutish frame of mind. Just a few minutes in a strange situation shows how readily human weakness adapts itself to a foreign attitude, or elaborates whatever new molds of morality are suggested by the circumstances. An American in a typically Japanese situation will react as does a Japanese who has been used to a life of privilege when he finds himself in the same situation. It is so natural to want to spare oneself the suffering of the masses, even if it means more suffering for them.

Americans are annoyed by the ceremoniousness of the Japanese—the fancy talk, the elaborate servility, the awkward "hiss, haha," which is really an affectation of embarrassment to flatter others. But while we joke at the bowing and scraping, we are not apt to resist the temptations of caste and privilege which lie behind it, and are often annoyed if the privileges are denied us.

I was a little slow to learn, as many other American servicemen did, the sure way to avoid the terrors of ordinary train travel. It is to ride in the motorman's cab, which is clean and pleasant on an electric train, or in the baggageman's special compartment This privilege is ordinarily reserved for railroad employees or personal friends of theirs, but no objection is made to an American availing himself of it. Nothing is ever denied an American who is aggressive enough.

Thus, one day when I wanted to go down the coast to Mishima, I rode with the baggageman. We talked about many things of little interest, and only when the train had almost reached Mishima did I mention my reason for making this trip. It was to see the wife of a prisoner I met on Okinawa, and to tell her that her husband still lived. Although I am usually very cautious in talking about prisoners to people who might know their families and gossip about their "disgrace," the baggageman was going through to Nagoya, and there seemed to be no danger in confiding the prisoner's story to him.

I was mistaken, however, for the news was out by the time I had passed through the station and stopped to ask someone the way to the city hall. A station employee came running up to say that he had heard the whole story from the baggageman and would gladly guide me wherever I wanted to go. My response was not very cordial. Annoyed at my own indiscretion and the swiftness with which the gossip had been passed on, I hoped somehow to discourage this man from prying any further into the business. It would be enough, I said, if he just told me how to find the city hall. Still he persisted, saying that the place was difficult for a stranger to find and that he wished to help the American who had done so much for an unfortunate fellow countryman.

I resigned myself to his company and we walked quickly through the main part of town, while he told with enthusiasm how overjoyed the prisoner's family would be to hear the news. He repeated many times his own gratitude for American kindness toward captured Japanese soldiers. I would have liked to respond with equal warmth to his friendliness, but my mind was still uneasy, suspecting that his ingratiating remarks were prompted only by curiosity and the hope of further injecting himself into the matter. When we finally reached the city hall, however, he made no attempt to prolong his usefulness to me. While I was talking to the desk clerk, my guide slipped unceremoniously out of the building, without even waiting for my thanks. Then, too late, I was convinced of his sincerity and reproached myself for having been so suspicious of him.

You may wonder why I went straight to the most public place in town on an errand which I regarded as so confidential. Oddly enough, the city hall was the only definite address my prisoner could give me for his family. His wife was the mayor's daughter. He guessed that she had returned to her own home during the bombing of Tokyo, and told me what a fine man the mayor was, how he had spent many years as a consular official in New Orleans and Havana, spoke good English and Spanish, and had a knowledge of the world rare among Japanese.

There was a great commotion when I asked for the mayor. A roomful of petty officials and clerks stared at me and at each

other, seemingly unable to answer my inquiry. A girl was sent
scurrying upstairs. She came down a few minutes later with the
assistant mayor, who told me that the mayor had gone to Tokyo.
I realized then that the people had probably thought I came on
some piece of occupation business and would be infuriated to find
the mayor gone. They were relieved when I explained that
Rinko-*san*, the mayor's daughter, was the one I really wanted to
see. The assistant mayor quickly sent someone for his hat and took
me to the daughter's home.

Rinko lived with her father-in-law, not her father, in a frame
house connected to a small Buddhist temple. There was no priest
around and they seemed to act as caretakers for the temple. At
the entrance, I was greeted by Rinko herself, a woman just on
the brink of middle age with a sweet smile and tired eyes. I
introduced myself and sat down to take off my shoes, while I
explained the reason for my visit. The news of her husband was
naturally a shock to her. She did nothing more than look search-
ingly at me, speechless. A Japanese bringing the same news
would probably have prepared her for it by involved introductions, or he might even have had a good friend of the family
ease her into the matter. But this sort of approach was impossible
for me, and I was actually relieved by her stupefied expression,
since it showed that she at least believed me, even if the news
was unbelievable.

After a few seconds, I was taken inside to wait while tea was
being made. I waited a long time and wondered why Rinko
did not come back sooner, impatient to hear more of the details
about her husband. When the door at last slid open, the prisoner's
father came in and sat opposite me at the low table. Rinko came
and sat at one side, serving. For the next twenty minutes I did
all the talking, remembering everything I could about the
prisoner's capture, his starved, wild appearance on first arriving
at the stockade and in what good health I last saw him. I told
them about the English classes we had organized while I waited
for orders back to Pearl Harbor; Rinko's husband was the instructor for the officers. I described the stockade, the food, the
little patches of sweet potato and onion cultivated under the tent

guy ropes. I finished with a description of the battle for Okinawa, and then waited to hear what else Rinko and her father-in-law wanted to know.

Rinko smiled, but said nothing. She was embarrassed because I had been speaking more to her than to the head of the house. For his part, the old man chose to ask nothing more about his son, asking instead innumerable questions about me. From these he turned to talking about himself and his career as a teacher and writer of history. It was only when he left the room to find a tract he had written on some obscure point in Japanese history that I had a chance to talk to Rinko again. She showed me a book of family photographs taken in New York, New Orleans and Havana—pictures of herself with American and Cuban girls, pictures taken at the beach, aboard ship, on hotel verandahs and in the luxurious landscapes of southern places. Rinko was a happy, smiling schoolgirl then, and she still had one of those little autograph books in which schoolgirls keep the farewells of their companions: "Here's to a pal, here's to a friend, here's to a girl who is true to the end." In Spanish and German were tributes to Rinko's goodness, more eloquent than the typical American variety. They were all dated in the early twenties, proving that Rinko could not be as old as she now looked. Her sad eyes followed mine as I leafed through the souvenirs of her youth abroad and saw how many unkept promises that happy life in the Western paradise must have made her—the freedom, comfort and security that might have been hers, if she had not been a Japanese woman, if the war had not taken away her home and husband and left her almost a prisoner of his father. I closed the photograph album and she said, with an effort to remember her English, "It is just like a dream."

My visit with Rinko was short, for it was already mid-afternoon and I had a long train ride ahead to reach Tokyo that night. She and the old man walked me to the station in order to bring back an umbrella which they insisted I take, since it had been raining most of the day. As we passed through the narrow lanes, along drainage ditches spilling over with clean rainwater, the sun came through a clearing sky and made the dripping town sparkle. Rinko's spirits seemed to brighten with the weather. She joked about American gallantry when, automatically, I stopped to let her go first between the big puddles in the road. At the station neither she nor the old man showed any embarrassment at associating themselves so conspicuously with the only American on the platform, perhaps because they did not suspect that anyone else knew the secret of our friendship. While we were waiting for the train, however, I noticed standing in a group of men across the platform the guide who had earlier taken me to the city hall. I was suddenly afraid that he might intrude to embarrass Rinko with his knowledge of the secret, but he made no move to join us.

When the train pulled in, I stopped at the second-class entrance and turned to shout a last good-bye. Rinko may have wondered why, at the last minute, I waved to someone behind her. She did not see my guide wave back at me with a great smile on his face.

Ted

◆ ◆ ◆

FROM SHERRY MORAN IN TOKYO
TO DON KEENE IN TSINGTAO

November 14, 1945

Dear Don,

A few days ago I made a tour of the Kanda section in search of the books and dictionaries you asked for. I could have picked a better day for it. When I left work in the afternoon, it was raining; there were no jeeps available and I would probably have done much better for myself by going home and warming up with a bottle and a couple of army blankets. All but a small part of the Kanda section was burned out. Its few remaining stores had only trade/school texts, popular bilge about the co-prosperity sphere and art photographs at impossible prices.

On the way back I fell in step with a young man wearing a sporty Swiss fedora. His name was Kōnō (rhyming with Oh, no!), and since that day my acquaintance with him has flowered into a steady round of engagements, at his invitation, through which I have met many of his friends in their own homes. As a result of this intensive campaign to show me around, I feel a little like a freshman during fraternity rush-week. There is nothing insidious in his motives, and I cannot blame him for having to entertain me in the homes of others since his own was burned down, but it does seem odd that he should have gone to the trouble of making so many engagements for me in such a short space of time. Until last night the engagements always included supper. I enjoy dining out, but with food so scarce I find it unpleasant to go into a Japanese home and eat more food than a month's ration would normally provide. What I am given, of course, actually comes from the black market, but that fact only makes me more uneasy, since I am eating at the expense of many poor Japanese and not simply at the expense of my host.

Last night I avoided this unpleasantness by resolving to break off my visit well before dinner time, but I doubt that I shall ever try to be so considerate again, and I certainly would not have had the courage to go through with it this time unless Tavey Thorlaksson had been along to support me against the horrified protestations of our host.

It soon became apparent that I would regret cutting our visit so short. Upon our arrival, Kōnō introduced us to an extremely alert and active businessman who had somehow managed to write a great deal for newspapers and magazines. He was a man with pronounced views on public questions and has been regarded by the Japanese as an authoritative commentator—Kōnō introduced him as "Mr. Sumida, the Walter Lippman of Japan." I was immediately impressed in his favor by the fact that Sumida did not try to follow up this introduction with a song and dance about being a liberal whose hands were tied during the war and who was now rejoicing in a new-found freedom. He admitted freely that Japan had erred in going to war, but he doubted that democracy could succeed in Japan and had much to say in criticism of the medicine we were offering the beaten Japanese. He had none of the ordinary Japanese liberal's hazy notion of what liberalism meant, nor did he show an uncritically joyful acceptance of Americans such as I have found in many other Japanese.

Sumida dominated the conversation, and I found this to my

liking, because it prevented awkward pauses from arising due to our slowness in speaking Japanese. He first told us about himself. He was a member of the International Steamship Company, a small firm which had specialized in high-speed runs between New York and Japan. Ever since his boyhood in Kure, the seaport and naval base, he had been engaged in maritime enterprises, and he felt that his country should always be a maritime power. The idea of Japan having to rely solely on other countries' ships for overseas trade was extremely repugnant to him.

One of Sumida's reasons for thinking Japan entitled to a merchant marine of her own was his belief that Japanese seamen are superior to American. He admitted that Japan had misjudged Americans in many things, before and during the war, but his own experience convinced him of this superiority. Japanese seamen were much better behaved in port, better disciplined and more conscientious aboard ship. They liked the sea; in most cases they had grown up, like himself, in communities of sea-going people. And the average Japanese was not only proud of his country's merchant marine, but regarded it as a privilege to travel in other parts of the world, where he was quick to learn what he could about other peoples. Americans, on the other hand, were disorderly in foreign ports and never seemed satisfied with their work at sea.

I felt sure that in the back of his mind Sumida was thinking of the fact that American merchant seamen are unionized and therefore less docile in the hands of people running steamship lines. But I let the matter pass, since it does not pay to get too controversial with a man like this—you would have less time to learn his opinions on other subjects. Sumida continued.

"There were, however, many points on which we misjudged you Americans. We thought your lack of native culture meant that you were weak. We thought your easygoing ways showed lack of moral stamina, and that your treatment of women indicated an exclusive preoccupation with sex. We did not know that you could be so tough, could make the sacrifices necessary to beat us.

"I first began to change my mind about Americans when I had occasion to notice the endurance of some B–29 pilots in a prison camp. They saved even the orange peels from their meager rations. This demonstrated a will to live which I had not expected of them. No Japanese in a prison camp would go to such lengths to preserve his strength and keep himself alive."

Sumida then launched into a discussion of the dangers facing our occupation. Although our troops had been well received and there were no open signs of hostility, Sumida thought we would be mistaken to assume that there was actually no resentment against us. There was, first of all, deep disappointment over the defeat itself which would be directed against us as living conditions grew worse for the Japanese, and as the Japanese became used to the unferociousness of the GI—something which now is a great source of surprise and respect. Sumida did not expect actual fighting to break out, but he was sure that the first wave of our popularity was bound to subside and that resentment would be manifested in minor incidents. He asked me if many Americans were not taken in by the docile behavior of the Japanese, and deceived into thinking that everybody was glad to see the war over. I said I couldn't generalize on anything as broad as that, but if he meant there were no Japanese who were glad, then I was sure GIs were being duped and I among them.

"I wonder," Sumida said, "if many Americans do not share our apprehension over the rising tide of communism. Of course there must be free elections, freedom of speech, freedom of this and that. But isn't MacArthur going too far in letting even the communists share this freedom? What will you do if Japan goes communist in the next elections?"

I tried to avoid a direct answer. "We do not think a communist victory very likely. It seems odd that you, and many other Japanese to whom I have spoken, should be so afraid of the communists. How can they win if everyone is opposed to them?"

"You do not understand how fickle the masses are. In a bad situation, they might be as easily swayed to communism as they were to militarism—particularly if the communists had money from Russia to work with."

"We do realize that," I replied, "but in the present situation, we are more interested in establishing democratic processes than we are worried about the communists."

"That seems strangely unrealistic for Americans—to be more interested in processes than in results. One election could wipe out all you had accomplished."

"That's true," I answered, impressed by his reasoning and anxious to meet it with arguments that would not put too much of a strain on my poor Japanese. "In America, where democratic processes are already established, we concentrate on beating undemocratic parties at the polls, instead of denying them the same rights we enjoy. That is what we hope you will do."

Sumida did not seem much comforted by the example of America, so far from Russia, so wealthy and so powerful. He emphasized that Japan was beset by many problems we did not have to face, problems which had already prompted the Japanese to try violent solutions. Population pressure, for instance. He repeated the old argument for Japanese: that the home islands could not support such a large population. I replied that, although the U.S. did not have this problem, many other nations in the Far East did, and it was no real solution to expand Japanese territory at the expense of people who needed it just as badly. The argument became deadlocked, with Sumida insisting on the injustice of making the Japanese live in an area the size of California. Finally he conceded at least this much to the Americans: that they had not taken advantage of the war to expand their own territorial holdings.

"But the Japanese people will never forget Korea lost, Sakhalin and the Kuriles ceded to Russia, Formosa and Manchuria given to China. After all, those are Japanese territories and eventually they must be given back to us."

I could not help but smile at the pretension that Manchuria was truly a part of Japan. I visualized maps of Japan with Sakhalin, Korea, Manchuria and Formosa marked in bright red: "Remember the Four Stolen Territories." When I was in Peking in 1935, almost every student's room at Yenching University had a map showing the four stolen provinces of Manchuria marked in the same way.

Sumida guessed what I was thinking, and said that he realized the rest of the world did not see it as the Japanese did, but that as a fact to be dealt with, the average Japanese would never forget.

As the time approached for us to go, however, Sumida attempted to reach some common ground by saying, "These problems will eventually work themselves out in a natural way. Culture is like water; it seeks out the lowest level. With free intercourse the advantages of American culture could flow to us. Similarly there is much that is good in Japan which will flow to you."

I was somewhat annoyed by this neat teacupful of phoney tolerance, just as I am irritated by people who say with an air of patient endurance, "I will try to explain to you our feeling about the emperor. When you return to America, you can explain to your friends what the emperor means to us, because you have lived here and understand our true feelings." I am well aware that most Americans do not understand what the emperor means to the Japanese, but it would do the Japanese just as much good to consider our attitude toward the emperor, or just toward emperors generally, as to make us understand theirs. And it would also do them good, I explained to Sumida, to realize that most Americans do not give a damn now about Japanese culture, except as it proves susceptible of reform. To many Americans today, Japan means nothing except a nation of war-makers who have brought death into their families.

It was, of course, too much of an outburst, and you may wonder why Sumida did not just throw us out of his house. I think, however, that he wanted me to be frank with him, and understood that I was not really condemning all aspects of Japanese culture. I just wanted to warn him against assuming that Japan's recent enemies were now ready to welcome her back into the family of nations without any hard feelings over the past. Many Japanese simply do not realize how much hostility they will have to face abroad; they talk of wanting to travel in the States and learn American ways, which would be a good thing, full of rewards for the individuals who did so, if they waited a few years to do their traveling. But can you imagine a delegation of "cultural ambassadors" going to the States now?

Sherry

◆ ◆ ◆

FROM DON KEENE IN TSINGTAO
TO TED DE BARY IN TOKYO

November 15, 1945

Dear Ted,

I wonder if there isn't something in the air or the buildings of certain towns that makes them good or bad, little devils or angels who can make an identical building seem so different a hundred miles away. Returning to Tsingtao yesterday I suddenly felt the difference. Was it the remembrance of Tsingtao's faults brought on by the sight of the begging children or the sailors reeling down the streets that imbued the buildings with the drab, sallow look of the foreigner in China? Or the cheap signs fronting newly painted dance halls that returned to me the weariness I had forgotten for over a week?

Tsinan was different. When I told people I was going there, those who knew the town shook their heads and warned me, "There is nothing interesting in the whole city. Except maybe the lake, and that is so dirty. The city is filthy, not like Tsingtao." From the air I could feel nothing toward the sprawling black mass on the brown countryside. I had left Tsingtao in a dive-bomber and had watched the Shantung countryside go by for an hour or more, the little, black, walled villages polka-dotting the drab landscape. Occasionally, on the top of a hill one could see a monastery, and here and there a pagoda towered over lonesome trees, but mostly there were the villages, some seemingly separated by a few hundred yards at the most, each a tight little entity. Probably two such little villages, divided only by a stream any mouse could jump across, were violently antagonistic, spoke entirely different dialects, and considered one another a barbarian menace to the way of life they were fighting to preserve. Tsinan seemed a larger village, with a red fringe of brickyards and new factories. It wasn't until we had arrived in the city from the airport that any impression was formed at all. I had left the hotel, a shaking remembrance of the German occupation, and was walking down a street when suddenly a loudspeaker phonograph started to play "Valencia" with a determined frenzy that carried all before it. This sudden intrusion of the West quite possibly should have struck a jarring note in so Chinese a city, but it acted rather as a catalytic agent in dissolving Tsingtao's burden of a spurious West. I knew that I would enjoy Tsinan tremendously, that it would not betray me.

I discovered very quickly after my arrival that people thought that I had something to do with Marshal Ho and Major General McClure, who had arrived earlier in the morning on a kind of inspection tour. There were banners and archways and posters in every direction, proclaiming the city's joy in welcoming the supreme commander. General McClure did not pass unnoticed. "Welcome Kindly General McClure," one purple and green banner shouted from a wall. Further down the street, "General McClure is the Kindly Leader of the World," and on a building at the Provincial Government, "General McClure is the Kindly Guidance of the World." "What a wonderful place Tsinan is," I thought. "They have found out the truth about a problem which has long worried me, and they have proclaimed it to the world. At last I know who's responsible for it all." (Later, when I met Miss Tsui, she praised General McClure in no uncertain terms. "I like General McClure. He is so . . ." "Kindly?" I suggested.) I saw a picture in the newspaper of the general. I would have known him anywhere by his twinkling eyes, his rosy cheeks (a trifle smudged in the printing) and the genial chuckle that I could divine rather than see. I knew that I would be secure in Tsinan, that I need not worry about any Eighth Route Army interference with my plans.

In Tsingtao I had been one officer out of many (*e pluribus unum*), but in Tsinan I was almost all of the American armed forces in one semi-integrated whole. My mission was not exactly clear to me, but I determined to find out as much about the city as I could and write a report that would astound by its volume, its quality and its joie de vivre. After paying my respects to the Chinese in the form of leaving my card at the general's headquarters, I went back to more familiar ground, the Japanese consulate. In a few hours I was sitting in my accustomed place of honor at a *sukiyaki* [Japanese dish of beef and vegetables cooked in soy sauce] dinner, listening to the usual exclamations of delight at my proficiency with chopsticks, my ability to eat Japanese pickled spinach and my general remarkability in being able to sit with crossed legs for an hour or more without writhing in agony.

At dinner the conversation developed mainly along the lines of an interview, with myself as subject. As the first American with whom Mr. and Mrs. Mori and their guests had ever spoken, at least since the outbreak of the war, I naturally was an object of considerable interest. Someone asked me about the university I had attended, and when I answered, Mr. Mori interrupted with, "I used to know a fellow who graduated from Columbia. He was a Nisei from Hawaii who couldn't even speak proper Japanese and had returned to Japan just before the war so that he could go through a Japanese university as well. Once the war started, he was cut off from funds at home and was unable to make any money for himself. I met him quite by accident one day, noticing his shabby clothes and his hungry look. I gave him money and clothes a few times, but then I was sent to China and lost all track of him.

"Early this year when I went back I saw him again. He was in the uniform of the naval air force. It seems that he was unable to stay out of the service any longer because of his poverty and because of various pressures to which he was subjected. He went off to train in Korea. The next time he came to Japan was in May of this year. He arrived from Genzan, in Korea, with a wonderful big fish and some other food that was impossible to get in Tokyo. When he met me he said that he wanted to have a big party that night, a great celebration. I asked the occasion for such festivity and he told me that he was to take off the next day on a suicide mission off Okinawa. That night we had a wonderful party, much drinking, much singing. The Nisei sang Hawaiian songs and danced a hula. Naturally no word was said about what was to happen the next day. I think that the party must have lasted until three or four o'clock in the morning, we enjoyed ourselves so very much. We shook hands and said good-bye without any special display. I was told later that he took off that morning."

When Mr. Mori finished his story we drank a little and the subject of conversation changed again. Mrs. Mori, unlike most Japanese women who habitually shrink from any share of the social activities of their husbands, took an active part in our talk. She asked me if I would like to marry a Japanese woman, to which I replied that I found them too retiring. "Not my wife!" laughed Mr. Mori. "She's a regular tomboy!" Mrs. Mori answered with, "I'm in favor of women's rights. I would like to stand up in the Diet and tell the people there, 'Hear ye! Hear ye! The reason Japan was defeated is that the Japanese women were made fools of.' " She didn't mean it, of course, but I was delighted to hear her say so.

The ten days in Tsinan were remarkable for me in the vast amounts of food I consumed of every type, for the varied people I met, and, most of all, for the new identity of Captain Keene, the mysterious powerful being who could summon airplanes from out of the sky or cause the flames of hell to lick high over the head of any transgressor. My name appeared in the headlines without any explanation, as if everyone knew that Chin Tang-na (my name in Chinese) was President Truman's vicar in Tsinan. There were rumors that I was the forerunner of large bodies of marines. I upset economic conditions; I caused the wicked to tremble in their shoes and brought deluding solace to the good.

The people I met included Governor Ho Ssu-yuan, General Yang Kung-yeh, a Mr. Tsui, who, my interpreter Lieutenant Friendly Wang assured me, is the governor's "supreme advisor," and a number of Japanese of varied qualities. Governor Ho has studied in the United States, France and Germany. He said with a smile, "Little did I ever think when I was studying philosophy that I would ever be leading a band of guerrilla troops or that I would become governor of Shantung." I was favorably impressed with the governor, even when assured by some wise old rumor-monger that he had five wives, and even when I was informed that all of the so-called pro-Chungking guerrillas in Shantung had co-operated with the Japanese to the point of having close liasion with them in their campaign to crush the communists. Governor Ho, in his description of his frantic rush for Tsinan which followed the end of hostilities, failed to mention the fact that the outfit he was leading into Tsinan was surrounded by the Eighth Route Army and was saved only by the intercession of Japanese troops. The picture he painted of the loyal and courageous supporters of the Generalissimo fighting enemies of all kinds and on all sides was so appealing to me that I was almost ready to accept it against evidence. The pro-Chungking troops have had so sorry a record here. A Japanese officer told me that the Central Government troops would not have lasted a week in Shantung had they not been protected by the Japanese. The Central Government troops and the Japanese did not engage one another in fighting except by mistake. It must have been a difficult decision for Chinese to make that resulted in their fighting with the Japanese against fellow Chinese for ideological reasons; why the communists should have appeared more dangerous and distasteful than the Japanese is apparent only when the parallel experience of France in recent years is compared. It is almost impossible for me to see what persuaded Chinese to join any one of the "loyal" guerrilla bands. There could certainly have been very little conviction about General Chiang Kai-shek's policies or the necessity of a unified China, at least in the minds of the rank and file. If money or food was the sole consideration, the puppet troops would have been a better choice, for the Japanese army with its comparative abundance was always within shouting distance as support. I should like to have asked Governor Ho just who his followers were, if they resembled the Peace Preservation Troops who stalk moodily through the streets of Tsingtao. Talking to Governor Ho, I found it impossible to believe that he could actively have been a collaborationist. Almost impossible, anyway, for in conversations with Colonel Kato, an old Japanese artillery officer who was head of a kind of liaison mission between the Japanese army and the Chinese puppet government, I felt for the first time the power of the arguments of the Japanese propagandists.

If you can think of China, not in the terms with which you are familiar, but as an independent government in Nanking attempting to found a nation which would have its proper place in a great league of Asiatic nations, but hampered by the activity of various bandits and foreign-supported rebels in its efforts, you have a Japanese picture of the situation in China during the war. How many Chinese they were able to persuade of the cogency of their arguments I do not know, but it would be a great wonder to me if any large group of people could have looked with longing eyes to the

Chungking horizon. Colonel Kato even now speaks with much emotion about the desire to create a "fine, self-respecting government which would contribute to a lasting prosperous peace in Asia and the world." The argument is not entirely nonsensical. Granted that the puppet government (which Colonel Kato called without irony "a sovereign nation which must be respected as such") was but a tool of the Japanese, and that the Japanese were seeking to create a prosperity sphere which would redound mainly to their own interests, the idea of such a league does not seem to be a bad one to me. The nations of the Far East represent an economic group which is virtually self-sufficient as a whole, but which falls into a number of disjointed parts if separated. If some nation with a more intelligent way of acting, a better sense of process than Japan possessed, had undertaken the job, it is possible that it might have been more successful than we will be in creating a "new order."

For Chinese who thought about the matter, there must have been indeed some cause for hesitation. Most collaborationists will tell you that they were forced to act so for economic reasons. The present government must believe them, for only the very top men of those who were in office have been replaced; the bureaucrats go on. Aside from such persons, however, there must have been a number of Chinese as susceptible of conviction as hard-bitten old Kato. No, possibly not, for ideals are a rather new thing for China as a whole, and Japanese rule might not be the best way of germinating them.

When I was in Tsingtao before going to Tsinan, the Eighth Route Army—the Palu—meant only a group that was tearing up the railroad and doing similar mischief, scarcely the same people about whom Edgar Snow wrote. One day, when Henry Luce was here and expressed a desire to meet a communist and have a chat with him, a special group was sent out north of the city to find one. After several hours' travel the mission returned unsuccessful. (Chinese rumor the next day had it that an American colonel had gathered together two thousand five hundred communists at a secret rally.) The communists have thus been unreal, more nuisances or bogeymen than a tangible menace. I was warned solemnly to look out for the Palu at Tsinan. I answered that I would rather like to be captured by them just to see what they were like, a foolish answer in view of the fact that the Palu has reportedly killed several American aviator prisoners in the recent past. After talking with all the Japanese experts on the subject of the Palu while I was in Tsinan, I was switched back to my old views on them, the Edgar Snow vein if you like. The Japanese said that the first act of the Palu directed against the mass of the people had been the cutting of the railroad, which has meant also the blocking of coal and food supplies for everyone. Unlike the Chungking solidiers, who were dreaded for their robbery, rape and looting, the discipline of the Palu had always been excellent. The communists have opened schools in the villages, for the purpose of propaganda perhaps, but with the desired result of raising markedly the standard of literacy. They have stirred the farmers into forming a militia of proven loyalty. There is some question about Palu connections with Russia and the Chineseness of their intentions, but there is no doubt as to the fact that they have been far and away more successful than any other Chinese military organization in winning popular support for their ideals. To gain their weapons they have had to fight with superior troops. Their bases have been ravaged by the Japanese in "pacification" campaigns, but the communists have grown ever stronger. Listening to the stories told by the Japanese (who incidentally were strongly anti-Palu as a rule), I could not help feeling that if any group deserved Shantung, it was the Palu. The communists have fought for the province and they have won the people. They are so close to Tsinan that one can almost see them from the center of the city, while they are just across the bay at Tsingtao. If the Japanese are disarmed and no new Chinese troops come in, the communists will swoop into these cities from their strongholds. Even if they are pushed back at the entrance to the cities they will blockade them until economic life is at a standstill. And, if a really large and powerful Chinese central army comes in, they will go back to the hills and fight their traditional "raiding warfare." A Japanese officer told me that they would then be stronger than ever.

To be fair, one must listen to the pro-Chungking side, but there is almost nothing to be said except that the "bandits" (the new official name for the Eighth Route Army) are ravaging China and harming her by continuing resistance. This is almost exactly the picture of a year ago—an organized central government harrassed by guerrilla warfare which it terms "bandit attacks." The government of the Generalissimo is undoubtedly much more Chinese than its predecessor, the puppets, but it is scarcely as representative as the communists are. The latter, of course, may be acting in much more direct communication with Russia than is usually supposed. There have been reports of planes dropping supplies to the communists and of Russian equipment in Eighth Route Army hands. From persons escaped from Manchuria come tales of horror about the treatment given to Japanese civilians there by the Russians. The latter appear to have refused to allow Chinese government troops to enter parts of the province even though they originally promised to clear out in three months. There is no news either from Russian Korea or from Dairen and Port Arthur, where the Chinese have also been refused admittance. Palu troops are reported sailing from the northern coast of the Shantung Peninsula for Manchuria. The Japanese say that Palu troops now in Manchuria are operating directly under the Russians and are receiving the superior equipment of the Japanese Kwangtung Army.

Governor Ho criticized the United States for having persuaded Mr. T. V. Soong to sign the agreement relative to the temporary occupation of Manchuria by the Russians. "It is all very well for the United States to expect idealistically that other nations will abide by treaties, but the Russians are conscious of no such obligations it would seem." Predictions are made freely on all sides that Manchuria or Korea will be the cause of a new world war. "President Roosevelt once said that America's frontier is on the Rhine. The new one is in Manchuria," Governor Ho remarked to me, adding that it was impossible that a democratic Korea could be established south of a certain line and a communist Korea north of that line: a conflict in ideology similar to the one between the United States and Germany was bound to occur. If there is any deep connection between the Russians and the Palu, Shantung may be the first wedge into China. Success here would enable the communists to march south to their real strongholds, the industrial cities of central China.

While talking about the communists with various people, I came across one Japanese who had operated a large number of spies and agents directed against the Palu. His special mission was to apprehend Palu agents and convert them into Japanese spies, sending them back to their headquarters for further information. My informant told me that he had been investigating the Palu for eight years and was well acquainted with its methods. I should think he would have been! On one occasion he went to the very heart of communist territory disguised as a representative of the Asiatic Culture League. He managed to plant some of his own men in key positions in the communist military and political organizations, thus permitting the Japanese to learn in advance all the Palu plans for attack. He himself on another occasion broke up the local communist ring by skillfully using the wife of one of the officials. In every village he had his agents, usually the most respected persons in towns, the ones whose opinion would be believed. Every merchant or traveler who passed through communist territory reported to him under penalty of never traveling again. Railway employees, postmen, teachers, all those people who were in a position to furnish information were in the employ of the Japanese. By "employ" is not meant that they received money, for there were almost no funds or commodities at the disposal of the Japanese. Rather, they were accorded what favors could result from Japanese influence such as civil service positions or preferment for other jobs over which the Japanese had control. I was told, however, that most did not even seek such rewards, that they helped the Japanese because they had been persuaded of the Japanese views. This was hard for me to believe, but I was assured that this was the principal, almost the exclusive, method used in obtaining agents for the Japanese side, particularly in converting communist agents into Japanese ones. "But weren't you afraid that such agents would work against you, that they would report the Japanese situation to the communists or falsify the communist situation to you?" I asked. "We could assume that most of our agents worked at least forty percent of the time for the communists. They had to, for the communists knew which persons had been in contact with the Japanese and were most eager, of necessity, to obtain information about us. We expected this kind of double-dealing and it did not bother us, for it was infinitely more important that we should know about the communist situation than it was dangerous that they know about ours. We could always implement our knowledge with action, while they usually could not. As for agents giving us false information, we of course checked all reports in the light of the testimony of many agents. Such occurrences were rare, however. We were too successful in persuading them of our views to permit treachery."

The successes of this Japanese were almost unbelievable. Undoubtedly his face or even his name must have terrified many Chinese. At least one came to tell me of the horrors suffered at his direction. Usually when it was reported that there was a communist agent in town, such reports coming from a "contact man," a few persons would be dispatched at night to the quarters of the supposed agent. If their report indicated that he was actually a communist agent, the chief himself would come the following night to persuade the man to change his views. Once successful, and I was assured that success occurred in almost every case, the turned-back agent would be directed to contact someone higher in the communist circles. This was repeated until county magistrates or even brigade commanders were reached and converted. It was explained to me: "You see, only the very top men in the communist forces are real communists. The rest are attracted because they like the methods of the Palu as contrasted with the Chungking or guerrilla forces, particularly the treatment of the farmers. If I can convince them that the Japanese desire to effect the same reforms and that Japanese rule has the added advantage of peace, all but the fervent communists will do whatever I ask." After the interview with him, this master agent wrote a manual for me called, "An Outline of Methods to Be Used in Obtaining, Educating and Training Superior Spies."

The danger is that I will see them all with too jaundiced an eye.

After talking to this Japanese, I felt again my hopeless inability to distinguish the good from the bad by speech or actions before me. The tendency is to distrust them all in self-defense, which I suppose is as great an error as open trust. It is true that I have been forced to work with the worst element of the Japanese in the interests of my work. Occasional visits to the Japanese on whom we must place our hopes for a future Japan might help me to see more clearly, but China is not noted for the quality of Japanese residents. There are a few such as Mr. Yokoyama here or some I met in Tsinan who have shown the goodness we would like of Japan, but most Japanese here came for profit only. How to tell them apart? How to be sure that the fellow who nods sympathetically to my most radical statements is not the consummate hypocrite? Or that contrition expressed for Japan's faults is not the lie of a moment?

One beautiful, clear, sunny morning I sat on a little hill overlooking the Tsinan Japanese Shrine with Captain Kusama. In the distance a Chinese temple crowned the highest of the barren brown hills. Silence waved over the landscape with the light breeze. We then could see a woman walking on the path up to the steps which lead to the shrine. When she reached the stone of the steps her *geta* [wooden clogs] clacked to our hill. She climbed the stairs and then walked across the court to the rail in front of the shrine where she bowed deeply, clapping her hands in between bows. Captain Kusama turned to me and said, "I have never done that." "And yet you undoubtedly instructed the men in your company to do so?" "I taught them that they were born to die for their emperor, that there was nothing higher." "Was that your belief?" "Surely even in your nation it is held noble to die for one's country. That I believed. The rest . . ." Kusama shrugged his shoulders. "But how can Japanese like yourself maintain superiority to old customs and habits as being barbaric or for the masses only, and yet indulge in unparalleled barbarism yourselves? You who sit here and can tell me of your independence from the doctrines you yourself have preached are no different perhaps from many other well-educated Japanese, some of whom, surely, must have been responsible for the horrors of Nanking or the South Pacific?" "I have not heard of them. What things may have happened were naturally not communicated to us." I told him of some of the Japanese atrocities, in the face of the beautiful morning and the slow clack-clack of the woman's *geta* as she walked back down the stairs. I told him of these things because it was inconceivable that he could have done them himself. Not gentle, merry Captain Kusama! I do not think I am mistaken in him.

The second time that I recited the revolting deeds of the Japanese was at dinner a few days later when the question of the basic nature of the Japanese came up. I had gone after another, and as usual, overwhelming Chinese dinner to the home of a friend of one of the Japanese officers I had met. The friend had a large collection of porcelain of various periods, mostly Sung. I could see how proud he was of the cups and dishes that bore for him the unmistakable genius of the period. We had gone together to inspect the porcelain stores within the walled city and had both been disgusted with what they had to offer there, my disgust being mainly a product of his knowledge. He would pick up a piece and exclaim, "Now this fellow isn't Sung—you can tell that he isn't by the weakness of the lines. This is bad, a very bad piece." But the night of which I am speaking there was a greater authority present, a Buddhist priest who came attired in full Japanese robes. His round, shaven head had a kind of intellectuality that was certainly not mere scholasticism. We sat about a table, the priest across from me, Lieutenant Fujita in black Chinese clothes sitting far back into the sofa, Mr. Nagao, the owner of the bowls at the corner, and a Mr. Nakayama at the end of the table. Nagao's two sisters were just outside the circle, able to interrupt only once in a while with a giggle or a little cry.

Mr. Nagao showed one piece after another to the priest for his criticism. The first pieces were all undoubtedly Sung, the reddish brown porcelain slip over a white clay. These must have been the utensils of peasants or the lower classes, for they bear the mark of underestimation of their value in the carelessness with which they were piled together, leaving the mark of one cup on the center of another into which it had been placed when still hot, or the trace of sand into which a cup had carelessly been dropped. The priest looked these over approvingly, pointing out little distinctive features of Sung cups, like the sharp point given to the clay at the bottom. Then Nagao presented the priest with a piece with a black lacquery finish saying hopefully, "They told me that this fellow was picked up at the same time as the last one, but . . ." The priest frowned and said, "This is bad. Very bad. This couldn't have been made more than a few hundred years ago. No Sung workman would ever have been so careless. Occasionally one finds little lumps where an excess of the porcelain coating has formed, but it always looks natural. This is a fake, a crude attempt to reproduce the carelessness of the original." Then followed a series of pieces, each greeted with the same observations, while Nagao's face dropped lower and one of his sisters giggled, "And we believed everything elder brother told us about porcelain!" Or, sometimes Nagao would say, "I am sure that this fellow isn't very old, but . . ." The priest would look at it and declare it better than any of the others, to which Nagao would reply, "Yes, one can really sense something strong in the lines."

The priest picked up one piece and examined it carefully. "There is something about pottery which makes it more personal than most of the arts; that is, it has a more direct relation to the human body. The hand of the man who made it is forever preserved. The few strokes with a comb which he may have given for ornamentation are a more spontaneous expression of the instinct for beauty, and thus closer to the man than one finds in other forms. There is a story of a man who made surpassingly beautiful pottery. When people tried to find out how it was that this particular man was able to create such masterpieces it was discovered that he was lame in one leg and this physical factor may have been important in determining the final product. The imprint of the thumb of a man turning a piece on a potter's wheel is the result of the action of his entire body.

"It is particularly true of pottery that the physical is reflected in art, but one may find the same tendency in sculpture or painting. You know that oriental art is almost entirely planal, whereas Western art is solid. For example, a Japanese image of Buddha is not meant to be seen from the rear or the side the way a Western statue may be viewed. It must be seen from the front. In painting this is obviously true in the lack of perspective or even in an attempt at it. It is also true of pottery, but it would take a long explanation to show just how. I wonder if the planal aspect is not a result of the features of the Orientals themselves. In the case of Westerners, the ears form a part of the face and represent part of the three-dimensional effect of the face with its hollows and angles. The Oriental's face is planal, flat. The ears are not a part of the face, but are well beyond the line of what may so be regarded. The result is that in reproducing in art the image of the face one section of the world was led naturally to planal image while the other developed a solid, three-dimensional effect."

There was some discussion after this about the meaning of planal and solid, particularly by Lieutenant Fujita, who is a gay fellow, little accustomed to serious discussion. Nakayama then, from the end of the table, talked a while about the potters at Po-shan where he had once lived. Nakayama has long, beautiful hands and an intellectual face. The short, wild hair was a clear indication that he had recently been discharged from the army and was permitting his hair to grow again. After a little pause in the conversation he looked up and asked the priest, "Chinese friends of mine tell me that there is really no Japanese art as such, that everything is merely a copy of what Chinese genius has already developed. What do you say to that?"

The priest moved on his chair, brought his feet up from the floor and sat cross-legged on the chair, looking very wonderful, like an old Japanese painting. "I have been asked that question a great deal by boys at the school recently. I have told them that they need not feel ashamed of their country, that wherever the art may once have originated, its present and past have been glorious in Japan. For example, the Hōryū-ji is a perfect example of a T'ang building. There is not one such in all of China. The reason is that the Japanese long ago revered Chinese art and sought to preserve it. They could appreciate its worth while the Chinese saw fit to destroy everything that remained of their great civilizations. Today in Japan there are craftsmen in Kyoto who are carrying on the great traditions of pottery and painting.

There are none such in all of China. A few years ago there was an inquiry by which it was shown that there were only 120 Chinese who made a living by painting, while in Japan this number reaches 20,000. In all of modern Chinese art there is only one figure whose works bear a second glance, Chi Pai-shih, and he is eighty-five years old. There may be others, but I have not seen their work. Japan has preserved the greatness of Chinese art and has developed it. In the world there are now only two countries whose art really shows greatness, France and Japan. To dismiss Japan's art as mere copying would be the height of narrow-mindedness."

Nakayama interrupted, "I know, I know all that. What I want to know is if there is anything that Japan has produced which is her own and not a copy, no matter how skillful or in what number."

The priest rearranged the folds of his robe and then answered, "I know how you feel now. Years ago I passed through a similar period when I thought that there was nothing in Japan but slavish copying. China was the only thing in the world for me and I could not rest until I came here, only to be disillusioned in one way or another. I could tell you a number of points in which Japanese art differs from Chinese, definite creative steps which show as much genius as any similar Chinese discovery. For example, in Chinese sculpture one always has a symmetrical image. If the statue is cut in half vertically the two halves will be mirror images. The Japanese sculptors broke up the regularity and had their figures sit with one leg crossed and one leg hanging down, or with the head resting on one hand. This represented a step of great daring and shows a freedom from the Chinese originals which does not accord with any idea of slavish imitation. But there is something even more unmistakably Japanese in all Japanese art. Look at this statue." He opened a book to a photograph of one of the masterpieces of the Nara period, "Look at the curve of the shoulders. That is something peculiarly Japanese. It is the curve found in the *haniwa* [clay funerary figures], the oldest of Japanese art objects, and in the *magatama*, or curved beads, which are the earliest of Japanese creative efforts. It is the curve that one finds in the faces of the Japanese themselves. Here we go back to the physical aspect of art. Chinese and Japanese girls look very much alike, but they differ in that one respect of their faces. That is unmistakably Japanese. If we do not make the single comparison of Chinese and Japanese but ask also what there is of English art or German art or French art which is more distinct from Greek or Roman or Italian Renaissance originals than Japanese art is distinct from Chinese art, we may have an answer. There is a Japanese basis for all Japanese art, whether it be in the selection from Chinese or other arts, or in the physical differences of the Japanese people."

Nagao brought out the prize of his collection then, after a pause while we all sat around thinking about what had been said. The priest looked at the beautiful pale green of the Sung bowl. "There is nothing finer than this in Chinese porcelain." Nagao smiled in gratitude and then mentioned the fact that I was going to buy the bowl, at which I made my apologies for carrying off so beautiful a treasure. Someone interrupted then with the usual argument that it was better to give it to me than to have some ignorant Chinese misuse it. While this is a statement perhaps intended to make me feel better, it usually has the effect of irritating me and making me ask if the behavior toward the Chinese shown by the Japanese would justify requiring the Chinese to demonstrate any particular consideration. When I put this question before them in so many words, there was a little confusion. The priest was first to answer. "I understand what you mean. When I was first sent to Peking I was filled with the conviction that Japan was anxious to impart its present cultural benefits to the Chinese. I had thought of Japan's mission in China as something very noble and was proud to participate in it. Once I came here I saw the true state of affairs. Japan was here to make money. The Japanese living here, with few exceptions, had no interest in China except in so far as profits were concerned. The benefits that Japan gave to China might best be typified by the air raid shelters she built—shelters that collapsed the first time they were used."

I brought up the question of atrocities again and they all listened with grave faces. When I had finished, Nakayama, his face very sharp in the yellow light of the candle, said, "When

I hear you say these things I do not want to believe them, but knowing the Japanese I realize that they could very well be true. What is most heartbreaking of all is to hear you tell of officers who had graduated from universities and who were presumably capable of understanding how terrible the acts were that they were performing. Ignorant soldiers might not have known any better, might be led by any stronger comrade or unprincipled officer, but university graduates!"

One of Nagao's sisters spoke up then, "Is it true that there was printed in the magazine *Life* a picture of a skull of a Japanese soldier which was sent by an American soldier to his girl back home? Japanese were all very horrified at this story." Fujita interrupted with, "No, of course not. That was just a propaganda story circulated by the Japanese authorities."

I was forced to answer, "Unfortunately, it was true. Americans were likewise horrified. When I speak of the terrible things that the Japanese have done, I am not saying that individual Americans are not capable of acts of wickedness themselves. I am certain that the American who sent the skull back home did not cut the head off the body of a Japanese and then wait for it to reach a suitable condition to send back home. It was quite possibly not a Japanese soldier's skull after all, but just one he picked up and sent back home with that description for the sake of impressing his girl. But that is not the answer to your question. If you want to know if Americans haven't done the same things of which I have accused the Japanese, I will say that they have indeed committed some of those atrocities, but always individually and not as part of an organized program of immorality. There is no parallel to the savagery shown by the mass of Japanese soldiers at Nanking or at various other places in China, or by the Japanese *kempeitai* [military police]."

"Yes," Nakayama took it up, "I hate the *kempeitai* worst of all. It was impossible to say or do anything except as prescribed by the authorities. No one, soldier or civilian, was safe from their intrusion. That is another one of the benefits that Japan will derive as a result of being defeated—the end of the terrorism of the *kempeitai*."

The priest continued, "Japan's defeat has been a blessing in disguise. The darkness in which Japan has been plunged will give way to the light of a better understanding of other peoples."

It was by now quite late and growing cold within the room. The electricity had long since given way to candles, which lent rather the air of a conspirators' meeting to our conversation. We arose and started to leave. Somehow I felt that I would like to say something to Nakayama which would give him the reassurance in Japanese art which is certainly necessary if Japanese are to continue with their glorious traditions. If I had been speaking English, I might have succeeded by the words and the tone, but I was forced by my inability to use Japanese flexibly to say, "I can think of at least one thing the Japanese invented—the fan. Surely that was a contribution to art." "Oh, yes. They also invented the rickshaw and numerous other such devices. No, Japanese craftsmen for all their individual skill have never learned to work together to turn out a sustained piece of art." "What about the Tōdai-ji and the Hōryū-ji and the many other famous Japanese temples?" "The pattern was foreign. The workmen were also usually foreign. The Ise shrine is Japanese, that's true. That is, if it isn't Polynesian or some other such thing."

My efforts were unsuccessful, but when I finally left amid all the bowings and polite expressions of contrition at having been so impolite, I suddenly felt impelled to stick out my hand and shake the hands of the others. The warmth with which we did so showed me that at least in this respect I had succeeded. We understood one another.

Tsinan meant many dinners and many conversations as well as the daily round of people to be seen. I was crammed with Chinese food and then, as I barely staggered down to my car, I was taken to a Japanese dinner. It is too bad that, unlike the camel, we are unable to store up for the long desert stretches of canned meat. I had dinner twice with my interpreter Wang's relative, to whom he referred sometimes as a cousin and sometimes as a brother. The cousin-brother is a wonderful, quiet man, all the charm of the old China that the new China has succeeded in destroying but not entirely replacing. I admit that

I still find it a little less than charming to have people spit on the floor or toss bones, shells and stray bits of food before them, but it is infinitely more pleasing than the strangulation of the "modern" Chinese room with its rigid square of furniture and the pre-sweetened tea on the table. Wang's relative said to me, "You have not come to my place for two days. Why do you eat outside? I will be waiting for you tomorrow." But that tomorrow we had lunch with General Yang, and the day after with someone else, so that when I felt a tug at my sleeve as I sat in the Chinese opera wondering, "Just who does fill up the theater?" I felt at once a sudden recognition of him and unhappiness that I should have disappointed this real old Chinese. There is something precious about a Chinese who still goes to the opera and enjoys it, not with the third eye of an outsider, but with his own.

I felt this when invited to the home of Mr. Tsui where I had a *sukiyaki* dinner. Mr. Tsui had studied in Japan and not only speaks Japanese but also looks exactly like one's preconceived picture of a Japanese baron, with his long gray mustaches and his yellowed teeth. To have a Japanese dinner at his place was not exactly a shock, but it certainly seemed an unwelcome step in the direction of cosmopolitanism. Miss Tsui, his daughter, studied in Chicago for a number of years and spoke good English. She is obviously the leading female of Tsinan life and is present at every gathering. Her poem greeting the arrival of Governor Ho hangs on the wall of the gubernatorial mansion, while her calligraphy decorates many another wall. I discovered that she was a member of the Tsinan smart set, which also included a number of persons connected with war transportation, all of whom bore the title of general, regardless of age or profession. When with them I wished desperately that I could understand more than the most simple and banal of statements, for one can obviously learn very little about China without a knowledge of the language. The decline of China, of which the Japanese spoke so much, was a question which I was unable to answer to my satisfaction on the basis of the conversation of the "better elements" of the new China as I painfully attempted to follow it. Of course Tsinan was not the place to discover what young China was doing, for everyone worth his salt must have tried to escape to Free China, but the conversation even so seemed sterile and mundane. To so large a degree it seems true that these Chinese have sold their souls, probably after considerable haggling.

One more person I must mention in Tsinan is Dr. Scheer. As part of my general survey I looked up the Germans (the only foreigners) in Tsinan to see to what degree the Nazis were still in control. I visited Mr. Schwardtmann, the head of the Nazi party in Tsinan. His story, as I could have guessed, was that he had become party leader merely as a favor to his friend, the former leader who had left for Manchuria. "The Nazi party in Tsinan was just a kind of social club where German people got together once in a while to talk a little and drink a little beer. Most of the members are over fifty years old and none of them has been to Germany in ten years. Surely this doesn't seem a very dangerous organization!" I found myself agreeing with the statement that an organization of nine or ten people in a city of perhaps eight hundred thousand was not very impressive, but I couldn't help disliking Schwardtmann, a heavy, stupid man with bloated lips and squirming eyes, and his nephew, Lichtfuss, a thin, cold person who looked as if he belonged rather in some dead society than in sprawling, noisy Tsinan. Lichtfuss told me, "I am the only recent arrival here. I came from Shanghai a few months ago. The others have been here for twenty years or more." Then, with an ironical grimace, "Tsinan is so beautiful it is hard to tear oneself away."

I met Dr. Scheer later that same day. He was Tsinan's leading anti-Nazi, permitted by the Nazis to exist only because he was the sole foreign doctor. He had lived in a state of virtual isolation from the other Europeans for almost ten years. I asked him about Schwardtmann. "I am perhaps not the best person to give information on the Nazis because I refused to speak to them for so long. My only contacts with Schwardtmann were when he divided up the coal the Japanese allotted the German community. He would take twenty tons for his brandy factory and give me one for my hospital. He is a fanatical Nazi like most of the Germans here. To make everyone come to his house he decreed that beer could be consumed there only. Thus, if one wanted a glass of beer, and most Germans, as you know, are very fond of beer, one would have to attend the party meetings. No one dared oppose him, or almost no one, for Herr Schaefer once fought with him."

Herr Schaefer I later met. He is an example of the German version of the "old China hand." He had come to China with the first Germans, when Germany acquired Tsingtao and the Kiaochow Bay area at the end of the last century. Schaefer still retains the manner of the period, down to the imperialist mustache and vandyke, like King Ferdinand of Bulgaria. In his speech, too, he showed that his forty years in China had left him with the vocabulary of another age. "My first quarrel with Hitler was when he signed a pact with those horrible Japanese. I thought to myself, 'It is all right to rebuild Germany, but the emperor of Germany has no right to side with the Japanese.' When I voiced this objection to Schwardtmann, he grew furious. At every meeting our relations grew worse until finally I asked him if he was the party leader or the party tyrant. He stood up and screamed at me, 'I have absolute control over every German in Tsinan. I can crush you!' When I still refused to submit to him, refused even to drink beer at his house, he sent to Tsingtao for Ihlenberg, one of the big Nazis there. Then, one day my wife and I were sent for. Schwardtmann and Ihlenberg were seated at the end of a long room and made my wife and myself stand while they read the accusation of my disloyalty. I asked to allow my wife to sit down for she was not well, but Schwardtmann refused. Ihlenberg then announced to us that our relief money was being cut off and that we could starve. Oh, you don't know what kind of monsters they are! If it had not been for friends whose names I will not mention, we would be dead now." Schaefer's little goatee danced with fury.

Another German who visited me was a party member named Jungmann, a person of little authority, typical of the Tsinan German community, most of the members of which have no apparent means of support. In the case of Jungmann, it was almost impossible to imagine how so frail and vague a person could have lasted in China. He addressed me in a whining tone, a little insanely, "I know that I have been called a Nazi, but I am really not even fully a German. I was born in the Saar, in Saarlouis, a town founded by Louis XIV, and my brothers have worked for the French. I am really almost French myself, you see, for the Saar is so close to France. You couldn't really call me a pure German." I thought to myself that racial superiority had here its most curious denial.

Dr. Scheer took me to see my last German interviewee, Frau Imhoff. To reach the convent school where Frau Imhoff was living we had to drive through the walled city until the car could go no further because of the narrowness of the streets. Then we walked through streets and wet alleys wide enough for only one man to pass. Stores and houses crowded up to the streets so closely that one felt that they sought only the little additional that would permit them to push together. We saw donkeys turning mills, women working bellows, children struggling under heavy carrying poles, and merchants measuring peanut oil from great vats. Dr. Scheer then opened the gate into a high-walled compound. Inside were gray buildings and never-ending courtyards connecting to other courtyards. From one building we could hear something being sung in Latin. Three little Chinese girls dressed in the blue convent school uniforms looked out of a window at us. Dr. Scheer then led me into a cold building of great plainness, no decoration at all except for a crucifix at one end of the room. Frau Imhoff entered a moment later, a pale woman with disorderly white hair. I was told by Dr. Scheer that she had been a repatriate from Java and was on her way back to Germany when the United States entered the war, forcing her to remain in China. I asked her about her experiences in Tsingtao. Her face was empty and frightened. Dr. Scheer assured her that it would be best to speak to me. Her words then came out in a great rush. "Almost since the first day in Tsingtao they persecuted me. I sent a postcard to a friend in Japan saying that the boat trip from Shanghai to Tsingtao had been unbearable. The consul at Tsingtao called me down, and in front of everyone denounced me as a traitor worse than the people around Hitler who attempted to take his life. They called me a rumormonger and all the women in town were advised to have nothing to do with me. Then when I attempted to move from the pension where I was living because everyone was sick there and I was afraid for my health, Dr. Schmidt informed the consul that it was unnecessary for me to move because there was sickness everywhere. Later, I tried to obtain some medicine for a friend. This was discovered and I was denounced again as a meddler. The consul and Herr Ihlenberg then ordered me to appear before them. When I did, I was told that I was being sent at once to Tsinan. I asked to be allowed to go to Peking where I have friends, but they refused me. So I came here where I knew no one, and have lived most of the time at this school."

I asked her about her experiences in Tsinan, but her answers were confused and contradictory. Dr. Scheer told me as we left that she was probably afraid to speak about people in Tsinan for fear that her allowance would be cut off. I thought to myself that this might be the explanation, or it might also be that Frau Imhoff, who is not an anti-Nazi in any ideological sense, had less reason to complain of the Tsinan Germans than of those in Tsingtao.

On the way back, Dr. Scheer and I went shopping, an activity in which his most charming qualities are shown off in the masterful and delightful manner with which he jokes with the Chinese. In one silver store which specialized in trinkets for Chinese children he joked with the owner for a while until the latter asked him, "How long have you been in China?" "Seventeen years, How about you?" "Fifty-six years." "Have you been to Germany? No? Well, in the next life you'll get there." Or, to a Chinese who asked him how he was feeling, "Not very good. I haven't eaten in three days—as of the day after tomorrow." I am sure that Dr. Scheer's medical talents must be strengthened by his warmth in dealing with the many sick of China.

The last night before I left Tsinan there was another party at a former geisha house. The geishas have all left, but the rooms are still beautiful. I ate with three Japanese officers dressed in civilian clothes. I really felt very sorry to leave, but I was ready to return to Tsingtao, imagining that I might soon be able to break away and leave for home. I am still here, alas, in the midst of my work and the confusion of Japanese repatriation.

Don

FROM OTIS CARY IN TOKYO
TO DON KEENE IN TSINGTAO

November 20, 1945 (?)

Dear Don,

You must remember the exceptional POW we captured on Saipan—one of the four survivors from Admiral Yamamoto's party of two planes shot down at Buin in April, 1943. The memory that POW displayed in recalling almost verbatim the entire Combined Fleet Secret Operation Order No. 1 was amazing, simply amazing. It is pretty accurate, too, from all I've been able to gather here. The one thing the POW didn't feel he could tell us accurately was the quality of the strategic decisions that were made when the final plans were being drawn up, and just how good the intelligence was upon which they were based. He, like us, was a lad snatched from college, and although he was a good smart boy who had to become a yeoman instead of an officer, he did not pretend to be a military strategist of any proportions. He told me many times, when we would finally reach a blank wall in trying to remember details of the planning for the Pearl Harbor attack, that he had had no idea that what they were planning was going to take on the proportions it did. He was more interested in getting as much liberty as possible and in kidding with the coffee girls than in plugging for the Naval General Staff.

Recently I have been fêted by many ex-members of Admiral Yamamoto's staff, who have been in and out of the Japanese Naval General Staff, Combined Fleet and the Imperial General Headquarters all through the war. When I displayed the knowledge of facts and personalities I had received from our POW friend (he had been a writer on the Combined Fleet Staff and also with the Naval General Staff), rather than shying away, they accepted me with open arms. Actually meeting some of the personalities in the planning, of whom we had talked so much, was rather fantastic, considering how much time we had spent months before trying to recall everything they had said, thumbnailing character sketches of them, figuring how they would act in the emergencies which were arising as the iron curtain drew tighter around the home islands. It was just as fantastic the first time I went to the

Naval War College, where all the top men of the Japanese fleets, the Naval General Staff, and the Navy Ministry had assembled to draw up the plans of the attack. In order to get the POW to remember as much as possible, I had taken him large sheets of wrapping paper, and we had drawn the floor plans of the first and second stories of the Naval War College and the printing plant in the rear. We had traced his movements from one room to another, identifying each room and its occupants for the vital ten days. I knew the place well before I went there—then to see it! It is being used for something else now—a foreboding, brick and stone godown type of building. It looks capable of the dastardliness we ascribe to the Pearl Harbor attack.

Stars and Stripes out here daily carries the latest in the Pearl Harbor inquiry going on at Washington. One of the men who had been high up in the planning of the attack was laboriously reading these articles. He said to me the other day, "Why do they go on with that foolishness? It was the fault of the Japanese that the thing happened. We planned it and executed it."

This man, a rear admiral on the Naval General Staff, and I had talked at some length at a couple of geisha parties he had thrown for me earlier. From the POW at Pearl through all the Navy Ministry and Naval General Staff, people up to this rear admiral all had quite a different slant on the Pearl Harbor attack from that which we attribute to the Japanese. Some of the most interesting points, as I was able to put the story together, I'll try to tell you. Everything they said is fascinating and of great historical importance. I wish I could remember every detail.

The Japanese navy, up to the outbreak of war and all through the war, knew it was a matter of time before their supply lines would be cut and the homeland bombed. Yet they could not restrain the army. The only direction the army had been looking for years was toward Russia. They knew little or nothing of America or Britain or the Pacific. Admiral Yamamoto, the leader of the strategic thinking in the Japanese navy, realized long ago that in the event of war Japan's supply lines to the Netherlands East Indies would last only in proportion to the impotency of our fleet, and that sooner or later the two fleets would have to meet. He ordered (doubtless we had men working on the problem of where best to attack Japan) Rear Admiral Ōnishi (after the end of the war he committed suicide) to make plans for a possible attack on the American fleet in Hawaii. This plan was the basis for war games at the Naval War College as far as Hawaii was concerned. Years earlier Admiral Yamamoto had kept Ōnishi from being thrown out of the Japanese navy on grounds of dishonorable conduct, and Ōnishi was devoted to him. Ōnishi was an airman and *kichikōkūtai* [air base] staff officer at that time. Our POW told us that security measures taken at this time at the Naval War College were nil. Anyone with a half official air could have walked in. He and another yeoman took the completed orders down to Kure with them on the train, tied up in a couple of *furoshiki* [wrapping cloth], with no further precaution.

But the intelligence upon which the strike at Pearl Harbor was finally based is incredibly meager. I was able to get ideas on this not only from the staff point of view but also from men in the attack and the man who led the first wave, Captain Fuchida. Three possibilities were considered up to the very end, and they were briefed on two of these right up to the last minute. They knew the American fleet would not be on the West Coast—we had said so with fanfare. It would be either: in Pearl; anchored at Lahaina Roads off Maui (an anchorage used for years by the navy); or at sea. The main target was the carriers which they thought were in Pearl till they got overhead and could not see them. They expected to get all the carriers and perhaps two battleships—five capital ships altogether. They expected to lose one-third to one-half of their striking force, that means two, perhaps three, of the six carriers they came with, to say nothing of the same ratio of battleships, cruisers, and destroyers, etc. The last actual dope from Hawaii they had was an American news announcement by radio and press that the fleet was in on the 4th or 5th of December, and word from their own submarines the night before that the fleet was not anchored at Lahaina. Anybody who had kept up with the papers in Hawaii for the past three or four months could easily see the regular, methodical pattern with which the fleet went on maneuvers. Every other weekend at least, and as a matter of fact usually every weekend, it would be found in port.

In a cabinet meeting on the 1st of December, war was decided on for the 8th or after (of course their 8th is our 7th), but it might be called off any time up till then. Such word was passed on to Admiral Nagumo commanding the task force which had already set sail from the Kuriles. Between that time and the time of the strike only two communications were sent to the striking force, the latter reporting the latest news announcement of the fleet's being back at Pearl. As you know there was absolutely no sabotage in Hawaii by the Japanese or those of Japanese ancestry. The stories of arrows cut in canefields to guide the Japanese airmen and little hissing junk dealers who turned up on Sunday morning in Pearl Harbor with machine guns on their carts become even more ridiculous when you talk with these men. They knew nothing of the mysterious phone call from the *Yomiuri* which discussed types of flowers as though they might be meant to be types of warships. They did tell of an assistant to the naval attaché, a lieutenant commander named Kaneda, who briefed the pilots up in the Kuriles. He had come back from Washington, but by ship, and it was only background dope he gave as he knew Hawaii well.

I think what we fail to understand more is the poor liaison in the Japanese government itself. It is not excusable for a minute, of course. For instance, nobody in the Japanese army had any conception of the possible proportions of the attack they had forced the navy to plan. Even on the highest levels just a few of the top flight army people vaguely knew there was going to be a Pearl Harbor attack. It was not discussed with them or explained to them. Also there was poor liaison between the Foreign Office and the army and navy. With no particular attempt at heroics Admiral Kurojima told me that after the first reports on the results of the strike had come in from the task force, Admiral Yamamoto had asked, "Did the [diplomatic] word get through?" Of course, it was an hour and twenty minutes late getting delivered from the Japanese embassy to the State Department in Washington. Furthermore, it was merely a note breaking off the conversations, not diplomatic relations, and it was not a declaration of war. In good Japanese style this task force was not handled from Tokyo (as our B–29s were under the direct command of Washington), but through the usual chain of command, the commander in chief of the Combined Fleet, Admiral Yamamoto; but he in turn was not aware of just what was going on diplomatically. He was down in Hashirajima, the Combined Fleet anchorage in the Inland Sea, at that time. It had never occurred to the men I talked with that the plan was laid around the fact that the attack was going to take place before war had been declared. Certainly Admiral Yamamoto had not conceived of it as that, although he had made the decision that Hawaii would have to be attacked. What convinces me further on this count is that none of the men I talked to either had objectively thought of, or had felt it necessary to bring up, in the planning stage the strength and unity America would gain from the phrase "Remember Pearl Harbor." From the Japanese army you might expect such poor planning as that because of their lack of knowledge of the United States. But the navy had many men who knew their America pretty well. A man of the caliber of Admiral Yamamoto would not overlook such a point either. Yet it never seems to have been brought up. If they had planned the attack as a sneak attack, certainly they would have looked into that point in deciding whether a surprise attack would have been worthwhile. It seems to me that the army, which wanted the war, the navy, which was going to have to strike the first blow, and the Foreign Office, which was to declare war, all should have gotten together a little better. If they had, we probably wouldn't have had a war.

In all this talk with these ex-navy men one point seemed to be pretty obvious—Admiral Isoroku Yamamoto was an astute and outstanding leader. I don't doubt that both as a man and as a commander he is one of the great military men of this war, in a class with Nimitz, Marshall and Eisenhower. You doubtless knew that the statement he is alleged to have made about dictating peace terms in the White House is the grossest pulling of words out of their context. What he actually said, and it was in a letter to some friend, was in effect: unless they could expect to dictate peace terms in the White House in Washington it would be folly even to consider war with the United States.

He was a keen man but outspoken. He loved bridge, *shōgi* [Japanese chess], *go* [a Japanese board game], in fact they said any kind of game when I asked. They tell the story of a meeting of oil magnates at which he and Tōjō were asked to speak before the war. They were to emphasize the need for oil. The distinguished war minister got up and made his usual long, bombastic speech. It lasted close to an hour as he flailed the big oil men for not realizing the need for oil, the country's lifeblood. Yamamoto then got up and said: the need for oil is no greater than I have been saying to you for the past several years, and sat down. And he had been as outspoken as that for many years.

These men who composed his staff said that before the war Yamamoto had said many times that in the event of war they would be able to hold their own for two years at the outside; after that anything might happen. When he left Japan for what proved to be the last time he told one of his good civilian friends, whom I met, "I shall never see Japan again." He went on down to Truk and later on an inspection and morale-building trip to New Guinea and the Northern Solomons, where his plane was shot down. Captain Ōmae said that he (at that time on the staff at Rabaul) had advised close fighter escort for the last fatal hop to Buin, but they didn't really think anything would happen. After the word of Admiral Yamamoto's death had spread around, there was much concern over how we had found out. Native spies were, of course, suspected. They never seemed to have considered seriously that we might be breaking their secret codes, for they continued to send all their operational messages by dispatch. (If they only had known how every man in every radio intelligence outfit from Noumea to Washington claimed himself responsible for Admiral Yamamoto's death!) However, they were concerned over some high-ranking imperial observer coming the next month, who was touring all the forward areas to report back to the emperor. If he were shot down, it would be a terrible thing. However, they had plenty of time to get the details of his schedule through by courier mail, much to their relief.

Admiral Yamamoto must have had a great faculty for drawing forth the best in his officers and men, much like Admiral Nimitz.

Admiral Nimitz, untrue to the usual navy tradition of bringing all your own team with you when you take over a new command, arrived at Pearl Harbor on Christmas Day, gathered together the staff, told them he was sure they knew better than he what the trouble had been, and continued to operate with Admiral Kimmel's staff, getting terrific results from them as well as saving much time. I imagine that Yamamoto did the same sort of un-orthodox, un-navy-like thing, but got results. He would listen to hardworking younger officers and let them try out their ideas. Commander Arima was given a free hand to go ahead with his midget submarines using the *Chiyoda* as their mothership on a top-secret project. Commander Genda and two other fliers developed much of the navy air strategy, accounting for the basic three-plane fighting formation they used, because Yamamoto gave them a free hand to go ahead. Men such as these would often come in and argue with him spiritedly on many points, *and* he was always accessible to them. He would help out men like Ōnishi who became devoted to him, but he was always devoted to all those under him. Once, after a big geisha party had been thrown by a number of his friends, more or less in honor of him, they found the bill already paid when the end of the month came around. Finding out that it had been paid by Yamamoto they went around to confront him with it. It was quite a bill to have to pay from one navy officer's salary. His only explanation was that he was so overcome that they wanted to celebrate for him that that was the least he could do.

A final story about Admiral Yamamoto and I'll let him rest in peace. Admiral Yonai, when he relinquished the navy min-istership, gave a high school classmate of Yamamoto with whom I was able to talk an explanation of why Yamamoto had not succeeded him as navy minister. Although Yamamoto had been Yonai's vice minister, and it was logical for him to become min-ister, Yonai said that making him navy minister would be sure to result in his being shot by young, hotheaded army men. So he was succeeded by an old nonentity, Oikawa, and Admiral Yamamoto was sent to the Combined Fleet as commander in chief.

I think that we could have used Admiral Yamamoto and, from what I saw, many of the men he chose for his staff on any of our own staffs as operation officers or chiefs of staff. They are definitely some of the coolest-thinking and most capable men I've seen in Japan.

Otis

◆ ◆ ◆

FROM HISASHI KUBOTA IN OSAKA
TO DON KEENE IN TSINGTAO

November 24, 1945

Dear Don,

I am now in Osaka. I first came here several weeks ago, but this is the first free time I have had long enough to do a little uninterrupted writing. The masterminds of my outfit, taking into consideration the fact that the Osaka-Kobe area was one of the greatest industrial districts of Japan both before and during the war, decided to make it the subject of one of their investigations. I was chosen to accompany the party as an interpreter, and one dark night (the nights are really dark in Sasebo) the Osaka-bound group was assembled and given final instructions. Everything went off as though we were going out on an operation the next day, and about the only thing missing was a final synchronization of watches.

Early the next morning we rolled out of bed and lugged all of our belongings down the steep concrete steps onto a waiting truck. When the truck reached the railroad depot and was unloaded, we discovered to our dismay that the coach we were to board was on a different track a couple of hundred yards away. The leader of our group, a commander, saved the day. He sent for the stationmaster and made me explain to him that when the train was about to leave, it should reverse to our track and stop until we could load our baggage aboard. The stationmaster became all flustered and insisted that such a thing was impossible, but the commander stood firm and would not budge an inch. Meanwhile, it was getting close to the time of departure, and the stationmaster in desperation offered to have his men tote the baggage.

This was evidently what our commander wanted, but he, with magnificent control, gave only a weak assent. There and then we discovered one of the mightiest tools at our disposal when we have manual work to be done.

There was one thing I noticed on the train ride which struck me as being rather interesting—the blinds placed in front of all munitions plants. Such blinds may be anything from concrete walls to wooden screens, with the one apparent purpose of shielding vital war plants from the direct gaze of train passengers, who could get a momentary glimpse at best. The Japanese appear not to have been too sure of their vaunted national solidarity. Another thing I noticed from the train windows was the havoc wreaked by the recent typhoon on the rice fields. The rice was weighed down and about to be harvested when the storm struck, drowning entire fields. Even the fields which best survived the disaster will probably yield but half of what they would have in normal times. This is another tough break the poor will have to take, but I am convinced now that they can take anything.

When we reached Ōmura we went to an airfield and waited there for three days for a plane that was supposed to take us to Osaka, but we waited in vain and had to return to Sasebo. We started out again, on a destroyer this time. I shall long remember but hate to recall most of the trip to Wakayama. After leaving Sasebo we headed for Nagasaki where we anchored overnight. The voyage from Nagasaki started innocently enough, but once we were out in the open sea the steering gear went haywire and the ship went around in circles for a while. After the steering gear was repaired we ran into a small storm which drove me below deck for cover. For the next twenty hours it was all I could do to hang on and not be thrown from my bunk to the floor. I had originally thought the ship would go to Wakayama by way of the Inland Sea, but it is still unnavigable because of pressure mines; hence the discomforts of the open sea.

We went ashore at the fishing village of Wakanoura, which serves as the fleet landing. It was late afternoon and blue-clad sailor boys were gathering at the boat pier to return to their ships after liberty ashore. Immediately after landing I saw the first obvious differences between occupation in a marine-administered and in an army-administered area. Here the rules of occupation seemed to be much more liberal; there were more shops, more people in the streets, more fraternization—an overall atmosphere that was much lighter and gayer.

We drove through Wakayama, which is largely destroyed, and were let off at the terminal of the line between Wakayama and Osaka. While waiting at the station for our train, I was approached by several civilians and plied with all kinds of questions and requests. At first I had an awful time trying to pick up what they said because they talked so fast. One kid wanted to know the cost of taking a course in electrical engineering in the States; another asked if I knew his brother, who was presumably in the American army; several asked to be let into our coach if we had any room to spare. It was a good thing that the train finally pulled in, for my resources were being taxed to the utmost. We had been able to commandeer a whole coach for our party, but actually took up little more than a third of it. Since there was such a large crowd waiting outside, the leader of our group generously offered to let the civilians fill up the rear half of our coach. As soon as the word was passed, the crowd gushed in, some even through the windows. We had cause to regret our offer because the crowd began to push into our half, and it was only after threatening and forcibly pushing them back that we had any room left for ourselves. I learned a valuable lesson in dealing with Japanese crowds—never give an inch, for the good you do is such a trifle compared to the evils that may result.

It was midnight when we pulled into Osaka. All the other trains had stopped running for the night, but the immediate vicinity of the entrance turnstiles was jammed. These were the people awaiting the next morning's trains. They slept on the concrete floor or formed circles and jabbered away continuously to while the time away.

It was about 2 A.M. when we finally pulled up to the New Osaka Hotel, which is not too bad by American standards, and damn good for this place. We went to sleep in the lobby, on chairs and sofas, but our sleep was not to be enjoyed too long. Along about five in the morning an excited staff sergeant woke us and begged us, the enlisted men that is, to make tracks as hastily as possible lest some irate general discover us enlisted trash sleeping on his doorstep. After several wild goose chases, we were unceremoniously deposited at the enlisted men's transient center located on the top floor of a department store.

The first night here three of us decided to take a look at the red-light district about which we had heard so much. Directions were readily obtainable from other soldiers and we easily found the place. Although we had heard the district was rather pretentious, we were not prepared for its vastness. Block after block was filled with establishments which all vended the same type of ware. The girls are listed on placards (sometimes illustrated with photographs), which are placed in the lobby of the establishment. One can ask for them in person but apparently a request for a girl does not necessarily tie one into filling out an engagement. I guess that I will leave out the details because all I know of the inner workings is simply hearsay.

At a couple of houses I struck up conversations with the madames. Their line of talk dealt strictly with business and nothing else. They wanted to know how many troops were coming altogether, how long they would stay, and so forth. One asked me the proper way to ask for a tip.

On one of the following nights I dropped into a cabaret for a drink. It has a crude dance floor, a number of tables and chairs, and a host of girls. It costs two yen or about thirteen cents for a dance which lasts a little over two minutes. The sociologist in me comes out every time I visit any of these places, and the first thing I do is to get into a conversation with one of the girls and ask her about her story. Most of the girls working at the cabarets appear to have gone through high school, and claim that they are there trying to pick up English. They are also out for all the money, candy and cigarettes they can get. The girls actually receive surprisingly little for what they take in, but by playing favorites they can expect good tips. That is why so many working girls aspire to be dancers.

One evening a friend of mine and I were stopped by two fairly good-looking girls who propositioned us thus: they would go anywhere, do anything, if we would in turn teach them to dance and also teach some conversational English. But not all of them are so enterprising. I asked one of the girls working in the department store downstairs to do my laundry, offering to supply the soap and pay her well. The girl makes only forty yen (less than three dollars) a month and could easily make as much by doing washing for a few people, but she refused. I was told later that she considered that taking in washing would not be in keeping with her job of salesgirl.

I was out with another girl last night who made a remark I had heard once before, but dismissed at the time as a crackpot's idea. Now that I have heard it again, I wonder if it doesn't represent the Japanese attitude toward the Nisei She asked me if I did not feel that I had been hopelessly entangled in the meshes of war when I was compelled to fight what she termed my "blood brothers." She went on to express pity for us Nisei for having to do what we did. To her and other Japanese (as well as certain Americans, I suppose), everybody must forever remain what his ancestral stock was, and cleavage from that origin is considered impossible. It would be a terrible blow to my reasoning and would make my behavior a hopeless contradiction if they were right. The only comfort I could derive from the remark the girl made was that she had retained the ability to pity me in spite of the want and suffering she may have gone through and in spite of the obvious advantages I enjoyed.

When I first learned that I was to be sent to Osaka, I said to myself, "Here is your chance to visit Suemori's folks." When I was working at the prisoner of war camp on Guam, Suemori had asked me to look up his parents, and I was only too glad to do so, for he was so extraordinarily interesting a person that I was curious to see from what kind of Japanese home he could have come. Before going to his home I had stayed up nights trying to figure out some appropriate way to introduce myself and approach the delicate matter of prisoners of war. I had still not hit on anything suitable when I knocked on their door. It was about ten in the morning on a weekday, not exactly the most fitting time for a dramatic scene. A middle-aged lady came to the door and stopped. I hesitatingly asked if this were the house of one Kakuzō Suemori, a person to whom I had been entrusted with a message. She answered that it was, and I continued, "Please forgive me my rudeness in speaking to you, but I am an American and am not familiar with the correct words to be used. I have come to tell you that your son Takeo Suemori is alive and well. I saw him last in a prisoner of war camp."

When I finished the sentence there was a moment of silence. I was afraid then that the traditional Japanese attitude concerning prisoners of war had proved stronger than parental love. But there was no need for me to have had any doubts as to how she would receive the news—she gave me such a relieved smile, and asked me in. Over the customary tea which she insisted on spiking with a few drops of whiskey and the more-precious-than-gold sugar, we conversed slowly. Mrs. Suemori was obviously overjoyed. "I could never believe that he was dead. When they announced that Okinawa had fallen, they failed to say that all the defenders had met honorable deaths as they usually did when one of our islands was lost. Everyone assumed that the entire garrison had been annihilated, but it seemed strange that, if all the troops had fought to the death, they had not been credited for their determination. As you know, anytime there is any doubt, idle minds begin to turn out rumors. In this case there was a story circulated that the troops were not all killed, but that some had been captured. And so, although all of us with relatives on Okinawa more or less assumed that they were dead, there was still that small hope that they might have been saved."

Later in the day, I went with a friend of mine to a drinking place he knew of which is set in beautifully landscaped grounds. As soon as we had entered, we were invited by another party to join them, which we did. I was amazed at the variety of food and the amount of liquor flowing. The revelers were young businessmen of obvious means. They told me, "Yes, we knew we couldn't win, but we were helpless. It was a case of do what you are told or suffer the consequences. We in business suffered the most because we lost our stock step by step and our business was then all but taken from us. We could not operate unless we complied strictly with the laws handed down to us. Now that we have lost the war, our leaders have left us holding the bag. We knew we couldn't win. They started the war twenty years too soon." And these unfortunate businessmen, eating and drinking at a cost of about one hundred and fifty dollars a head, continued to pour out their troubles to me: "We are rather fortunate as compared with the average man because we can still eat regularly, but we certainly miss our tobacco. If there is one thing you can do for us, it is . . ." I excused myself at that point.

That evening I returned with my friend to the Suemori's. We brought along a case of beer and a bottle of sake, with which we would be welcome anywhere, to liven up the evening. I met the rest of the family then, including another one of the Suemori sons. This one had just been discharged from the army a few weeks previously. He had been a first lieutenant in the Shipping Engineers and was on one of the last ships from Manila and Okinawa. He was on the deck of a ship at Ujina when the chain reaction took place at nearby Hiroshima, and his face was burned. At the first sip of sake, the area of the burns was tinted pink. The outline of his cap visor and his collar showed very clearly. His father, the elder Suemori, had been importing radio parts from the United States for ten years or so and spoke surprisingly fluent English. As the evening wore on and the drinking progressed, my friend and I found ourselves more and more outspoken, and we were soon telling them what was wrong with Japan. And then, as usual at Japanese drinking parties, we got around to singing. I finally heard for the first time the famous song, "Umi Yukaba" which was sung to Kamikaze pilots before they took off.

One week after coming to Osaka, I was sent out on a trip to the end of the Wakayama peninsula to aid in the inspection of naval defenses there. We traveled the whole way by jeep, no mean achievement considering the roads. The typhoon last month had washed away parts of the road, and we were the first to test it. At one fishing village, the whole town including the women turned out to fill in a gap in the road for us. Going by car had its advantages, however, for we were thus enabled to see parts of the scenery which I imagine even local inhabitants must be unfamiliar with. I guess that no matter what part of Japan one may go to, the most striking thing is the natural beauty of the scenery. Some people say, "These people don't deserve such lovely surroundings." My own feeling is rather different. I cannot help but wonder why a people living amid such beauty could ever nurse thoughts of conquest and world domination. If ever natural beauty could bring contentment, it should have been brought to the Japanese.

We stayed at a hotel near the beach. In the evening we would sit by the sliding windows, sipping tea and watching the fishermen draw in their nets to the cadence of a slow and strange chant. We could see the sun set behind the pines along the beach, the small craft threading their way between the rocks in the bay, and the gulls and hawks scavenging for their food. In the meantime, serving girls kept pouring hot tea. After dark, when we were about to turn in for the night, the girls would come in, set the bedding on the floor, and giggle a hurried good-night before bowing silently out.

We were the first Allied people through this area, and the roads we went over were lined with women who stood at a respectable distance, waiting to bow in unison to their "liberators." The one sure indication that no American troops had preceded us was the fact that none of the kids cried out for "cigaretto" or "chocoletto."

In addition to the scenery one is thereby able to view, travel by car has the other advantage of permitting one to avoid the railroads. The trains are now loaded with soldiers returning from overseas. Seeing them I realized what a miserable thing it must be to be a soldier on the losing side. The Japanese tradition of soldier-worship is certainly a thing of the past, for these returned soldiers are now neglected and even despised. It is no wonder that many discharged veterans have turned to armed robbery and banditry. I suppose such lawlessness must be one way of easing the pain of frustration. I would think, though, that after all the misery and suffering that some of them have been through (particularly those who starved on the bypassed islands) that the people at home would be more sympathetic to them.

The other day I saw a rather motley group of Japanese servicemen getting aboard a train. Most of them were wearing parts of American uniforms including ponchos. Curious, I inquired of one of the Japanese Red Cross girls, who was helping an injured soldier, who these people were, and I was told that they were some of the first contingent of prisoners of war returning from Leyte. They who had vowed never to return, who swore that they preferred death to the disgrace of going back to Japan as prisoners, had finally come home. I wish that I could have predicted this to all the prisoners with whom I have ever spoken. These prisoners were returning in a manner no different from that of those who had not been captured, and were meeting with essentially the same reception.

I met some other repatriates, a family that had just returned from Korea. They had escaped by the skin of their teeth and considered themselves very lucky to have come back whole. They declared the Koreans to be an unruly lot and very vicious. When I suggested that maybe the Koreans were just getting back at the Japanese for the treatment they have received for the last forty or so years, these people immediately went on the defensive. "Yes," they admitted, "the Japanese have been pretty rough in some instances, but such actions were necessary because the Koreans are such a stupid lot. We ourselves, however, tried to be as nice as possible to the Koreans whenever we felt it was safe to do so. When we escaped, it was our Korean friends who made it possible. Ever since the end of the war we have been kept alive by the food they smuggled to us at night at great risk to themselves. When we think we have loyal friends like that, we believe that we are only fair in saying that we have not done too much wrong." There was not much point in my trying to make an issue of the matter, for after all, I had not been there.

I have visited several airfields in this area and have seen at each several first-line fighting planes in serviceable if not good condition. It seems that the only reason these planes were not committed was the shortage of fuel. Antiaircraft defenses here are pitifully inadequate. One reason that more antiaircraft guns were not emplaced by the Japanese was their fear of setting fire to the cities with their own AA shells. I have also come across several boys who admit that they were in the Kamikaze force. They seem to be very glad to be alive, and most of them now declare that it would have been foolish to have died in the usual Kamikaze manner. Yet all of them said they would have gone out on a suicide flight had they so been ordered, for there was no turning back. The one trait they usually retain is the lusty drinking habit developed during their training period. I have always wanted to meet some of the girls who wrote the letters found on the bodies of Kamikaze pilots fished out of the water off Okinawa. I wonder if the worshipful admiration they expressed in those letters has given way to some other feeling now that it is only too apparent that their heroes died in vain. Perhaps, instead, it is all the stronger.

Hisashi

◆ ◆ ◆

FROM DON KEENE IN TSINGTAO TO TED DE BARY IN TOKYO

November 25, 1945

Dear Ted,

The other night I was invited by a friend of mine to have dinner with a group of Koreans. As you know, the reputation of Koreans is the very worst possessed by any foreign group in China. Koreans have been used by the Japanese as opium peddlers, undercover agents and pimps, and have gained especial notoriety as the merciless interpreters for the Japanese *kempeitai*. Many persons report having been beaten by such interpreters, apparently without direction or even suggestion by the Japanese officers concerned. In Tsingtao a group of little over a thousand Koreans has kept us as busy with its problems as ten times as many Japanese. When I was in Tsinan, an important Chinese official told me that the first people who had to be cleared out of the city were the Koreans; they were the most offensive. You can see why, then, I hesitated to accept the above invitation, being very little inclined to mix any more than necessary with such people. My friend, Bill, was quick to see what was passing through my mind. "Oh, no, you're mistaken," he assured me, "these are very special Koreans. I picked them out myself. Nothing but ministers of the gospel and schoolteachers."

The dinner turned out to be a most delightful one. The variety of dishes was so great that Bill told me that he could think of only one typical Korean specialty which had not been included. I tasted again for the first time in several years the Korean hot pickled cabbage, *kimchee*, the pungent flavor of which recalled with the utmost vividness days at the Korean prisoner of war camp in Hawaii. On holidays or special occasions I would stop at one of the little Korean stores in Honolulu and buy *kimchee*, bean curd and whatever delicacies I could find. At the camp we would eat the food together, each bite recalling for the prisoners, I suppose, dinner at home in Korea. On this evening, however, it was my turn to be nostalgic. All the Korean expressions I knew came back to me, even the song "Arirang," which is almost an anthem to the Koreans although it tells only of a lover who would walk thirty miles to be with his beloved.

The conversation at table was unusual in that it was the first time I had ever been present at a gathering of Koreans when the words "Korean independence" had not provoked a violent argument of one sort or another. The only subject discussed which led to any controversy was that of Russo-American relations, an issue which is naturally peculiarly pertinent to Koreans at present. It is very difficult, whether over a dinner table or in a lecture hall, to persuade everyone that America and Russia have no quarrel and can get along in a world at peace. The old words "ambition" and "designs" came up over and over, words I attempted to combat with the no less traditional "mutual interests" and "certain catastrophe." In such a discussion one must take a side (either that of Russia or of America if one wishes to be intelligible), for life in China has taught people to distrust the word "cooperation" as we might distrust "collaboration." These Koreans, who had braved severe punishment by listening to American shortwave broadcasts during the war, thought it only logical that America in return should help their country against the Russians, about whom they have the gravest apprehensions. A solution based on cooperation is viewed as out of the question. All they can see are two different factions in Korea, each striving to win all; cooperation in such a case they would consider betrayal.

The next day when I thanked Bill for having invited me to the dinner, he replied that the Koreans had enjoyed my company as much as I had theirs. "Since you get along so well with Koreans, why don't you go down to the brig and interview Tsoi?" Bill asked. I had heard a great deal about Tsoi, the famous war criminal, the fiendish agent of Japanese brutality, but was unprepared for a request to interview him. Jokingly, or perhaps half-seriously, I asked, "Will I have to look out for his fangs?" Bill laughed, "Not at all. You'll find him very pleasant." When I was sitting in the brig office later in the day waiting for Tsoi to be brought to me from his pitch-black solitary cell, I felt the gravest doubt about my ability to interrogate a hardened war criminal. I wondered nervously what I would do if he were to refuse to answer my questions or if he snarled back obvious lies. I was half-tempted to tell the warden to call off the interview when Tsoi entered, bowed, and then stood at attention waiting for me to speak. My astonishment at his appearance could have been no greater. Instead of the furtive or oily individual I had been expecting, I discovered Tsoi to be a person of great physical charm. He is tall and well built with handsome features; his eyes were exceptionally beautiful. When he started to speak I was amazed at the purity and grace of his Japanese, so unusual in a Korean. (I found later that he was equally fluent with Korean, Chinese and Russian.) His manner of speech was also engaging, just a little ironical, with a half-smile as he formed his words.

Before I questioned Tsoi, all we knew about him was what had been told us by various White Russians he had threatened, beaten or robbed at one time or another. As chief of the foreign section of the Chinese police, he had been personally responsible for many of the indignities inflicted on the White Russians, particularly for the beatings which took place on August 13 of this year. On that day a large number of White Russians, plus a few French, Czechs, Poles and others were arrested and examined by a committee consisting of Tsoi, Lieutenant(jg) Shimagawa of Japanese naval intelligence and a Russian named Mezhnikoff, Tsoi's successor as chief of the foreign section. The testimony of the victims and of doctors who later attended them indicated that they had been beaten mercilessly, or almost so, for one woman said that Tsoi had spared her right leg when she told him of varicose veins. Other statements mentioned Tsoi's having extorted money from shopkeepers in his official capacity, and of his having threatened with a sword a White Russian mistress whom he suspected of having taken money from his room. Local White Russians speak of him with greater hatred than of any Japanese. On the other hand, the Koreans appear to like him, for they appointed him head of the propaganda section of their "liberation army," while the Chinese admit that he never molested any of them, even declaring that he was known for his honesty. The Japanese regarded him with some suspicion because, unlike everyone else in town, he took no pains to conceal his dislike for them and because, one exception among many Korean conformers, he had refused to adopt a Japanese surname, being known only as Tsoi. His brutality appeared confined to the Russians.

The first questions I asked him were routine, about his boyhood in Harbin, his schooling at Korean, Japanese and Chinese institutions, and his coming to Tsingtao as a marine engineer. "Then the Japanese gendarmerie somehow discovered that I knew Russian and informed me that there was a job with the Chinese police that I had to take. There was no possibility of refusing and attempting to live in peace in any territory where the *kempeitai* was in control. I was forced to take the job. I tried to quit it any number of times, but did not succeed until April this year. Even while working for the Japanese, however, I was acting as a member of the Chinese secret service as I can easily prove. My younger brother is in Chungking now, working for an independent Korea, and it is with that hope that I have been helping the Chinese, too." Then, looking up with his half-smile, "When are you going to let me out of here?"

I had decided not to ask Tsoi directly about any of the crimes he was alleged to have committed. I asked instead about the local Russian community, in particular about the Anti-communist League that the Japanese had founded and to which all White Russians in the community were compelled to belong. Tsoi was well acquainted with the organization and described it in great detail, telling of the members, the military drilling, and most interestingly, about the leaders. "The Japanese wanted to put someone in charge who had above-the-ordinary prestige and who would still be amenable to their orders. Malkoff proved just the man. A former general in the Russian army, he fled to Peking and eked out a living there as a violinist in cheap cafes. Chased from Peking for some reason or other, he went to Tientsin, and eventually drifted here. Tsingtao is the last stop on the line for White Russians; once they come here, they can't drop any lower. The Japanese decided that Malkoff was just the man to lead such people.

"The White Russians, or so-called White Russians I should say, for almost every one of them would be overjoyed to accept Soviet Russian papers, are a contemptible bunch of liars and cheats to a degree which you are unable to realize. I can understand how they became that way. The necessity of earning a living, somehow, forces men to do strange things. Even though this is apparent to me, I can feel nothing but disgust and repulsion for them. The best one can say about any of them is that he is innocuous. Most of them are the kind of people who would betray their parents for an extra cent. They are inhuman. Utterly!"

Tsoi, as he spoke, grew more excited. He stopped for a moment then, and looked me straight in the eyes. "I suppose that you have been told all kinds of things about the arrests on August 13?" I made a noncommittal gesture. "Those damn Russians are always making a big commotion over nothing. I didn't want to go in the first place, but Shimagawa came to my apartment and told me that I had to help in the arrests. When I refused, saying that I was no longer connected with the police, he declared that it wasn't so easy to get out of such work. I recognized the threat and went along. Shimagawa then gave me a list of people to be arrested; I had nothing whatever to do with the compilation of the list. Everything that followed was his idea, not mine. In any case, those Russians deserved to be arrested, most of them, for having attempted to influence the gold market by spreading wild rumors. One day they would circulate a rumor which was designed to make prices go down. When that succeeded they would buy gold, only to sell again when the market returned to its normal level. I needn't tell you how susceptible the Chinese are to rumors of this kind. The Russians managed to undermine the entire money market in Tsingtao by such practices. Then, just when they were in jail, the war ended, causing the price of gold to drop again. Do you know why they are making such a row about what happened on August 13? It is just because they lost a great deal of money by being in jail at that time and want to get even. They're a disgusting lot. Did you know, by the way, that Malkoff, as head of the Anticommunist League, declared war on the United States and had pledged to send the recruits who were drilled here to the front in case of any action? That's the kind of servile, untrustworthy people they are. They really don't deserve your sympathy. Not in the slightest!"

Amidst much that Tsoi said which I found difficult to believe without qualification, I was especially disturbed by his references to Shimagawa. I had heard before that Shimagawa was present the night of the arrests, but assumed that he had been there only because of his position as head of the foreign affairs section of naval intelligence. It had not occurred to me at all that Shimagawa had been the motivating force behind all that went on. From the first he had seemed the most likeable of the Japanese officers. His easy behavior and amusing frankness set him off from most of the others, who are either stiffly polite or overly desirous to please. I felt unwilling to let Tsoi's accusation go by uncontested. I asked, "Aren't you a little unfair about Shimagawa? He seems like such a pleasant fellow."

"The kind of pleasant fellow who could eat human liver and boast about it!" I looked up at Tsoi. "He told me all about it, just a few months ago, in August, over tea at the Lucky Asia

Restaurant. I could scarcely believe my ears, that a person, however wicked, could eat the liver of another human being, but Shimagawa was proud of it, and told us how human liver increased one's sexual prowess. That's the kind of simple, innocent example of young Japanese manhood that Shimagawa is!"

"Are you sure of this? Wasn't it just a joke?" I asked.

"When I heard Shimagawa tell me of having eaten human liver, I was, as I said, horrified, but one of the others at the table, Sergeant Muranouchi of the *kempeitai* chimed in with as much enthusiasm in an account of the value of human liver as a medicine. This was all I heard about the matter until recently when I was talking to some of the Koreans who were discharged from the Japanese navy—there are about a hundred of them in Tsingtao. Some of those who were stationed at navy headquarters on University Road witnessed a number of executions of men described as communists, but who were actually random persons picked up, briefly examined and then thrown in jail. They were kept in a cell from several days to a week without food or water. This was to cause the liver to contract and harden. Then they would be taken out to the mountain behind the university where they were tied to trees or crosses. They were then bayoneted to death by young Japanese sailors, whose fighting spirit the officers wanted to harden. Once a criminal was executed someone would invariably rush forward to cut out the liver. It must be cut out at once or else it spoils. The livers thus obtained were hung out to dry and then were made into a medicine. Every month from five to twenty persons were executed to keep up the supply of liver. It was supposed to be good for all ailments. The officers, particularly the high-ranking ones, regularly took this medicine. Can you imagine human beings sinking to such depths?" Tsoi shook his head.

"Who else was involved?"

"They were all involved, all guilty, because they knew just what they were doing. But that's what the Japanese are like, every last one of them in that nation that prides itself so on its code of honor. Sometimes I wonder if anyone can do the things they do and still remain a human being. Eating human liver! Demons!"

I sent Tsoi back then with a request that he write up everything he had told me. I was unable to take any more. What affected me most was that the crimes, if indeed they had been committed, were the work of people I knew well, people with whom I would drink tea or exchange jokes, people who would complain to me about the meanness of the Chinese, and with whom I would smile in understanding. To think that once when I received a good letter, one so good that I couldn't keep its pleasure to myself, I felt so in rapport with Shimagawa that I showed it to him, to share some of the pleasure! My amiable hosts of a late afternoon were cannibals, not in the way those hunted creatures on Guam were, but cannibals who could be proud of their gentlemanly traditions, cannibals who would raise their hands in horror if they heard that some Peace Preservation Corps soldier had taken away a Japanese gentleman's coat.

As I walked back to the office, kicking at every stone, I tried to examine Tsoi's story dispassionately. It was possible, of course, that he was lying. There was no real reason to believe accusations made by a man who was considered a war criminal himself, but his words were impossible to cloak in qualifications thick enough to insulate their horror; every step I took I kicked more savagely.

The next morning the colonel ordered me to find out the entire truth about Tsoi's accusations. I felt that however distasteful the job might be it had to be done. Ships were arriving to repatriate the Japanese, and unless quick action were taken, persons guilty of the alleged crime would be allowed to return to Japan, to be lost in the confusion that must be prevalent there now. I was uncertain as to the correct procedure to be followed, at length deciding to investigate first the Koreans who had been in the Japanese navy as the eyewitnesses most likely to be willing to furnish information.

The room in which I questioned the Koreans was so cold that I found it almost impossible to sit still and my teeth were chattering so badly that my words came out in little jerky syllables. I had the shivering Koreans sent in one at a time, asking each more or less the same questions: "When did you enter the unit at University Road?"; "What kind of work did you do there?";

"Did you ever witness any executions?"; and others of the sort. Most of the ex-sailors were poorly educated and could not seem to understand that I wanted direct answers to the questions asked and not rambling accounts. Surprisingly enough, however, none of them tried to excuse himself for having served in the Japanese navy or to excite my sympathy by reciting mistreatments by the Japanese. Nor did they seem anxious to embroider on the facts and make up details in the hope of supplying me with information I wanted to hear, as Koreans often seem so inclined to do.

The first few I questioned had each seen the same execution in July of this year. I asked, "How were they killed?"

"The officers lined up about fifteen trainees for each man to be executed and then each trainee stabbed the man in front of him two or three times with his bayonet."

"What happened then?"

"The company commander cut off the heads of two of them."

"Was anything done to the bodies after that?" I hesitated to ask directly if the livers had been cut out for fear of suggesting the answer they thought I wanted to hear.

"No, they were just kicked into holes."

I felt relieved, thinking that Tsoi's story must certainly have been made up largely of pure hearsay, or perhaps even his own animosity toward the Japanese. The next Korean came in very shyly after bowing awkwardly at the door. He looked like a boy of sixteen, with a round dewy face and eyes which did not leave the floor. I asked him, "Did you ever see any executions?"

"Yes, I have seen about twenty-five men killed myself. I heard that many more have been killed, as many as one a day on an average. They were usually killed by being bayoneted to death by the primary enlisted trainees, but sometimes they were just beheaded."

"Was anything done to the bodies?"

"Once I saw a man come out just after an execution and slit open the bellies of the dead and remove their livers. I heard that they make medicine from the liver."

"When was this?"

"After Japan was defeated, maybe a week afterward. These

weren't communists like before. I think that they were ordinary thieves, who had attempted to steal a car. I saw this execution myself. None of the Koreans was supposed to go, but I saw some petty officers heading for the execution ground and I went with them. There were just a few people present including some nurses. I kept thinking how strange it was that the Japanese should be doing such things even after losing the war."

The testimony of others who filed into the cold room confirmed the boy's story, and Tsoi's. Two or three had seen the livers cut out. One of them knew the name of the man who had leaped out with his short sword and cut open the executed. Another had seen liver drying in a corner of his barracks. Several had heard Japanese sailors boasting of having eaten human liver. There was no note of anger or excitement in the voices of the Koreans narrating the details of the executions, except that one might end his story with, "This was the first time I ever saw an execution and I couldn't watch to the end." I had thought that the Koreans might have made up the story in order to bring trouble to their commanding officer, but most of them could not even remember his name, and only a few were sure that he had ordered the executions. When I asked one of them why the company commander had had the Chinese bayoneted to death, he answered, "Why don't you ask Lieutenant Mochihara?" in all innocence.

The next day I drove out to the suburb where the Japanese navy is now awaiting repatriation. The colonel had authorized me to arrest Mochihara and any others I thought might be connected with the crime. All kinds of doubts made it difficult for me to take any such action. I was not sure of the reliability of the statements made by the Koreans or of Mochihara's individual responsibility. In addition, I hesitated to arrest him at this moment when he was undoubtedly anticipating return to Japan, for if I kept him here it might mean that, even if innocent, he would be unable to go back for a long time. I was really very disturbed by the thought of pronouncing the words, "I arrest you," and every possible doubt presented itself to me in an effort, I suppose, to make me put off the actual arrest.

I found an empty office and had Mochihara sent in. He sat

down opposite me and answered my routine questions. I felt immensely relieved when I heard him speak in a squeaky voice, a little saliva drooling out of his mouth. I felt that there was no longer any danger that pity would prevent me from making the arrest. Finally, after staring at him in silence, unable to find anything else to ask him, I informed him that he would have to come to town with me. I did not use the word arrest, assuming that Mochihara would understand, but he asked innocently if there would be a place for him to stay, and reminded me that the ship he was to board would be sailing in three days.

The drive back was unspeakably gloomy with sporadic attempts at conversation killed for each of us by what it was impossible to talk about. Along the way, kids standing near the road cheered the jeep and then stopped to stare at Mochihara in his blue overcoat with the rows of brass buttons. When we reached town it was dark and the few lights shone on empty streets. There was a final moment of hesitation on my part before I conducted him into the brig.

I was impatient to talk with Mochihara, but was afraid that my lack of experience in dealing with such matters might cause me to do the wrong things. I tried to recall what I had read about the use of psychology in the interrogation of prisoners. It had never been necessary when interrogating Japanese prisoners during the war for me to resort to much more subtlety than asking what I wanted to know with a rising tone at the end of the sentence, confident that I would be given the right answer. In a case like this, however, it might be necessary to try all the tricks I had heard were used on German prisoners, or by the Germans on Allied prisoners, involving casual references to seemingly unimportant matters, lightning thrusts, and the quick catching of a contradictory phrase. As I set out for the brig later in the evening I lost heart and confidence in my ability to do the job, and called on a friend of mine who is a lawyer to help me out. The two of us were subtle with Mochihara for three hours, Steve asking the questions while I contented myself with interpreting. At the end of the long session, Steve turned to me and said, "Let's try again tomorrow. It's obvious he isn't going to talk now."

Steve and I met in the morning and started again. "Were Chinese ever kept at the University Road establishment for punitive reasons?"

"No, that never happened."

"Was there any place to keep such persons there?"

"No."

"Well," in desperation, "weren't there any Chinese ever punished by the navy there?"

"No." Then a pause, and Mochihara's face broke into a grin, "Oh, you mean executions don't you?" He had obviously been unaware as to what we were driving at, but he was perfectly willing to speak about the executions, the one thing we thought he would have hesitated to discuss. We pressed him for details. He could remember four or five executions in the past eight months with an average of four men executed each time.

"How were these criminals executed?"

"They were either beheaded or bayoneted to death."

"By whose order?"

"Mine."

"Why did you order your men to bayonet the Chinese?"

There was a kind of giggle, accompanied by a salivation, "I thought that it would be good practice for the younger men."

He giggled again. "God damn it, what's so funny?" Steve shouted at Mochihara in English. Mochihara shut his mouth. "How did they bayonet them?"

"I ordered my men to form a line in front of each criminal and to jab him with their bayonets."

"Was this your own idea or were you told to execute them in this manner?"

"It was my own idea. Lieutenant Kamimizu, the legal officer, would call up and say that he had a couple of criminals he wanted executed and ask me to do him the favor of having them killed. I would then send a truck to pick them up. When the execution was accomplished, I would telephone Kamimizu and inform him, but I did not tell him or anyone else of the method used. That was my responsibility."

"What happened to the bodies after the criminals were killed?"

"Sometimes I would cut off their heads with my sword, but usually they were buried as they were."

"Was there any mutiliation of the bodies after the criminals were killed?"

No answer.

"Was the liver ever cut out?"

"Yes, once. An interpreter from the naval courts-martial ran out and cut open the body and took out the liver."

"Just once?"

Mochihara thought a minute, grinning and drooling with his head cocked to one side in the typical Japanese attitude of thought. "No, another time when I led an expedition to the tip of the Shantung promontory, the same interpreter cut out another Chinese's liver. We had captured a man who had been looting a shipwrecked Japanese vessel. I questioned him through the interpreter and then, when I was satisfied that he was a communist, I ordered him executed. He was tied to a tree and bayoneted to death. The interpreter then cut out the liver."

"Did he ask your permission?"

"Yes, I gave it."

There were a few minutes of silence then during which Mochihara stared at the floor. I felt that we had too much evidence; what should have been obtained only as the result of great pains fell to us without effort. I thought that Mochihara must be telling the truth, for I could not see any reason why he should have told so much to incriminate himself and yet persist in falsehood on certain matters. Of course, the possibility existed that he was lying to protect someone else, either his commanding officer or junior officers, but unless his drooling, his high-pitched voice and his inane giggle were elaborately contrived devices, it seemed almost certain that Mochihara was not entirely sane. The kind of mind which could originate live bayonet practice is almost impossible for me to realize. Even if one can encompass the idea of a bayonet clash between two men, each murderously inclined, it does not seem possible to imagine the moment of thrust into the body of another man tied to a tree. You must remember the beginning of Malraux' *Man's Fate* when Tchen is unable to strike through the mosquito netting at the sleeping merchant, wishing only that he would stir and thus permit action. How is it possible to stab a man who stares helplessly from his cross or one who is already bleeding or dead from twenty wounds? It seems to have no connection with military prowess. It is sordid brutality—worse, utter degeneracy. I thought, looking at Mochihara, that he was probably capable of it.

We resumed our questioning. "Have you ever eaten medicine made of human liver?"

"No."

"Do you know anyone else who did?"

"My predecessor as company commander, Lieutenant Makuda, was supposed to have eaten human liver, but I don't know for sure. I have never seen any myself."

There was another pause, and then I began, "Tell me, did the sailors in your company bayonet the Chinese readily?"

Mochihara looked up from the floor with another grin. "About half didn't seem to want to take part in the bayoneting, but naturally no one complained. Every man took his turn." After more silence during which we stared at Mochihara, attempting to divine from the lines of his face or the movement of his hands what could possibly be going on within him, we sent him back to his cell. "Nice guy!" Steve remarked shaking his head.

Even though Mochihara had taken sole responsibility for the executions, it was still necessary to check his story, and also the other accusations Tsoi had made. I sent for Shimagawa and Kamimizu and ordered the arrest of Fujimoto, the petty officer the Koreans had named as the man who had cut out the livers. When Shimagawa came into my office he smiled at me saying, "This place is very familiar. Before the Americans moved in, this was our chief of staff's office." I was unable to answer him in a similar manner, but tried to guess from his movements if he knew why I had sent for him. I attempted to speak to him coldly, but his interested, sympathetic face which betrayed to me no guilt made me start over again.

"Up to now we have spoken as friends. I would have liked this relationship to continue, but my duties now make it necessary for me to speak to you in a different way, and for you to answer me accordingly." Pause. "Do you understand?"

Shimagawa nodded, "I understand."

I tried to think of some way of starting a line of questioning which would terminate logically with the important thing, but my mind would not work. I could hear the clock ticking in the office and the newsboys out in the street shouting the names of their newspapers. Shimagawa continued to look at me expectantly. Then the words came out in crudest form, "Have you ever eaten human liver?"

Shimagawa started. "Human liver? Never."

"Have you ever said you did, even in a joke?"

"No, never."

"Do you remember eating at the Lucky Asia Restaurant last August with three other people? Didn't you mention it then?"

Shimagawa smiled embarrassedly, "I do remember now having told some kind of dirty story in which I said that I had heard that eating human liver made it possible to go to a brothel a great many times in one day, but I never said I ate it myself."

I showed Shimagawa the account which Tsoi had written for me and which repeated the accusation of Shimagawa I had first heard. Shimagawa read it over, shaking his head. He asked hesitantly, "Was this written by someone I know?"

"Yes."

"By one of my close friends?"

I thought for a moment that somewhere I had read that it was effective to make a suspect doubt his own friends, but I felt incapable of answering more than the one word. "No." That was all I said to Shimagawa then and I have not spoken to him since. Subsequent evidence has neither proved nor disproved Tsoi's charge; Shimagawa is being held until it can be verified.

Kamimizu, the legal officer, was to follow Shimagawa in, but Lieutenant Ishihara managed somehow to come into my office in between the two others. He had a farewell present to give me, a kimono, before he left for Japan. Ishihara is so naively pro-American that I find him very winning usually, but coming at that moment he was certainly not suitably greeted. As I went back to my desk, guiltily bearing the present, the mark of Japanese kindness, Kamimizu knocked and came in. Kamimizu had been the judge presiding over the naval courts-martial, and should have known how many Chinese had been sentenced to death and what type of trial they had been afforded. When I sent for him and placed him under virtual arrest, I had felt more or less the same reluctance as in the case of Shimagawa, for my relations with Kamimizu had been very cordial. I remember in particular one Sunday when Kamimizu escorted me through the grounds of the Tsingtao Shrine. The shrine is the most enduring symbol of Japan in China that I have seen, sweeping up a hill along pine-covered slopes and dominating the entire city. That day Kamimizu and I climbed the hundred and thirty steps until we came to the shrine itself. He pointed apologetically at the sign, "*Datsubō*," "Take off your hat." We approached the railing before the shrine uncovered. There he made a deep bow. Standing beside him motionless was an act of nonparticipation which seemed to divide us as no other gesture could have. The ways in which we might be similar, the things we enjoy in common seemed at that moment of infinitely less importance than his motion of worship in a religion which for me is no religion.

We took pictures later in the day, while crowds of Chinese children stared at us. As we walked, I asked, "As a lawyer, what do you think of the problem of Japanese prisoners returning to Japan now that the war is over?"

"To answer not necessarily as a lawyer, but as an ordinary Japanese, the idea of becoming a prisoner is extremely distasteful to me. It strikes me as an outrageous thing for a man to expect to be treated well and given food and shelter because he has surrendered while his comrades are still fighting and dying." I unfortunately made the mistake of asking a little sarcastically if he knew what modern fighting was like from firsthand contact. He answered, "If I didn't go to the front it is not because I did not wish to do so. As a legal officer, however, my requests for combat duty were invariably turned down. I would have been proud to fight at the front. I would not have surrendered."

"But there are many fine men who were taken prisoner, some of whom surrendered, and many of whom were captured when badly wounded or even unconscious. What do you propose to do about them?"

"For the enlisted man it will not matter so much. People will cover things up. But for the officers it will be as in the past, when some friend would come around and say, "It would be better for you to die," and they will undoubtedly kill themselves. There will be some loss to Japan in that way, but it is worth the loss of a little if traditions can be preserved."

It had been unusual to find any Japanese willing to state opinions which contradicted my own, and I had been glad to know Kamimizu for that reason. When he came into the office for questioning, I prefaced my remarks with a statement of attitude, as I had done with Shimagawa, and then asked much the same questions. Kamimizu professed to be entirely ignorant of the practice of consumption of human liver "except once, long ago, before Mochihara and even before his predecessor, Makuda, there was a company commander who was said to have eaten human liver."

I asked, "Is there any penalty for cannibalism in the Japanese navy?"

He thought a minute, "No, I am sure I have never seen any reference to it in law books. I imagine that it was never even considered a possibility. Is that sort of thing common in the American navy? Do you have regulations about cannibalism?"

Naturally, I had no idea, but answered that cannibalism while virtually unknown in the United States, was punishable by death. Kamimizu remarked that Japanese law had apparently not foreseen such a contingency. I asked, "What about the method of execution? When you sent prisoners to University Road did you tell Mochihara how they were to be executed?"

"No, I did not. When first I started turning over prisoners to the University Road unit I told Makuda that they should be put before a firing squad, or, if that was impossible, that they should be beheaded. I assumed that he told Mochihara of my instructions when relieved of command. Shooting is the normal method of execution, but beheading has become more common here because of the shortage of bullets. You may find it hard to believe, but we were really so short of ammunition that we could not afford to waste any in executing criminals."

"Would there be any penalty for executing a man in an unorthodox manner, such as bayoneting him to death?" I asked this because Mochihara had stated that Kamimizu was present at one execution at which this had been done. Kamimizu answered that he did not think so. Other questioning brought forth his guess that a total of eight or nine men had been sentenced to death in the past year. The figure he gave was obviously far from correct, but I decided to postpone discussion of it until I had additional evidence.

My third examination of the day was of Fujimoto at the brig. When I went there I was accompanied by two Koreans who had witnessed Fujimoto cut out the livers of the executed Chinese. Fujimoto proved to be a dumb animal, a beast with ferocious little eyes and an empty masked face. He had been in the navy for many years, but had only recently been promoted to petty officer, an indication of his general deficiencies. His answers to my questions marked him as an illiterate capable only of crude expression. He recited without emotion the part he had taken in a bayonet execution, remarking only that he had been so ordered. He had seen one other execution. That was all he admitted, denying ever having seen a human liver.

I ordered the Koreans brought in. Cheng, the baby-faced one, identified Fujimoto as the man who had cut out the livers. Fujimoto glared at Cheng, brute power and dumb hatred in his eyes. "You are lying."

Cheng started to sweat and turned his head away from Fujimoto, unable to meet the ferocity of his eyes. The other Korean, Han, stood placidly beside him, taking comfort from the fact that he had not accused Fujimoto himself. "Is it true?" I demanded of Cheng, but he could only stammer a few incoherent sounds, his eyelids fluttering. I turned to Han, but he excused himself saying that he could not be sure. I looked at Fujimoto in the eyes for a few seconds without speaking. The perspiration was pouring down his face and his tongue went over his lips. His jaw was thrust forward defiantly and his little eyes narrowed. Suddenly I shouted at him, "Well?"

Words started to tumble out of his lips all at once. "Once after we bayoneted some Chinese, I saw somebody with something. It had a funny smell. 'What's that?' I asked him. 'Here, I don't need it,' he answered, and gave it to me. I didn't want it and it stank so I threw it away. They said it was a liver, but I don't know. It stank so much that I didn't touch it. I don't know what it was." I immediately threw questions at him for details, but he stopped talking all at once and then denied he had ever seen a human liver. In a rage, I ordered him put on bread and water in a solitary confinement cell. He bowed stiffly and left the room.

When he had gone Cheng found words again. "That's the man who did it. I am positive." Han joined in with, "Did you notice how he changed his story? First he said he had seen a liver and then he said he hadn't." Cheng ignored this, but went on, "I saw him go from body to body, slitting open one after another, putting his hand inside and pulling out the liver. I thought how small they looked. He's the man who did it."

Mochihara and Fujimoto are, at present, the only ones in jail, although I have put others on detention arrest, which means they cannot return to Japan with their units. Among these are the warrant officer I interrogated who admitted having dried a human liver in his barracks. He stated that he did not know just what it was he had been drying until much later and that, in any case, it had disappeared one day before he could use it to help his delicate constitution. I have also detained an old crone who was employed as a maid of all work at the junior officers quarters. She seemed amazed to be under examination and answered every question with, "Do you mean me?" The woman admitted, however, that she had received a piece of something, "I thought it might have been a bear's stomach," from Lieutenant Makuda, the former company commander. She made a broth out of it which improved her health greatly. Once when she heard of some men dying of a hopeless sickness she gave him some of her medicine. He was cured in three days.

I have also interrogated the ordinary sailors who did the bayoneting. One of them, a boy of sixteen, was utterly matter-of-fact in his recitation, although he claimed to have been reluctant to thrust his bayonet into the Chinese criminal. "I stuck my bayonet in twice, aiming at vital parts. Then an officer said "O.K." to me and I went back to clean my bayonet." Others have willingly admitted this participation, saying they were under orders, but no one, not even the interpreter twice named by Mochihara as having cut out the liver, will confess to having done so.

I have spoken at great length with Captain Okabe concerning the case. I think it has helped to shake his faith in the gentlemanly traditions of the naval service. He explained, "We all knew that there was something wrong with Mochihara. He spent one year, you know, in a sanatorium, and he was always on the verge of some mild type of insanity. He had highs and lows, good and bad periods. One of the lows was just after the end of the war when, in disgust with the way things happened, he disobeyed his superiors' orders repeatedly. We all knew this about Mochihara, but there were no replacements available, and besides, he is a naval academy graduate and there are so few of them." I asked Okabe about Makuda, Mochihara's predecessor. "Makuda joined a suicide boat unit and was killed at Okinawa. I guess that Mochihara will soon be joining him in hell!" Okabe said this with a laugh in which I did not feel inclined to join.

I asked Okabe what he thought of the crimes themselves. He answered, "Eating human liver is a thing I long associated with the Chinese. When I was a little boy I was always frightened off the streets at night by the story that I would be caught by a Chinese and have my liver taken out. The Chinese were always the bogeymen for us. I have heard it said that there is a medicine used by the Chinese called Six Gods Pills which contains human liver supposedly from Japanese children!" He laughed at this.

"What about the executions themselves?"

"I can scarcely believe that there were so many without my having had any knowledge of them, but I suppose that they might very well have taken place. There are a great many evildoers in China, you know."

"What about the method of execution, bayoneting?" I asked, a little disturbed by the pat finality with which he answered.

"Naturally in Japan we use humane methods of execution such as the gas chamber or the electric chair. When I read that General Yamashita is to be hanged I was greatly shocked, for that seems a most barbaric form of execution to me. Here in China, however, we have adopted of necessity more military methods, shooting or beheading. Bayoneting I have never heard of. Although I must confess that if I were a sailor ordered to bayonet a criminal, I would have a hard time getting myself to comply. I think that if the man with the bayonet aims for a vital part the first time, the whole thing can be done quite simply." Okabe lit a cigarette and then continued, "We expected an American landing imminently. Our naval troops here were mostly young boys with no knowledge of war and no particular feeling of combat spirit. Something had to be done to ready them for the battles in which they were soon to engage. At least, that's my supposition, for as I have said, I had no knowledge of the matter until you spoke to me of it."

I am still working on the case, but do not know where it will lead me. Mochihara signed his confession this morning. When I showed it to him for his signature, he read it over carefully, remarking at the end, "There are some mistakes." My heart sank at the thought that the work would have to be done all over, or even that he had retracted his statement of a few days before. There was no cause for such alarm. Mochihara wished merely to correct the characters which had been used for his name. He signed the confession in typical Japanese schoolboy fashion, "M. Mochihara." "Do you want my seal, too?" he asked.

This afternoon while writing this letter I have been interrupted by the visits of various people who have been detained in connection with the case. They are panicky at the thought of not being able to return to Japan and have come to beg me to change my mind. The horror of the case has now worn off; we now even make jokes about liver-eating. The Chinese have finally gotten around to sending a war crimes man here and I have determined to turn over the entire case to him as soon as I have finished my report. I wonder how shocked the Chinese are going to be.

Don

◆ ◆ ◆

FROM OTIS CARY IN TOKYO
TO DON KEENE IN TSINGTAO

November 25, 1945

Dear Don,

The letters that were recently sent on from the POWs at Pearl Harbor caused the same reaction all over again in miniature that the first ones I brought did. I never really had a chance to tell you about my first experiences of "bringing the boys back to life" before their families what with the rush of those first few days and the uncertainty of where we would be and what we would be doing.

I brought about twenty-five letters from the POWs I knew best, which I promised to deliver if circumstances permitted. The entire problem of the Japanese public's point of view on POWs was still indeterminable, so I decided to try a couple of test cases to see how some of the POWs' families would take it. At least it would give me an idea whether to peddle as many of the letters as possible, or whether it would be more of a favor to burn the letters and let the POWs do their own explaining in their own way when they got back. I can recall, at stunt nights at more than one POW camp, POWs putting on pantomimes of their return home. If a POW lived in Tokyo he would make his way immediately upon landing to the point in the home islands farthest from Tokyo. In a year he might possibly make a quick trip through Tokyo. In another six months if there was reason for him to go to Tokyo, he might just possibly go. Perhaps in the course of this business trip he might drive through his home neighborhood in a taxi with dark glasses on. If nothing happened he might go through a little slower again on the streetcar. Finally he might hurriedly go by his old home on a bicycle, then on foot. After inquiring around as to the general conditions at home at the corner tobacconist he might, if reports had been favorable, present himself at the door. This was a hilarious sequence to the POWs and never failed to bring down the house. Yet there was something tragic about it to me who had a chance to see home life there in Hawaii occasionally, even though I was so far away from mine myself.

I selected the letters of the two POWs I had known best who knew their families would only be glad to learn of their safety. I figured that they could give me guidance on what to do in the other cases, too. It turned out to be the closest thing to playing Jesus I would ever want to try.

You recall Oyanagi, editor of the *Niigata Nippō*, who was captured on Iwo. I delivered his letter to his brother-in-law first. His family is an old newspaper family and he knows everybody in the news game. His brother-in-law is president of Dentsū, one of the big advertising services and printing agencies of Japan. The letter was to him, addressed through Mr. Furuno, president of Dōmei, now held as a war crimes suspect, in case he had been burned out. I went to see Mr. Furuno, who sent me right over to see Mr. Ueda of Dentsū in his car. After being introduced to Mr. Ueda by Mr. Hagihara, who had made it possible for me to see Mr. Furuno and had brought me over to the Dentsū building, I gave him Oyanagi's letter. He read it quickly and half-aloud. I was able to hear most of it. It was masterfully written, for that is one of the many things Oyanagi can do and Mr. Ueda laid down the letter and his glasses at the end and smiled with great benignity. He seemed to accept it easily, but not to lose my chance I started to follow up with all I could tell of Oyanagi since he had left Japan, during the fighting on Iwo, his capture, his life at Pearl, etc. We talked for close to three hours, Mr. Ueda waiving company business aside. The army and navy, which up till the end of the war had been overcautious about notifying families of the dead of the Pacific island garrisons up through Iwo, had suddenly started to notify the families of all the garrison forces indiscriminately, without taking into account, any more than they had during the war, the possibility of capture. Up until the end of the war the country was told that everyone had died heroically to the last man, but now individual notification was going out. Mr. Ueda had just been up to Oyanagi's official funeral. He was about to have to go up and settle his estate and didn't know quite how he would break it up. We made a date for the following night, including Mr. Hagihara, too, for he had known Oyanagi well. He had also been the head of the Dōmei news agency in N.Y. for a number of years.

Mr. Ueda seemed to have no trouble in grasping the idea that Oyanagi was not dead. The following night he told me that fortunately he had been able to get a line through to Niigata and had spoken to Mrs. Oyanagi. He told her to brace herself and then gave her the news. She said she and Oyanagi's kid brother would start down as soon as they could secure tickets.

Following this, I went out to find Yokota's brother-in-law out in Ichikawa, a suburb of Tokyo. It was the most packed "El" ride I've ever had. Dr. Shikiba runs a mental disease hospital out in that unburned and pretty suburb. I stood in line with everybody else for twenty minutes to buy a ticket, then, as I finally got up to the window, found one reserved for "Allied Military Personnel." Up on the platform I stood and waited again for almost an hour, missing two trains because they were so full. No one around me realized I could speak Japanese, of course, but in trying to push our way onto the trains the group around me and I got quite intimate. As it seemed to become painfully obvious that we weren't quite going to be able to push our way onto the third train, somebody in back yelled, "This one is for MacArthur!" obviously referring to me. I hollered back in Japanese, "All right! I'll take the job!" This immediately drew a hearty laugh from my "intimates" and seemed to give us the added push to land us just inside the doors before they closed.

I got out to Ichikawa and, with the help of the local gendarmerie and a passing Japanese army truck which I hailed, I got quite close to the Shikibas' hospital and residence. After inquiring at the hospital I got to the house. There I asked for Doctor Shikiba and he came to the front entrance. I handed him Yokota's letter written a scant ten days before. He took some time to read it. (Yokota was a newspaperman of some experience in China and Manchuria for Dōmei as well as a photographer for the *Asahi* before he got drafted.) He finally asked me in. We talked for twenty minutes or so, but didn't seem to get anywhere. I kept telling him that Yokota was all right, but it didn't seem to get through. He thought I had seen Yokota before his death and was kindly delivering a note he'd written before he died. The date on the letter was 15 September 1945, not the Japanese Shōwa 20. (Putting the thing together later that night we found out why we hadn't got together. Only a few days before, in this home too, word had come through from the army that Yokota had been "lost" the previous September. Indeed, they showed me his obituary in that evening's *Asahi*, Japan's best newspaper and the one for which he'd worked. Doc Shikiba in his haste had thought my message was dated the year before.) He excused himself for a minute, went out back and read it again checking with a calendar on the date. This time we talked much more coherently. It was supper time and they asked me to stay. The word got around fast. All the family, two or three households' worth, gathered. Doc Shikiba's younger brother is there as manager of the hospital. We talked till after one-thirty, about the war, about the B–29 raids, about the occupation, about the propaganda leaflets, but always the talk would come back to Yokota. They were to have his funeral within the week. In fact they were just about to send an enlargement of his photograph for the casket down to Mrs. Yokota, who lived near Nagoya. They were all overjoyed with the news and yet it was so incredible that only when I supplied detail after detail of Yokota's life in the service and as a POW did it really sink in that he was alive and well.

I had come to first of all reassure them of Yokota's existence, but also to ask their advice on whether to let others know. They came to understand the former gladly, but the latter was much harder to determine. It was decided finally that Doc Shikiba's younger brother should go down to the Yokota house two days early and break the news to Mrs. Yokota. Their first impulse at the Shikiba's was to call the whole thing off and expose the army. I had to caution them that it might be better not to be too joyous for a while because of neighborhood as well as official reaction. It was left, pending Mrs. Yokota's final decision, that they would hold the funeral with a business-as-usual attitude and see how many other people had "dead" men coming home. We joked the rest of the night about the "glad funeral" coming off. Since then I have become fast friends with the Shikiba family. They insist on doing my laundry every week and make it mandatory for me to come out every weekend. We inevitably talk till one o'clock.

I was able to meet Mrs. Oyanagi at Dentsū three or four days after I saw the Shikibas, and Mrs. Yokota came up to Tokyo after the funeral was all taken care of. Both of them had skeptically inspected what the army had painstakingly forwarded as their husbands' last remains in supposedly unopenable containers before I had brought any news. Oyanagi's contained ashes of lord knows who (or what?). Yokota's was some hair which was not even his own (he had told me so before I left Pearl). Mrs. Oyanagi was a dainty little thing, a modern woman but in the Japanese tradition, extremely alert and perceiving, but demure and coy. She drank up every word I had to say about her husband, and I found myself led on just by her passive attention. Mrs. Yokota proved to be quite the opposite type. Yokota loved his two children, and she was certainly the perfect mother for them. She brought the older son with her up to Tokyo. She had never given up hope of her husband's return, even when the (supposedly) official announcement came. She knew something was wrong as soon as her brother came down to her home before the funeral. She sensed it even before he called all the family together in the big room to tell them. It is rare to find a Japanese mother who will not pamper her children, especially male children, at even a whimper. Mrs. Yokota was one who didn't. The older son was only six, but he seemed to sense his father's absence. He had had a chance to get to know him somewhat, for Yokota spent much time with him. He had a conscientious streak in him somewhere which had him looking out for his mother and little brother, often in a manly, responsible way.

On the strength of these two experiences, although both these progressive families were only too glad to have the news and could hardly keep it from the neighborhood, we decided that on others it would be better to wait. If I could go personally to deliver the letters and also drum in the fact of the POWs' existence with many details of their capture and present circumstances during the course of a long visit, it would be plausible to other families. To receive just a letter from a veritable "ghost," no matter what explanation was enclosed, would be too much, we figured.

I later had a chance to go and see both Mrs. Oyanagi and Mrs. Yokota in their homes. This afforded me much more time to talk with them personally and tell them everything I could remember about their husbands. Mrs. Yokota told me how they all sat in the back row at the funeral so they wouldn't be caught snickering in the private funeral at the Oyanagis' (after I had broken the news); they doubled up on Oyanagi's mother's funeral along with his. The whole Oyanagi family prayed only at the mother's picture. Mrs. Oyanagi has a big home in Niigata where the Oyanagi family is one of the leading families. As a result of her joy over the knowledge of her husband's safety, she came to open up her home to many of the occupation troops stationed in Niigata. When she came to Tokyo a little while ago she asked me to meet and talk with a certain captain who had fallen for her and to explain to him her situation. I could not see him unfortunately, but I wrote the following letter.

Dear Captain,

Perhaps you have seen my picture at the Oyanagis' home in Niigata. I am on skis with my wife—a picture taken during our honeymoon. Mrs. Tami Oyanagi insisted on having it when I went up to Niigata for a visit. I am a naval lieutenant at present doing duty with the Civil Information and Education Section of Supreme Commander for the Allied Powers in Tokyo. However, having been born and raised in Japan and so being able to speak Japanese, I was attached to Admiral Nimitz's headquarters in Pearl Harbor throughout the war, going out from there on various operations. My specific duty was working with prisoners of war.

As you know, contrary to what the Japanese admitted, many Japanese prisoners were taken during the war. I participated with the marines and the army in the assault on Saipan. The latest figure of prisoners taken there was over two thousand five hundred, more than ten percent of the original garrison. Iwo Jima yielded about ten percent, also;

the last count was a little over one thousand five hundred. I got to know many of these boys well, for they helped us in countless ways. Many of them were mere civilians in uniform and could see no sense in the hopeless battles in which they were ordered to participate. One of the many men I got to know extremely well was an ex-newspaperman, drafted, and among the Iwo Jima garrison force. He was not well at the time we landed and the field hospital he was with was holed up in a cave. He was in there for more than a month. At last, though, they were rescued by some marines. He regained his health again and I first got to know him at Pearl, where he was under my jurisdiction for more than six months. He was editor of the *Niigata Nippō* and his name is Yutaka Oyanagi.

When I was ordered to Japan after the surrender I left him and others like him. I promised those I knew best that I would look up their families. In September, as it still is now somewhat, it was a problem as to how the Japanese public would accept prisoners of war. When I arrived in Tokyo and had some spare time and went to see Yutaka Oyanagi's brother-in-law, who is president of a large advertising and printing agency; he could hardly believe it. Luckily, I had a letter which I brought with me written by Yutaka Oyanagi.

Mrs. Tami Oyanagi is his attractive wife. I also had one written to her. Rather than entrust it to uncertain mails, after she got the news on the telephone, she decided to come down in person. I was luckily able to give it to her personally, not much later. She insisted that I come up to Niigata sometime, too, which I was glad to do for a weekend, to see her husband's newspaper plant and talk to his brothers and sister, and of course, wife.

Until he comes back, the secret is still being kept in the family, and down at the newspaper plant people have been kept in the dark. I only tell you this confidentially. They were just about to have his home funeral when I came with the news, and they went on with it just the same, for they didn't want to have undue commotion caused in the community. As you know the Oyanagi family is one of the leading families in

Niigata. They have been good to a number of servicemen in the best Japanese way. Mrs. Oyanagi finds it difficult to mention, and it would be typically Japanese to never say, anything about this to avoid causing you any embarrassment.

Only recently one of my friends, also a language officer, returned to the States and he was able to stop off and see Yutaka Oyanagi and some of the other POWs and send some letters on from them. Mrs. Oyanagi was overjoyed when she got hers. I told her to write a letter and it might be possible, when other officers who know Oyanagi go back, for me to get them to take it along. She came all the way to Tokyo to deliver it to me, and partially in the hope, too, that there might be a few more things about her husband that I recalled that I hadn't told her up to now.

Mrs. Oyanagi finds it difficult to talk on this subject with you and doesn't know how well she can express herself in English anyway, and so how much you are understanding. She asked me if I would meet you if possible, but that seems impossible while she is in Tokyo this time, for you are now in Niigata, so I told her I would be glad to write a letter as best I could. I hope sincerely that when you come back to Irumigawa that you come to Tokyo and look me up. I can tell you a good deal more of the situation. During the day I am in the Meiji Insurance Building with the U.S. Strategic Bombing Survey. My quarters are M407 Yuraku Bldg. almost next to Dai-ichi Bldg., where General MacArthur's offices are.

Mrs. Oyanagi is not too well, and she is all up in the air awaiting her husband's return. However, in truly Japanese fashion she cares not to show that to anybody. Her house has been thrown open to American servicemen on many occasions and the Oyanagi clan has been extremely kind to all of us so far from home. I hope that with this as a background you consider very carefully before you chase her. It quite confuses a Japanese lady and merely makes her more polite.

Hoping to see you in Tokyo,

Yours,
Otis Cary

What do you write in a case like this anyway? I just hope this didn't cause her further embarrassment.

One of the POWs nicknamed Gonchan, whom I got to know well, could not read or write. He was an amazing little fellow with a handsome cherry-pattern tattoo of remarkable restraint over his chest. He was an excellent gambler and mimic, but a boy close to the soil. He seemed to understand some things about life that many better-educated people don't. He stuck to promises he made. He had swum seven times between Saipan and Tinian during the fighting, carrying messages between the commanders of the two garrisons. I went out to see his family. They all looked just like him and talked just like him. His oldest brother wanted me to have his favorite sword. He was a petty contractor and bossed many minor construction jobs. He knew a good deal about blades and this one was an eight-hundred-year-old one. I had no use for the thing, but for the sentimental value, as it was Gonchan's brother, I did not refuse it. He said, "I realize it's not in good taste for a member of a defeated nation to offer you a mere sword, when we're supposed to have turned them all in, but it's a good one, one of the best of its kind. You must take it!" All this was as he was getting drunker and drunker. After listening many times to its life history and idiosyncrasies, I took it. During the evening I had to listen to a long argument about whether MacArthur was born in Japan or whether his mother was Japanese, "otherwise how could he be such a great man?" Suddenly they found out I was an officer, a *full* lieutenant. It overpowered them to think that I, a full lieutenant, would come to their hovel. It mortified Gonchan's oldest brother more, though, that I had not been able to show up in my jeep at work that day, or any day, just so that he could have been seen talking to me or showing me his present project. That would have upped his prestige thousands of percent.

I had come to tell them as much as I could about Gonchan, but I ended up listening to them mostly and playing the awe-inspiring naval lieutenant, which was pleasant and much more amusing. I got a true glimpse of the feudal part of the Japanese mind which exists all over Japan still, of course. It reminded me much of experiences in my childhood. That is the part of the Japanese mind which must be thoroughly enlightened. That is the part that makes it "fanatic," as we experienced in the fighting all over the Pacific. And yet that is the part that will accept MacArthur as great (so great that he must be at least born in Japan or have Japanese blood) and accept *me* as a lord. These "inscrutable people" can seem so simple every once in a while. Then the mist closes over all again and they are the two-faced people whom we say we can never really understand.

Mrs. Shikiba has helped me since in writing letters to all these twenty-odd POWs' families, saying that if that address reaches them she will send them a very heartwarming letter from someone dear to them. We feel that things have progressed to that stage. There is little feeling against POWs in Japan. The feeling will start when the boys from overseas who didn't get captured come back and start making the differentiation between themselves and the "cowardly" who got captured. As far as the people at home are concerned, everybody overseas now was a POW and if their loved ones are among them and safe, all the better.

I got this letter from a POW who has returned to Japan already; he worked as a doctor for us at Pearl:

> Dear Lt. Cary,
>
> I am glad to sent this letter to you.
>
> I am much obliged to your kind favour for us in long life in Hawaii. I heard, you have a good life and business in Tokyo, from Mrs. Matsudaira who is wife of my intimate. Most impressive thing of my long life in Hawaii is kindness of all interpreters, officers and medics. When I go away to Navy camp, I was disappointed to be unable to say "goodbye" and thanks for your kindness. But I can say it now. I thought I cannot see you again.
>
> About 3 weeks ago I visited to Mac-Arther's Headquater to see Lt. Gorham, but I disappointed because he was absent there. I returned to my home. My home is still standing; my families are also all healthy for God's favour. Jan. 21st. I tripped to Saga-City in Kyūshū to see my mother and sister. Now we are living in peasant house, farming vegitables

and fruits to eat ourselves. I'll return to my home in Tokyo to see my American friend. I want to speak everythings,— life of San-Francisco, Texas, the way home of ship trip, and our future, etc. Where is Lt. Szathmary? If he is in Tokyo or other place of Japan, I want to see him too.

I throw away all things of this war.

I have dreamed foolish thing, I awake now from frantic dream. I am proceeding with great hope as doctor. Medical studies of Japan were delayed from American or Europian medical investigations by this desperate war. We must catch up medicin of Japan with American medecin.

I wish to keep your favour.

Soon, maybe within 2 weeks, I can see you again. I'll visit to Takumi shop within from the 18th. to 22nd.

So long,
from your friend,
Jiro Ide

I think that letter expresses the feeling of many of the POWs coming back, although mild for what Yokota and Oyanagi feel. I am sure that out of this sort of feeling, out of men who have undergone the "disgrace" of being a POW and had to figure out what they considered worth living for, will arise much of the leadership for a new Japan.

Otis

◆ ◆ ◆

FROM DON KEENE IN TSINGTAO TO TED DE BARY IN TOKYO

December 3, 1945

Dear Ted,

Letters from you finally are beginning to cross over to China, in spite of all the obstacles and bafflements of the military postal system in the Orient. I was particularly delighted with the letter in which you describe the new political activity in Japan, for nothing of that nature has appeared in the local newspapers and all of us have been impatient for news. When I say all of us, I include the Japanese here with whom I associate, those members of the military who are now expecting repatriation. They are naturally curious to know to what conditions they will be returning, and anxiously ask my "opinion" about the future of Japan, the length of the American occupation, the possibility of their starving to death.

I showed the letter with the mention of Mikami's new political program to a group of Japanese soldiers, most of them privates, who form our translation staff. These people were culled from the ranks of the Japanese military because of their knowledge of English and are about as eccentric as any random group of Americans knowing Japanese would be. My first thought when I saw them was that if we had had a fight for Tsingtao, these would have been our prisoners; they looked so much like the ones we captured on Okinawa, smiling and bespectacled. The chief of the translators is a Corporal Ōmura who learned his English from the great Victorians and manages to translate matter-of-fact reports on Japanese troop movements in a way that suggests Thackeray's description of Waterloo. The other day he came to our office for some stationery saying, "You have given me much paper already, but, like Oliver Twist, I must ask for more." The others are of lesser caliber, but all painfully anxious to pick up any additional bits of English or American, so that they can take leave with a "I am very sorry to have caused you much inconvenience. So long!"

To return to your letter, the translation section was delighted with almost everything Mikami demanded. Occasionally one or two would shake their heads over something they disagreed with, but this was more than compensated for by the approving smiles and the occasional interjections of, "That's right!" Just then, the officer in charge of the section came over and asked to look at the letter. In ordinary times, I suppose, Japanese soldiers would have fallen flat on the floor if addressed by their officer, but the war is over now, and the translators consider themselves people of some position. They therefore showed no particular desire to surrender the letter to him, but handed it over with some sort of recognition of the fact that he would disapprove. He did indeed show his annoyance, by throwing the letter down on the table after reading a few sentences. There were a few moments of silence which I sought to break by asking the officer his impressions of the letter. By this time almost the entire Japanese army liaison staff was crowded about the table. When I failed to get any satisfactory answer from the officer, I looked at the throng of military and asked in a loud voice, "Isn't there anyone left here to defend the *gumbatsu*? Surely there must be one of you who has something good to say about them?" As I said this I looked straight at Captain Tabuchi, hoping that I could stir that real soldier at least.

"No," he answered with a laugh, "I am what you Americans are supposed to be—an isolationist." After saying this, he let out a roar of laughter which ended the discussion.

One part of your letters which is most interesting to me is that which mentions the famous May 15 Incident. Almost entirely by chance I have met and interviewed one of the "young navy officers" who took part in the assassination of the premier. One day when a Japanese was identifying for me the persons appearing in a group photograph he pointed to one face, saying, "This is one of those officers who shot the premier. He's still in Tsingtao. I saw him on the street the other day."

I heard this just at the time when the atrocity case was beginning to occupy all of my time, and I was therefore unable to follow up an investigation of the man. Later someone told me his name in another connection—Kakushi Murayama—and just recently Captain Okabe mentioned him. I asked Okabe what he knew about Murayama. He answered, "You will hear all kinds of talk about Murayama and some of it may be true, but underneath everything else, Murayama is a fine person. I have known him for a long time, since his days at the naval academy when I was his instructor, and I have watched him ever since. Naturally I could not agree with his ideas, but I have felt the greatest affection for the man himself."

I managed to get in touch with Murayama a day or so later and arranged for an interview with him. My first impression of him, unfortunately, was concerned with the trouble I had in understanding his speech. He talked in a provincial dialect with which I was unfamiliar, and he made comprehension even more difficult by his partiality for obscure words. He seemed to be willing to answer all my questions, but his replies were veiled by his speech. We only managed to reach a point of understanding when he resorted to writing characters for unusual words. I asked him about the circumstances of his coming to Tsingtao.

"After five years spent in jail I was feeling utterly exhausted, and I was unable to find any peace in Japan, where my every action was observed. I decided that I couldn't stand that maddening existence any longer and came to China. I was on the advisory staff of the Shantung Provincial Government at Tsinan for a while, but the work proved too much for me and I came here to Tsingtao for a rest. I worked for about a year with a shipping company, and was later connected with the exploitation of a graphite mine. I was forced to give this up because of unsettled conditions. In 1940, I started a company of my own called the Murayama Trading Company which later was called the Orient Company. I was able to obtain the confidence of both the army and the navy, and managed to become the general contractor for hemp, peanut oil and other such products. Then, in February 1944, I was asked by the navy to set up the 'Sea Organization' and I turned over my business interests to my associates.

"The 'Sea Organization,' as its name suggests, was concerned with the sea and the villages near it. As you know, most of the territory around Tsingtao was controlled by the communists during the war. Instead of encouraging the Chinese living along the coast to cooperate with the Japanese, the *kempeitai* had so restricted the passage of junks into Tsingtao that most of those Chinese preferred to deal with the communists instead. The navy viewed this situation with much concern, and asked me to help set up a self-government system in areas along the coast. Such a system would insure peace and order and would promote friendly relations. In addition, intelligence of various types could be obtained in this manner. However, hardly had the 'Sea Organization' started to function than I was arrested by the *kempeitai* and thrown in jail, presumably because I was suspected of having dangerous thoughts and because my opposition to Tōjō was well known.

"When they let me out of jail in Tsingtao, I attempted to start again from scratch. I heard that prices were cheaper in Korea and attempted to set up an import business in dried shrimp, water-chestnuts, carrots, medicine and other such commodities, but the war ended before I could get started. Since then I haven't been doing very much."

It is usually the case that the families of assassins have to live with the fading remembrance of the crime, the assassin having, in turn, been killed and his grave left unmarked. Here, instead, as a result of a different law, the law of military Japan, I saw the assassin himself, and heard him tell of his wholesale grocery business. Behind his words, however, was the one meaningful act, and his every employment since was based on that act. When he was introduced to others there must always have been the added whisper, identifying him and his crime. Murayama's face showed more of the essentially good nature that Okabe had praised than it did the essentially wicked nature that his actions and ideas would have indicated. The sensual quality of his face did not agree with my conception of what the fanatic, the hard young assassin would look like. Nor were his words the ringing tones of the man convinced, but came out instead in quick little volleys and died in polite endings to the verbs.

I asked this time how he had come to take part in the May 15 Incident. He had been expecting the question and answered as if prepared.

"It is clear from political and social histories that the middle twenties were the period of greatest corruption and degeneracy not only of the Japanese government but of the entire Japanese nation. I believe that one reason lay in the errors and inconsistencies which had arisen from the Meiji Restoration. The country which evolved as a result of the Meiji Restoration was a militaristic, imperialistic and capitalistic nation controlled by three classes: the class of special privileges (the *genrō* [elder statesmen] and the aristocracy), the *gumbatsu*, and the capitalists who worked hand-in-glove with the political parties. I believed that, in the light of world conditions, the time had come for a real change in Japan, and devoted my every effort in this direction when I was at the naval academy. After seeing America in 1929, I felt the urgent need of a revolution in Japan all the more.

"Then I thought, 'How should Japan be changed?' and the answer came to me that Japan must be made a moral country. My political philosophy, insofar as the building of such a moral country is concerned, owes a great deal to the 'philosophy of self-government' of my teacher, Seigo Gondō. Gondō was primarily a student of ancient Japanese institutions, but he belonged to the so-called people's school of scholars which generally has been under the heel of the government-sponsored scholars. My teacher preached the doctrine that the emperor was the spiritual center of the Japanese race, and that the people should not trouble him with problems of government. He explained that the people must govern themselves along lines consonant with the emperor's wishes. My teacher also believed that man is essentially good. Therefore, if everyone had enough to eat, sufficient clothing and proper shelter, the result would be good morals and a cultural development. Gondō preached self-government by the people. He used to attack the bureaucratic administration. He hated party politics and was grieved by the condition of the times and by what he called, 'the worst government since the founding of the nation.'

"We secretly organized a club and determined to build a national army which would travel the road to a moral nation and which could defend that road. This club resulted from our grief over the fact that the navy had degenerated to the status of a military organization run for the benefit of the zaibatsu and the politicians. When internal reconstruction was still not achieved, the country suffered the successive misfortunes of the Manchurian Incident and the China Incident. One calamity followed another, and with each came the growing conviction that unless the country were awakened at once, it would be in grave danger. Thus we were roused to inevitable action on May 15, 1932. The results, however, were not in the direction we had anticipated. What we had done may be likened to sprinkling salt on a fish which had already begun to petrify. The ruling classes continued to control the government and the way was paved for the February 26 assassinations which occurred three years later."

I started to ask Murayama about his part in the actual assassination which took place May 15, 1932, but he suggested instead, "I have a little pamphlet which contains an account of everything that happened and of my own testimony. My feelings and ideas have not changed since then, so you can accept the statements in the book as those I would now make. Is that satisfactory to you?" I felt little inclined to refuse, for the strain of attempting to understand Murayama was considerable, while one can always puzzle out a written text.

The pamphlet was delivered to me the next morning. It turned out to be a little volume published by a newspaper in Kyushu in 1933, apparently with the purpose of justifying the assassins. The editor, in his preface, traced the transfer of power in Japan from the military (the samurai) to the lawmakers, to the capitalists and finally back to the militarists with the outbreak of the Manchurian Incident. He calls upon the *gumbatsu* to consider its responsibilities seriously and thus effect a rebirth of Japan.

Leafing through the volume I saw Murayama's picture in formal clothes, a list of the defendants and their ages (under which Murayama had scrawled a few words for each, such as "student in Germany," "now in Tsinan," or "dead"), the speeches of the navy and army prosecutors, the testimony of the defendants, the decision of the court. I knew that Murayama had been found guilty and that he spent five years in jail, but could not discover in the book any reason for so light a sentence having been imposed. I opened to the speech of the navy prosecutor which began with these words, "All of the defendants were influenced and guided in their thought either directly or indirectly by the late Lieutenant Commander Hitoshi Fujii, and it would therefore be well to examine his ideas. Fujii, from the time of his student days at the naval academy, envisaged a union of Asiatic peoples, with Japan as the leader of such a union. Fujii condemned the outrages committed by the white race, and was a believer in a so-called Pan-Asiaticism, which was to spread its moral influence throughout the world. The defendants Kiyoshi Koga and Kakushi Murayama and others were guided by him, and joined with him in striving to spread these doctrines."

In reading this first paragraph it became clear to me why Murayama had been selected to head the "Sea Organization," for its object was precisely the Pan-Asiaticism which Murayama had learned from Fujii. The date the "Sea Organization" was founded was May 15, 1944. On that day the navy senior staff officer at Tsingtao introduced Murayama to a Chinese named Liu Ch'eng-lieh saying, "Today is the anniversary of the May 15 Incident, and I think that it is truly significant that on this day one of the old Chinese revolutionaries (referring to Liu) should join our ranks." The three of them then drank a toast to the new organization. Maruyama described his feelings, "I felt tremendously moved and overjoyed."

Probably the opposition Murayama expressed to the China Incident or to Tōjō was connected with the fact that war between China and Japan was diametrically opposed to Pan-Asiaticism and the implied united struggle against the white race. Murayama had not mentioned this aspect of his convictions, but there is no reason to suppose that he has changed his mind. Leafing through the book I noticed that he had underlined one passage, an excerpt from the testimony of one of the army officers who had participated in the incident. "Our first plan was something like this. On the day of the shooting, the two parties—the one which attacked the premier's residence and the one which attacked the residence of the keeper of the privy seal—would join together and go to the home of Admiral Tōgō. We would then have Admiral Tōgō go to the Imperial Palace and petition the emperor to declare martial law. We then planned to have Seigo Gondō invited to be minister of war and to take charge of leading the reform of the nation. The members of the Blood Brotherhood were to be released from jail and assigned to the best units."

Thus Murayama's teacher, Gondō, was to be assigned the key position in the reform of Japan along the lines of his philosophy. The members of the Blood Brotherhood (Ketsumeidan), the first group to attempt action based on this kind of philosophy, were to be honored as the predecessors of the May 15 conspirators. The boldness of the scheme to have Admiral Tōgō, a man of irreproachable reputation, act as intermediary for the terrorists appeared to have awed even them, for there was no attempt to carry it through.

Naturally, what was most interesting to me was the recorded testimony of Murayama. "The testimony of Ensign Kakushi Murayama was next heard. Murayama (aged 26) had been in close contact with friends in the army from the time that plans for the incident were first conceived, and he participated in the activity which took place within the premier's residence on the fatal day. When asked why he had participated in a national revolutionary movement, Murayama answered:

'My first ambition was to become a lawyer so that I could help the poor, and from this ambition has come the profound interest I have always had in social problems. I could see that all kinds of oppression had been rampant in Japan since the time of the World War because the nation had too closely imitated European and American capitalistic institutions after the collapse of our own feudal system. As a direct result, the communist party had sprung up. The reactionary Tanaka Cabinet only worsened the oppression. I felt deeply that a basic national revolution was imperative.

'At this time I learned of the existence of the Imperial Army Society and was then led to think that the first step taken in the direction of a new revolution would have to be the purification of the military forces which would return them to the spirit of the founders of our country. However, I did not have any concrete plans for such action. Then it happened by chance I was shown a copy of "A Proposal for the Reform of Japan." As I read it I thought, "That's exactly it! That's it!" I understood what was to be done.' "

Ensign Murayama in later testimony disclosed how he happened to have decided to take part in the assassination. "Ever since my days in the naval academy I have been particularly interested in the histories of the French Revolution, the Russian Revolution and the Meiji Restoration. I recognized the value of a coup d'etat, but it wasn't until I was serving on board the cruiser *Nachi*, in January 1931, that I realized the importance and value of individual terrorism. I spent several months organizing a plan in my head. First, the ruling class would be overthrown by individual action. Armed groups, taking advantage of the state of fear caused by such action, would carry out acts of terrorism in broad daylight. This would lead to martial law and the formation of a new cabinet. Then we would attempt a coup d'etat against the reactionary forces.

"This was just when the Hamaguchi cabinet was formed and started to carry out its deflationary policies. Farming villages were reduced to a state of utter impoverishment. Social conditions grew worse and worse. I felt certain that we had reached a point where there was no longer any time for mere words. I was at Shanghai at the time and managed to obtain there two revolvers and fifty rounds of ammunition. On March 19, after our triumphal return to Sasebo, I met at the Naval Officers' Club two of the others who took part in the incident. I suggested, 'It might be a good idea to go to Tokyo and attack one police station after another. That would certainly bring on martial law.' While my suggestion was being considered I was suddenly ordered to duty at the Yokosuka Navy Yard. I was worried that my connection with the Blood Brotherhood had been discovered.

"As soon as I reached Yokosuka, I met Lieutenant Koga and two of the other officers who participated in the incident. As the result of our discussions we decided to undertake the assassination of Makino, the lord keeper of the privy seal, on May 7.

Q: How did you feel when you realized that you were about to undertake the assassination of Makino?

A: I felt that I would certainly like to kill him.

Q: Weren't you dissatisfied to be sent instead to the premier's residence when you had been planning on killing Makino?

A: I consider that there were four cancers in the superstructure of Japan. These were the *genrō*, Makino, the police commissioner, and the *zaibatsu*. I felt that we had to get rid of all four and thought I would like to kill Makino, but when I spoke to Koga about it, he said, 'Makino is scared to death already, so we might as well let him alone.' "

(In his own testimony, however, Koga stated that the reason Murayama had been sent to the premier's residence instead of to Makino's was that he decided to send all of the Kyushu group, of which Murayama was one, to the former place. Koga was led to make this decision when others in this group remained at Sasebo and decided not to participate in the assassination. He apparently feared disaffection on the part of the whole group.)

Murayama was then questioned concerning some of the details of the assassination of the premier.

"Q: How do you feel now about the death of the premier?
A. Since coming to the prison at Otsu I have prayed almost every day for the repose of Premier Inukai and the others who were killed. It is my fervent hope that by the noble death of Premier Inukai the Japanese people has been saved from national ruin and that a new Japan can be established.
Q: What did you do with the revolver you had?
A: I stood with my left hand behind my back and I was holding the revolver in my right hand, ready to shoot and pointed at the premier's head. However, when I saw that the shots fired by Kuroiwa and Mikami had succeeded in killing him, I refrained from shooting.
Q: The shot you fired while in the garden in back of the premier's residence went through the arm of a policeman. How do you feel about that?
A: Now that I think of it, I realize it was a disorderly and unfortunate act."

Murayama had been one of four men who crashed into the premier's residence. At first they were admitted without question because they were in uniform, but then they were forced to use their guns. At one point a woman carrying a baby on her back appeared. From the testimony one can gather that someone must have raised his gun to shoot her, but at that moment one of the four cried out to her in warning. Another of the four stated in testimony that he realized then that the warner was the only one of them who had a wife himself. The assassins found the premier in the garden, shot him without a word and then fled. After committing other acts of terrorism they surrendered to the *kempeitai*, because they thought it would be a disgrace to be arrested by the police.

Murayama concluded his testimony with a statement of his views. "I would like to add this to the statement of my motivation for taking part in the assassination. At the time all I could see before my eyes was the spectacle of Japan being choked to death by the impoverishment of her farmers, the rapid increase of the unemployed, the bankruptcy of the national economy, the struggle between rural and urban elements, the rise of the communist party, the ambitions of right-wing groups, the destruction of self-government, the degeneracy of the political parties, the weakness of Japanese diplomacy, and the spiritlessness of the Japanese people. I felt most strongly that this condition was a result of the choking effect of the misguided capitalist ideology, and that it would be impossible to rectify matters basically if temporizing measures were used. I believed that the three sources of corruption and degeneracy—the privileged classes, the political parties and the *zaibatsu*—would soon have to be overthrown, and that a revolution brought about by a new sense of power and awareness among the people would result from the overthrow of those classes.

"Our actions were intended to act as a flare to illuminate these ideas. The reason we wanted to kill Makino was that he was acting in collusion with the leaders of the political parties in his capacity as an unworthy counselor of the emperor. In Japanese history, whenever the country's fortunes have suffered a decline it has been because of the counselors surrounding the emperor. It was to lay the foundations of a new and prospering Japan that we intended to cut down Makino in an unlawful way." Murayama continued his testimony with an attack on the Manchurian policies of the capitalists, declaring the capitalists to be traitors opposed to the emperor.

The Japanese have a somewhat different concern for the words "morality" and "loyalty." We Americans who do not appreciate idealism in the mind alone are likely to refrain from using these words. When the assassins declared that they wished to build a "moral" country, they meant just that, not a country with a higher standard of living, nor a country with the most powerful army, nor a country with any one particular group in power. Leadership was furnished the conspirators by teachers of morality and by Buddhist priests of the nationalistic Nichiren sect, not by economists or geopoliticians. The disgust with which young Americans view certain aspects of our government does not terminate in revolution or assassination because it is placed on a reasonable basis; we speak of economic inequalities, oppression of minorities, or the like, not of the lack of virtue on the part of our statesmen. We are more reasonable and more cynical. Our soldiers, victims of various necessary and unnecessary hardships, spoke with ironic smiles of our "war for democracy." The Japanese soldiers, suffering from hardships a thousand times worse, would cry as they expired, "Long Live the Emperor!"

I once talked with a prisoner and asked him how the Japanese people could stand for the domination of the *gumbatsu*. He answered, "If a child were playing by the side of a well and looked as if he were about to fall in, would not a person be justified in picking him up forcibly and carrying him to safety? The Japanese people was incapable of seeing the danger that lay ahead. The nation was disunited, each man seeking his selfish ends. We needed some stronger force to show us the just way, the moral way. We voluntarily blinded ourselves to everything but the one consideration of what it was proper for Japan to do."

It is true of course, that the Japanese do not act in perfect consonance with the ideals they profess—far from it. But I think it is important that they believe that they are following the path of righteousness. Once, when we were trying to find out if there was a certain person among a group of Japanese prisoners, we picked out a likely looking individual and asked him if he were not the man we were searching for. He stood up as straight as he could and cried, "Japanese never tell lies." I am convinced that he meant what he said, believed it without qualification, being capable of dismissing little lies, or minor infractions, as irrelevant. Another prisoner, Satō, about whom I may have written before, told me, "If you show a Japanese the moral way he will follow it blindly.

For that reason, in the event of an American victory over Japan, the Japanese will be willing to follow without question directives issued by the conquerors in the name of justice."

The Japanese fought the war self-consciously. There was a constant effort made to induce the Japanese people to think that the war was just, not only because the "ABCD powers" were allegedly strangling Japan, but because of the Greater East Asia Co-prosperity Sphere, Asia for the Asiatics, the end of white domination and others of the principles Murayama had once learned. If the country as a whole could think piously about Japan's mission, each individual was also conscious of his own responsibility. The Japanese soldier before he went on a *banzai* charge would write in his diary, "Here I am, a son of Japan, in my twenty-fourth year, about to end my life with the swiftness of the cherry blossom casting its petals at the height of its bloom. I offer up my life to the august virtue of His Majesty. Long Live the Emperor!" Occasionally one would find a note in crude English or in Japanese attached to such a diary, "To American Soldier. Please send this book to my family if you have the kindness." Not only did the individual soldier see himself self-consciously as the instrument of the emperor's virtue, but he wished others to see him thus.

If this is hypocrisy, it is unwittingly so. If what Sato said proves to be true, we shall probably have little trouble with the occupation of Japan, but the character of the Japanese people will not have changed, and it will not be too long before some group decides that cooperation with the Americans is not moral or virtuous. Then we may have another May 15 Incident, if Japan is no longer capable of war. Reeducation along the lines of doubt, and even cynicism, may be the only way of combating the crusading fanaticism of the Japanese.

The men on top were probably close enough to the facts to permit them to see clearly where their idealism led, but with a few exceptions—"the brains"—they were all apparently guided by their ideals and by a self-conscious fatality. Admiral Yamamoto, the night before he left on his fatal flight to Bougainville, had a presentiment of death no less sure than did the soldier who set out on a *banzai* attack. His staff officers pleaded with him not to go on the dangerous trip, but he was obdurate, fascinated perhaps with the idea of the falling cherry blossoms. He spent the night before his airplane took off answering letters from his admirers and writing them examples of his calligraphy, little mottoes about the holy war or the virtue of the emperor. These were for him the last diary entry, the justification to posterity of the suicide-sick soldier.

For some Americans, it will seem that the removal of the emperor and the restoration of free speech will prove all that is necessary to generate democracy. Does this mean that the image of the cherry blossom and the self-consciousness of the words, *Nippon danshi*, "A son of Japan," will vanish into the words of contention of political parties, or the song of democracy of some future Japanese poet? Rather it would seem to me that political parties will attempt to turn the existing tendencies to their own uses; the platform of Mikami's which you sent me is a perfect example of a call to the Japanese to follow on a new path of virtue. Parties which attempt to succeed with less emotional programs will speak unfamiliar language and response to them will be limited. We can turn to advantage the single-mindedness of the Japanese by causing them to strive for a new and virtuous Japan which will hate war, but I think it will take many years before the Japanese are in a position to choose calmly because they think something is just rather than because it professes itself to be so.

In the meantime we can only expect that there will continue to be young men who will find teachers to lead them to the kind of action of which Murayama was guilty. And it may be that only so long as there are such young men will the Japanese civilization we have known, for better or for worse, continue to make itself felt in the world.

Don

◆ ◆ ◆

FROM TED DE BARY IN KYOTO
TO DON KEENE IN TSINGTAO

December 5, 1945

Dear Don,

Kyoto, I am already convinced, has as much beauty and charm

as was ever claimed for it—and more. Five years would hardly be enough to see everything the guidebook and previous visitors recommend, or the long list of temples, palaces, shrines and gardens, any one of which some Kyoto resident insists that you see before leaving. I have done my best in five days, and thought this afternoon that I might have covered enough to make a fair sample of Kyoto's most highly prized treasures. Then a potter [Kanjirō Kawai] told me it was unthinkable to go without visiting Ryōan-ji and its rock and sand garden designed by the most famous of all Zen landscape artists. Late as it was, and unwise for me to risk getting lost after dark in the suburbs, I caught a trolley crowded with commuters and did not regret, after seeing the garden, having made such a great effort to do so. Much of the garden's artistic significance escaped me, of course, for I am poorly acquainted with both Japanese art and Zen philosophy, but the simplicity and quiet balance of its rock arrangement were suited exactly to my taste, somewhat jaded by a heavy diet of splendor and intricacy.

I decided quite early in my stay that it would be foolish to try to see everything, that one temple examined in leisure was worth a dozen given a few minutes apiece. With this in mind I set out one morning to see the Chion Temple, one of the oldest and most famous in Japan. Passing through a lane full of attractive shops, and beating down the temptation to idle over their silks, pottery, pearls and books, I finally reached the long stone stairway which led up to the temple on a mountain slope east of the city. The ascent was broken by a stupendous gate, the size and strength of which made it an imposing guardian of the sacred precincts within. This was the sort of place a Japanese soldier might have visited before his departure for the South Seas. His diary, found at Peleliu or still moldering on Choiseul, would have spoken of the gate, its grandeur, its enduring strength above the fleeting lives of those who passed beneath. A few lines would have wrung out the meaning of this great presence in the fateful life of a soldier:

> Autumn leaves scattering beneath the ancient gate,
> A young life falling for the dynasty of ages eternal.

I later regretted not having written down a few similar lines for myself. My potter friend sent some Osaka reporters around to my hotel, telling them I was a student of Japanese art—a GI with a soul, I guess. They wanted to know, in just a few words, what significance I attached to my aesthetic discoveries in Kyoto, just what these artistic treasures meant to me. Never having been asked such a question before, I was at a loss for an answer. Perhaps they simply expected me to say, "Gee, it was swell." I hoped they did not expect a novice like myself to hand out judgments with the ease of Dr. Johnson, but everything would certainly have gone well if I had stopped, somewhere in my sightseeing, to prepare a little poem for such occasions.

Instead, I climbed on up the stone steps to the temple, reading in the guidebook, "Under the southeast corner of the main hall is an umbrella, believed to have fallen there from the hands of a divine boy, which acts as a charm to avert fires. The corridor behind the main hall is so constructed that at every step the floor emits a sound resembling the song of the Japanese bush warbler." Despite the dampness of the weather, which inhibited the mechanical warbling, I heard the cricketlike song plainly as my stockinged feet pressed gently on woodwork more sumptuous than any rug I have ever walked upon. And when the warbler's song stopped, I could hear the chanting of monks in the Founder's Hall, "*Namu Amida Butsu, Namu Amida Butsu . . .*" ("All Praise to the Buddha Amida"). In the West it would seem incongruous to have a cricket-chirp incorporated by special design into the music and atmosphere of a church. In Japan, where the beauty and mystery of nature are so much a part of religion, such devices add almost as much to a feeling of sanctity as the chanting of monks, which itself seemed more natural and melodious than I had thought Japanese singing could ever be.

At an office next to the Founder's Hall I bought a ticket for a guided tour of the superior's apartments, in which were many magnificent screens painted by men of the Kanō school. The guide was an old man, who must have been saying the same few words of explanation to visitors for several generations. His monotone so strained my ear for Japanese that I had to make the tour twice to learn that he had even less to say than the guidebook. "This is the emperor's special room. Behind those sliding doors waited his samurai, ready to defend him in case of sudden attack." And so on.

When the second tour was over, I approached a young monk who had detached himself from the chanters, and asked him to tell me more about the screens and the objects designated as "national treasures." He was glad to do so, he said, but suggested that I first have tea with him and several of his fellow monks in the chamber adjoining. When introductions were made, I discovered that he and the others were all former pilots from navy suicide squadrons. They had just recently come here to make a retreat, after deciding to take up holy orders when they were demobilized. It soon became apparent that the monks were much more intent on learning what they could about me than on explaining either the artistic merits of the temple or the tenets of their particular Buddhist sect. With the exception of a devout female evangelist in Honolulu, I have not met a Japanese yet who was willing to talk about his faith with an American. No matter how eager he may be to learn, he is regarded as incapable of comprehending such elusive doctrines.

It was not until we had spent considerable time discussing the war and American intentions in Japan, that I finally persuaded the "Kamikaze" monks to show me more of the temple. Even then their comments were not very enlightening:

"The treasures in this case were shown to Ambassador Pauley when he visited the temple last week. The leader of our retreat, a college professor who had been to America and speaks good English, took Mr. Pauley through the chambers and heard him say that all these things would be sent to America as war reparations."

"That can't be true," I objected, "America is not interested in art treasures as payment for the war. I'm sure they are not on the list. We only care about removing war industries."

"But that is what Mr. Pauley told him, and we are all very despondent over it."

I could only repeat my doubts, and insist that the American people would never approve of such vandalism if they heard about it. We walked back toward the Founder's Hall, and just before I put on my shoes to leave the temple, the leader of the group came out to meet me. I asked him about the Pauley story, which he immediately denied. "Mr. Pauley took only a quick look at those paintings and said nothing."

The monks went back to chant their praise of the Buddha Amida and I sat down on the steps to lace up my shoes. Beside me a middle-aged gentleman, also preparing to leave, looked up and said with a smile in English, "What do you think of it?"

"The chanting? I think it is the finest music in Japan."

"I suppose so," he said with a faint air of condescension. "It sounds good the first time, but you would find it very monotonous after a while."

We started off down the steps together and the sophisticated gentleman, who was nevertheless of very ordinary appearance in his patriotic uniform, admitted that he had overheard my conversation with the head monk about Pauley.

"Those foolish young men believe anything bad they hear about Americans. They are always ready to start or pass on wild rumors. After thinking for years that you were monsters, they cannot believe what they hear these days about American generosity and kindness, and so they look constantly for something to justify their old notions."

The man's English was good, and he must have expected me to compliment him on it, so I did. "Where did you learn to speak English so well?"

"I have spent most of my life abroad, in Mexico, in the Philippines, and for the last ten years in Shanghai. I have known lots of Americans and knew they would prove a pleasant surprise to the ignorant, untraveled people of my country."

"Then you really think the occupation is a great success?"

He thought a second. "I think that you people have been much more lenient with us than we would have been with you. But that doesn't mean you are not also making some mistakes."

"What mistakes, for instance?"

"You are trying to change things too quickly. The Japanese cannot absorb it all that fast. And you are making a mistake to punish so many war criminals. The men who committed atrocities—I would not object to punishing them, because I saw in China what they did. But Tōjō and the other leaders are quite a different thing. Americans should understand a saying in Japanese: "Even thieves have thirty percent reason.'"

I understood him to mean that even Tōjō had "thirty percent reason," some good reason for what he did. Granting that men like Tōjō must have had reasons for going to war, I insisted that any old reasons were not good enough either for the thief or for Tōjō, that leaders were obliged to consider only the highest and best reasons for their actions, and that society could condemn those who acted on only "thirty percent reason."

"You mean," he replied, "to condemn them for a difference of opinion?"

"Yes," I answered a little weakly, not so much from lack of conviction as from a realization that it would take a long time to explain myself adequately. We had already reached the hotel, and feeling that I could not brush him off so quickly, I asked him to come upstairs for a while before lunch.

The discussion continued in my room without really advancing the argument any. On my cot the gentleman noticed a book I had brought down from Tokyo, an American book about Japan and the occupation. He leafed through it quickly, asking me what it had to say, and finally stopped to read what was written on the jacket about the author: "He represents the younger school of American experts who are not blinded, as are so many other older experts, by myths which even the Japanese do not believe."

"What myths is he talking about?" my friend asked.

"You can guess as well as I. He probably means myths about the emperor, about the Yamato race and Japanese society; myths which were used to maintain the present social structure of Japan and then to justify Japan's aggression."

"And the writer does not think that the Japanese believe these myths?"

"I guess not."

My friend got up to go. He looked hard at me and spoke with

conviction, "No one could say that who knew the Japanese people. You have talked to Japanese soldiers and sailors, to people in many parts of the country, and you must know how much this mythology means to them. Things may change in the next few years, but if the emperor were condemned as a war criminal tomorrow, I can guarantee that sixty million Japanese would volunteer to suffer his punishment in his stead."

After he had gone, I went downstairs to the dining room, which by this time was almost empty. Girls in bright kimono noiselessly brought in dishes prepared in the kitchen by army cooks, and then waited in little groups, repeating to each other funny stories about the guests, while I ate slowly and thought over the gentleman's remarks about Japanese myths and the emperor. Once before, in the ancient capital city of Kamakura, I had met a man very like my friend of that morning and had had a very similar experience with him. He was a young man whose mother had somehow been converted to Catholicism, and he himself had joined the Church soon afterward, taking the name Ambrose Elihu Kiyoaki Nakao. Ambrose was educated in America, at a Catholic college in the Middle West. Just before the war, he had returned to teach in a Catholic school near Tokyo. It is more a reflection on the propriety of most geisha houses than on the character of Japanese converts to Christianity that we should have met at a quiet geisha party given by a mutual friend. A few days later he undertook to act as my guide in seeing the shrines and temples of Kamakura.

There is one most unusual shrine in the city, erected near the cave in which an imperial prince had been imprisoned several centuries ago. About it my guidebook said, "Prince Morinaga was taken prisoner by the Ashikaga forces after an unsuccessful attempt to restore the rightful power of the emperors. He was confined in a stone cave, where, in 1335, at the age of twenty-eight, he was assassinated by his captors." The cave is a dismal hole cut deep into the rock of a damp and thickly wooded glen, which is, by contrast, landscaped to perfection with all the art and patient care of which Japanese are capable. As I peered into the darkness of the cave, through the bars of a heavy wooden gate, Ambrose said, "You should really have come here early in the morning, when people come to pray before the gate. They pray for the emperor's safety at the shrine of the imperial martyr Morinaga. Lately, more and more people have been making the daily pilgrimage, because there is so much talk in America about punishing the emperor and abolishing the throne. Many come as early as two in the morning and kneel before the cave until dawn. They come barefoot and in thin clothing, because they think that suffering in the winter cold will move Heaven to answer their prayers." I was much impressed by what Ambrose told me, for a great deal had been said in the papers recently about the increasing neglect of Shinto shrines. "That may be true elsewhere," Ambrose said, "but it is certainly not true here."

We walked back through the glen, out of the shaded grounds of the shrine and into a sunlit avenue full of playing children. Ambrose went on, "The devotion of these people is a remarkable thing to me, and disturbing, too. Think how hard we work at the school to convert a few young souls. And then, when they go into business, they lose their new faith very quickly. They do not go back to Buddhism or Shinto. They become, instead, agnostics and cynics, selfish, careless people.

"There is a great deal to be admired in those who come to pray at this shrine, in their selflessness and the firmness of their faith in such adversity. You can see how closely their devotions to the martyr approximate some of ours—the Stations of the Cross, for instance. And I often wonder how long it will take us truly to convert such people, not just to destroy their faith and leave them in a spiritual wilderness, but to bring them, heart and soul, to a better faith."

Ted

◆ ◆ ◆

FROM HISASHI KUBOTA IN HIROSHIMA
TO OTIS CARY IN KYOTO

December 14, 1945

Dear Otis,

When I was told last week that I could return to Hawaii for

eventual discharge, I decided that I would first visit Hiroshima and thus satisfy my parents' wish that I go there and light incense at the graves of my grandparents.

It was still dark and cold when I got off the train at Hiroshima, so I spent a couple of hours in what was left of the station sitting around a fire stoked by some railroad employees. These workmen repeatedly admonished the crowd waiting for the next train, declaring that fires might not be built in the station, but continued to put wood on their own. When it became light enough to see my way, I set out on foot toward that section of the city where my ancestors lived and where they now rest oblivious to the happenings of the world above them. In the early light and dead stillness the ruins of the city were dark against the sky, filling me with a terrible depression. Other cities have been destroyed as thoroughly and have yet managed to carry on. Hiroshima makes one feel as though everything and everyone had given up trying altogether. The city was struck by a flood last spring, and just when it had about staggered to its feet, along came the atomic bomb to crush it with finality.

My grandparents lived and died in the outskirts of the city. Their particular section of the city was protected by a hill from the direct explosion. Many of the more flimsily constructed houses collapsed as a result of the concussion, however, and there is not a single building whose roof is not perforated in many places. The first person I looked up was a woman who helped deliver me and who returned to Japan later to live there. She took me around to see my uncles and my aunts and finally to the graveyard where I paid my respects to the spirits of my forefathers. I had supper at her home in the company of her brother and his sons. When I returned to the depot at midnight, I was accompanied by two of them who claimed that it was dangerous for anyone to walk alone at night. Groups of demobilized soldiers led by armed Koreans are supposed to be systematically holding up all passersby in certain sections of the city.

Most of the people of Hiroshima seem to feel that they are martyrs and that the Americans, along with everyone else, should feel sorry for them. Everybody who was injured starts talking about his wounds at the slightest provocation, and ends by reciting all his troubles. I suggested to some of them that one atomic bombing might have been more merciful than repeated fire bombings in the long run, but they chose to ignore this possibility altogether.

People from Hiroshima formed the majority of the Japanese immigrants to Hawaii and the mainland of the United States, which accounts for the large number of Nisei in uniform looking for their relatives here. Naturally when these boys come to visit, they are not empty-handed, but bring whatever they can. In Japan, those who have anything keep it all, and the idea of sharing with neighbors is practically unknown. This attitude seems to have fostered a resentment of the Nisei on the part of those who are not receiving any gifts from them. This was the first time since I came to Japan that I have heard such resentment expressed outright. Even kids along the road shouted insults.

The refusal of those who have some form of wealth to share it with others seems typical to me. If one visits a Japanese home, the first and most lasting impression one will retain is of the rigid rules of etiquette which govern all conduct within the house. Every move made is accompanied by a gesture of apology to the others present. Yet when we remove these exactly behaving people from the atmosphere of their homes and transplant them to public places, they become individuals against the world. Each one of these individuals will do whatever is most profitable to him, regardless of what suffering it may bring to others. Someone remarked to me, "We are but children as yet, children who are well behaved at home, but who have no idea how to act away from home."

The Japanese desire to rescue some prideworthy fragment from every loss may be an example of such childishness. "Yes, we lost Guadalcanal, Tarawa and the rest, but we fought to the last man at each place. . . . Didn't you think our suicide charges were something? Didn't our Kamikaze planes give you a bad time?"

It is a terrible commentary on the Japanese of today to compare them with the vaunted ideals of their *bushidō*. The old proverb

"Even when a warrior goes hungry, he picks his teeth as though he had just finished a sumptuous meal" once could symbolize the pride and endurance of the Japanese samurai. Today's samurai picks his teeth only after enjoying a meal bought on the black market. It is often difficult to realize that the Japanese I see every day are the brothers and sisters of the stubborn fighters of the Pacific. I find myself wondering how this nation could have put up the fight it did, in view of the present sorry state of the people.

Perhaps I have been too severe in my criticism of the Japanese. Friends of mine who are now stationed in the Philippines, Malaya, China, Korea all write me that the Japanese are the people with whom it is easiest to get along of those they have met. It may be that I am so harsh because I have been exposed since my earliest childhood to stories of the excellences of Japan and her people, and what I find has disappointed me so. Perhaps when I return to Hawaii I will be able to see things in a better perspective. I hope to see you there.

Hisashi

◆ ◆ ◆

FROM DICK BEARDSLEY IN PEKING AND SHANGHAI TO DON KEENE APPROACHING PEARL HARBOR

December 18, 1945

Dear Don,

The weather grew colder each day after I last saw you in Tsingtao, and as the sun became smaller and chillier I hoped more fervently that I, too, could get away. In the ten weeks the marines had been wrestling with the problem, no progress had been made toward getting coal to supply heat, lights and water. We heard estimates that the last scrapings would be gone by Christmas. Merry Christmas! Black market coal, half stone and dirt, could still be found at 2,000,000 puppet dollars a ton (about 65 American dollars by this time), but I couldn't see how the honest marines would keep warm without drastic measures being taken. In any case, my main job of getting Japanese troops ready for repatriation had slowed to a temporary standstill, until new units might finish the three-hundred-mile march from Tsinan.

And they were being delayed by potshot skirmishes with the communists, who were still understandably annoyed that most of the Japanese were standing armed guard against them by Chungking order.

I saw no appeal in the prospect of marking time indefinitely in a cold and discontented city which had almost worn out its attraction for me, but I hardly dared hope to get elsewhere. You can imagine, then, how delighted I was to get temporary orders for Peking, the very place I wanted most to see. Even with orders in my hand, I started breathing comfortably only after the two of us being assigned were aboard the plane and in the air headed northeast for Peking.

From American forces all over North China, small groups of fortunates (not quite fortunate enough to be sent home on points) are taken to Peking for a couple of days' look at the capital city of the Manchu emperors and their Ming predecessors. I had meant to squeeze more than simple sight-seeing into my few days; but as the plane crawled above the plain toward the bare mountains in whose lee the city sits, I began to weaken. Our attention was still on the squared fields with their pocks of grave mounds and blobs of mud villages, when we were distracted by the sight of a tall pagoda standing like a lighthouse on the barren brown of an isolated hillock. The plane wheeled around it and coursed low over the city, sweeping first over the drab roofs of a multitude of houses interrupted by the fat line of a city wall, then directly over the heart of the city—the deep green and yellow tiled curves and the brick red walls of the great temples and pavilions of the Forbidden City. From that moment I was swept along with the ranks of everyday sightseers, sure that only the most compelling of affairs could divert me from spending every available hour among these extraordinary sights.

Peking is a large and busy city, whose people, in contrast to those of Tsingtao, seem as intent on their own affairs as on extracting money from Americans, and where large hotels burst with the brass of American and Chinese armies—reservations four days in advance, please. Although only one regiment of American marines is stationed there, a number of billets are arranged for servicemen on tour. Before we found a room at the famous Wagon-Lits Hotel, which divides its attention between aged and semidesiccated "steadies," who look as though they eat kippered herring for breakfast, and the newer batches of men and women in uniform, we were accommodated in one of these billets. It was once the Princess's Palace. Its elaborately carved architecture now encloses curio shops and the usual long chow lines of men, whose field shoes scuff the mats spread in teakwood-paneled rooms. We were to have the lesson reiterated several times that the precious charms of princesses and concubines are left to the past in this capital that is living in today. Everyone down to the stall merchant and the rickshaw man is anxious to have the Americans see all the worthy sites, but this is a crowded and busy city where a building is a building and will be used if necessary.

It is axiomatic that Peking stands supreme among the cities of China in the splendor and artistry of its monuments of the past. There might be many to deny that it is most alluring of all to the traveler in the quality of its entertainment, the goods in its shops or the food in its restaurants. The general sentiment of marines seems to corroborate my own feeling that one should go to Tientsin for nightclub life, to Shanghai for expensive luxuries or for the foreign colonies, and to Tsingtao, perhaps, for marvelous climate and scenery. But there is only one Forbidden City, and it is in Peking.

It doesn't follow that the Chinese invariably treat it as a priceless treasure. We were looking for a section of the Winter Palace one day. It was supposed to be sitting across the row of artificial lakes from the Forbidden City proper, but we could find no unbarred gates as we wandered through a grove before a high wall. Rather than recross the ice of the lake to inquire, we approached to try our Tsingtao accent on a soldier standing guard at a small adjoining gate. In the characteristic conviction that no foreigner can speak Chinese, he waved us inside to look for someone else.

There, inside, was what we wanted to see. Through tangles of grass and shrubbery we saw vaguely the galleries and windowed rooms of living quarters in classic style. A lieutenant on duty listened to us with a tolerant half-smile. ("These Americans! The wretched language they use, and the things they want to do . . . and yet they're Allies.") He accepted the strange fact that we wanted to visit his quarters instead of the authorized sights across the lake, called a boy-scoutish private and sent us off. The private's orders apparently were to lead us over all the main paths of the compound and he stepped out in obvious determination to execute them literally. As we wound across bridges, along paths and hallways, we would check him for a moment with a half-gestured question and gaze at the attractions while we listened to his answer. We gathered that this was a later structure for concubines added to the main palace. Plaster or now-ragged paper had been slapped over much of the wood carving and ornament, but the delicacy of the open galleries down which he led us was still apparent. Ignoring the unhesitant clumping of our guide's stolid feet ahead of us, we peeked into chambers and hallways. A few were empty of all but rubbish; the rest were crammed with piled boxes of horse fodder, rice, sauce or varieties of equipment, and it was hard, either looking left at the storage-room chambers or turning right to view the tangled garden, to conjure the romantic rustle of silken robes or to hear the echo of lute and mandolin. We were inescapably in wartime modern China, where soldiers and supply problems are of more consequence than reconstructing the atmosphere of a medieval court.

Ruins in America and, to a greater extent, the antiquities of temples and imperial palaces in Europe have been endowed with an artificial sanctity, so that people walk through them on tiptoe, viewing them with the unrealistic antiquarianism of the Renaissance and with something of the superstitious fear Christianity has felt toward the pagans. The Chinese are, in a way, more like the Romans of the fourth century or the Babylonians of a few hundred years before, to whom the ruins were just old buildings that were wearing out and should be torn down to make room for practical structures. The modern Chinese are about equally close in all but economic viewpoint to the inhabitants of the Forbidden City, so that there is not too great a span for the imagination to build to the past. Being close to the old ways and of conservative temperament, they are patient about old things, and they are economical to boot. They've set aside these great assemblages of walls, courts and temples as national monuments, but they're not averse to quartering troops—or horses or machinery—in them if they need the room.

It is true, unfortunately, that the exhibits which the Forbidden City houses are selective, and leave untouched large fields of history. I approached the displays of painting and porcelain with some skepticism, for museums in America are said to chuckle in secret over the vast number of original pieces which have come to them through the corruption of palace caretakers, leaving fakes in their places. Such fakes as there may be are masterful, however, and I was tremendously impressed with the beauty and abundance of the materials. When I had walked past case after case of exquisite porcelain and painted scrolls, and paused to reflect that I had seen the products of very little more than three out of a dozen and more dynasties, I arrived at a more concrete impression of the magnitude of Chinese culture.

I was once impressed by a detailed model of the great limestone altars, pediments and temples composing a group called Temple of the New Year and Altar of Heaven, which lies just outside the city wall of Peking. Perhaps I ought to have been more impressed by the original. These carved stone structures were sandblasted down to their pristine whiteness by the Chinese government a few years ago, and the flashing contrast between them, the tiled roofs, and wooden columns in brilliant greens and yellows, gives a quite unexpected appearance. The real atmosphere of the Forbidden City was impressed upon me later, when I walked outside the usual sight-seeing circuit across the grass-grown flagstones of a Forbidden City courtyard and found myself facing a temple whose carved wooden pillars were eaten away with rot, the intricate cloth and plaster cloud pattern of walls and roof weather-beaten and peeling in huge, gashed strips. Beside it, in more complete anonymity, were the total ruins of another building, represented only by the pit of its original foundation in the bottom of which a few rotten logs lay askew on the tumbled pieces of a carved balustrade. Here was a sight as ugly and as morbidly attractive as any skeleton in the closet, the unburied shell of an outworn age lying in the unloving embrace of a citizenry now engrossed in business and commerce. Within sight were temples restored at the whim of the modern government, which showed what artistic marvels of woodwork and lacquer once made these buildings beautiful. And around the corner of the world were the piles of stone rubble in the Acropolis, the Forum Romanum and the temples of Thebes and Yucatan—the final product of a disintegration process which I was viewing here in mid-stride. It seemed to me that this unfinished decay was not unique, that, majestic as its scale might be, it was only the latest of a long succession. With this thought I set my feet to moving again and left before I should be inclined to a soliloquy on the moldering fate of our skyscrapers.

The city is a series of concentric squares, with the Forbidden City's audience halls, apartments and temples forming the center-most, thick-walled square. Other temples and subsidiary palaces are in the Tartar City zone surrounding it. In the next outward zone, the Inner City, the chief monumental feature is the great city wall; and there are even a few ceremonial structures in the Outer City beyond the wall, which were once well out in the countryside. In every zone outside the Forbidden City, there is generally a green- or gold-roofed temple, a section of the wall or an archway across a street to proclaim Peking a capital city.

As a treasurehouse of monuments and memorials, Peking is uniquely advantageous to servicemen, since it costs nothing for any number of enjoyable days of sightseeing. Only at the gate to the Forbidden City itself do they ask apologetically for an admission price, which, since it seems to be at prewar rates, is no more than a gesture. As a city of dance halls, nightclubs and shops, however, Peking follows the usual pattern. Although a soldier's paycheck holds its shape longer than in Honolulu or any other place with American prices, the Peking merchants charge whatever the traffic will bear. There are too few Americans, however, to produce the frantically avaricious atmosphere that makes Tsingtao seem like the last, bare-shelf stage of the Christmas rush season. As a result, the merchants along Jade Street, Embroidery Lane, Brass Street and the like are still charitable enough toward a customer to reconsider a too-high price. And where Tsingtao had only hastily contrived imitations of hotels and nightclubs, there are enough genuine ones in Peking to make for comfortable living.

We climbed into rickshaws one snowy night and let the boys take us from one night spot to the next as they saw fit. From recent practice, they seemed more adept at this than they did at touring the temples, or were, at any rate, more enthusiastic in anticipation of more liberal cumshaw. We must have seen a dozen little clubs in quick succession, but each one was out of bounds to officers. When we finally found one with no restrictions, and were settled with our drinks, several men from the 28th Regiment drifted around to offer advice to us outsiders on how to enjoy ourselves in Peking. Like any nine out of ten overseas conversations, the discussion veered almost immediately to the miseries of low points or irreplaceability that kept these men from going home. But on the whole they thought pretty well of the entertainment set up at this station. For one thing, they agreed that the unusual policy of posting places "in bounds" to enlisted men was helpful. And, they added, the men were taken care of in other ways. "These girls, now," a corporal said confidentially, leaning over carefully to avoid spilling his drink, "they're all right, sir. You don't hafta worry about these, much. The docs inspect them regular." We suggested that we were interested in dancing; so, in the spirit of Arabian gallantry, he set down his drink and shoved through the crowd in front of the jukebox to show us a girl he had found who could dance.

It was less obvious in an "inspected" honkytonk like this, than in the courtyard of a Manchu palace, that we were in an unusual city. But there were many moments when we both sensed the infection of our spirits by a gently cordial atmosphere, which was less a feeling inspired by our release from routine on vacation than it was a quality emanating from the streets and people of Peking. It is difficult to describe how different I felt this atmosphere was from the spirit that filled Tsingtao. You remember how the people in that one-time seaside summer resort would exhibit all the Rotarian fervor of a Midwestern crossroads town as they pressed us for an admission that we found their city "just delightful."

They were seldom content to let the beautiful blue bay, the crystal air and the sharp mountainous background speak for themselves. I think of them as provincials anxious for assurance that their home was wonderful, an assurance never demanded of me in Peking. Peking is sure of itself in a way that never requires polite compliments from the visitor.

I cannot be sure, after one week here, that the hospitality of Peking is not just a result of the relative scarcity of Americans. I can remember how the Chinese of Tsingtao gave a riotously cheerful welcome to the marines before they set to work to make money. In later days, when the flocks of sailors landed for their single day ashore in China, roaming the streets in unswerving determination to take home some souvenir from China, they spent money wildly and uncritically. It would be foolish to expect the Chinese simply to be grateful for all this influx of American coin. No one likes to feel obligated for favors, and, even more, no one respects a sucker. So, if my feelings were chilled in the face of the growing rapaciousness and lack of decency, I have to hold Americans partly responsible. The marines and soldiers in Peking were spread more thinly and stayed longer, and they grew more savvy about prices. There were just too few Americans to encourage the pitiful layouts of junk that fringed the Tsingtao sidewalks. And it became evident to me that friendly social relations could be established better when overtures weren't accompanied by a gamin's, "Belly good, Joe . . . two dollah!"

Shopkeepers in Peking love to make money as much as their brethren in Tsingtao do; the difference is that they have something to sell and aren't falling back on Japanese porcelain bric-a-brac and the shoddy green and pink rayon clothing that is flaunted in gaudy masses along the cluttered streets in Tsingtao. Peking had a single "one-price" bazaar set up under city authority to accommodate American buying habits. Elsewhere, in small shops clustered along narrow alleys or at tiny stalls gathered under the great roof of a bazaar, it was again every man for himself. The merchant demands sixty dollars; you offer ten and end up paying perhaps twenty-five for jade, handwoven Peking rugs or porcelain vases (and nothing guaranteed). The Chinese method of merchandising can become dreadfully tiresome after a while, but as long as I don't have to bargain for each scrap of paper, each piece of soap and every bit of food I need, I can find it almost as exhilarating as the Chinese do.

I shouldn't imply that we found Peking all clean and sweet in its picturesqueness. Although the resident Japanese kept well off the streets, next to none had been evacuated up to the time of our visit. Coming fresh as we did from six weeks of worry over incidents involving the defeated nationals and their several conquerors, we could feel keen sympathy for those responsible in Peking, whose problems were all ahead of them. The Japanese wear armbands, but the considerable number of Koreans going about are, of course, unadorned, of them my rickshaw boys would say, "No good, all same Japanese." Then, just before we arrived, the Generalissimo, visiting the city, had interrupted his written speech to belabor the city fathers for their slackness. The streets needed sweeping, he said, and buildings should be repaired; now that the war was over, there should be no excuse for neglecting sanitation any more than for leaving factories idle. I wonder what he would have said had he inspected Tsingtao, for Peking was, by contrast, a well-kept, well-supplied city, where buildings were warm enough to sit in without a coat, where food was plentiful at a price, and where anyone with money to spend could find an abundance of things to buy. We were hard put to choose between tramping through historic sights and wandering through the stores. When we found ourselves too hungry or too cold to go on with our business, we would hunt up a different restaurant with the certainty of being able to gorge there on new delicacies. Peking roast duck, Mohammedan-style mutton, candied rice and fancy dumplings could be produced whenever our ravenous appetites called for them— at prices about two-thirds those of Tsingtao.

While shopping expensively through several of the choice bookstores that mark Peking as a thriving cultural center, I saw literary and scientific works with printing dates that continued through the war years. This made me increasingly hopeful that some men of note might have continued living in town clear through the period of occupation. I went to look up a famous paleontologist, whom, as a Jesuit missionary, I considered relatively aloof from disturbance. I ultimately located him in the rickety and underheated building of his society's scientific institute, where the warmth of his welcome made up for the scarcity of coal. He offered me an American cigarette from a package marked with the army stamp, and told how eagerly he and his associates were for Americans who could bring them news from abroad, apart from their pleasure at being occasionally able to get little luxuries as well as necessities since the Americans had arrived.

What I heard from him confirmed what I had seen in the bookstores. Although Westerners had been unable to move about for research in the field, they were not deprived of the opportunity to write and publish the unfinished research of earlier years. "Bothered by the Japanese?" he said. "China has been like that since I came many years ago. There have been fewer comforts and some restrictions, yes. But it is foolish to hope that this will vanish in a moment. It is most sad of all to see these people—one likes them, as one knows them—torn among themselves by civil war. And yet, in the past there has always been trouble. We do whatever work we can. . . . Yes, with Russia cooperating and Americans still interested, soon there will be great opportunities. But complete peace, no."

There was another question which I wanted, yet hesitated, to put to this missionary-scientist. While looking through a bookstall the day before, I had by chance reached for a folio on Chinese art at the same moment another man in civilian clothes put his hand on it. Youngish and casual in old overcoat and beret, he described himself after a few moments' conversation as a student of Chinese culture. It turned out that a close friend of his was the German archaeologist whose articles on old bronzes I had bought earlier in Peking. Since this was New Year's Day, he telephoned to arrange a visit before taking me to the archaeologist's home in the suburbs. It was a beautiful home, built in Chinese style within a walled compound, the interior tastefully furnished and colorfully accented with New Year's blossoming plum branches. It surprised me to find my author a young man, around thirty. I wondered that Germans as young as these two men should not have been called back to Europe before Germany attacked Russia, but it was archaeological shoptalk that engrossed us for the next hour or so, and I thought to ask about it only after I was being guided back to the hotel through the darkened streets by my friend of the bookstalls.

The Sinologist was describing to me some of the ramifications in the study of ancient Chinese music and marvelling at the quantity of interesting problems he had discovered in the short time he had been at work, when I broke in to ask him, "How long have you been working here?" "Since 1940," he answered. "We came from Germany across Siberia just before the war with Russia broke out. And, of course, who can say how long they will let us stay now?"

I sat a minute considering the meaning behind his question while, involuntarily, I listened to the steady pat-pat of the feet of my rickshaw boy in the fresh snow and heard the rustle of the German's bicycle beside me, invisible in the darkness. Why should he be dubious about being allowed to stay in China? It couldn't be that these two scholars, men of breeding and educated judgment, would be held equally responsible with the unprincipled and power-mad group that ran Germany for so many years. And yet, how otherwise could they have left Germany at so late an hour? I asked the inevitable question, and got the inevitable answer. "Yes, we both belonged to the Nazi Party."

But why? Now that the subject was opened, he was clearly anxious to explain, but as clearly uncomfortable and unable to explain. They had no idea, he said, of the things happening in Germany. They had been far away from home, heard and believed only the "truth" that the German radio told them and so were unaware of the concentration camps, the occupation terrors and other items of the real story. Any German—any human being—would be horrified at learning the things that had been done in their name. But they had not known. . . .

After seven years in Germany under Nazidom, they had not known! I have felt some sympathy for the various nationals who have lived for as many as forty or fifty years in China just to earn a living like any other men and who, because they are Germans or Japanese, are now being thrust out with scarcely more than the clothes on their backs. And there are others who, while not being lovable characters, have some excuse for following the mob into a vicious dogma simply because they lack the intelligence or training to think independently. But I was not yet prepared to meet highly trained scholars and students of society who must have been conscious that the dogmas of Nazism denied any value to the liberal tradition which gave their work a promise of usefulness, and who yet accepted Nazism. It bothered me that educated men could be persuaded to overlook and accept for themselves doctrines and actions which threatened their own existence. I wanted to hear a fuller explanation from this Sinologist pedaling beside me, and he appeared to want to carry the story further; but we had arrived at the hotel by this time. We agreed to meet again—an appointment he failed to keep.

So now I asked their fellow scientist in exile, the Jesuit paleontologist from Belgium, how he viewed this phenomenon. I wanted some comforting words to the effect that these men were students of society and not good Nazis, or vice versa; but more than that, I was driven to examine him by his own opinions. I wanted to see whether the same brush had tarred him. He showed no hesitation, no groping for thoughts as he leaned forward and began to develop his answer. There was, he maintained, a large kernel of truth in the system to which they had unfortunately clung. He reminded me that paleontology has helped to show that the progress of evolution has been continually toward more and more complex organisms of which man represents, by the extravagant complexity of his brain, the pinnacle thus far achieved. Now, he went on, we begin to see a further evolutionary advance in the urge to collectivism, whereby man, the most complex form, groups his members into a social organism. As the cells in an animal lose their independence to perform a function essential to the total organism, so individual humans will be submerged by the common need to permit the collective whole, the total state, to survive. The Nazi State started on this line of evolution, counting individual humans as nothing more than the cells of the collective social organism, but miscalculated which cells had to be eliminated from the new organism, and made the further mistake of attacking other budding organisms.

Since the father's time was short, I didn't venture a reply to this. In a few minutes I left him and returned to the street, brushing aside the hordes of rickshaw men who appeared, as always, from nowhere. I wanted to scuff through the snow on the sidewalks between the grey walls of the European legations and be glad that I was soon to be on my way home. The father's evident sincerity, his phrasing the argument in his own terms of evolution, showed me some of the force that had brought the two Germans to their present position. I couldn't answer for the motives of the Germans, but it seemed most charitable to imagine that life for them might have been pretty ugly unless they brought themselves to share the sentiments in which not only the papers and the mass of the people, but even their fellow students and teachers stood united. The missionary's position was a little different. The compulsions should not have been as great on him, and even in the last seven years in occupied China he might have seen people or read papers with different sentiments. But he was at the little end of the funnel, getting only a trickle of ideas just because he was a foreigner in China, and most of these ideas were probably totalitarian. I wondered how he might argue if he had received a larger flow of more varied thoughts. Surely someone would have pointed out to him that the highly regimented "societies" of ants and bees were already examples of the sort of "social organism" he anticipated, and that they exhibit flaws from our human viewpoint which his collective human society would probably duplicate. Theirs is an organization in which the inherited divisions between workers, drones and slaves are unalterable, allowing neither for the benefits of individual variation nor for the advantages of including outsiders. Given this argument, the priest might agree that a society which was low on internal organization and specialization, which was congenial to immigration and mixture, which encouraged individual initiative and moves off the beaten track so that any of its members might bring advancement without hindrance to others, might be a more adaptable society capable of faster "evolution."

I am glad to be finally going home, of course, because I have been homesick in greater or lesser degree ever since I came overseas. These meetings, however, give me another reason for wanting to get home. If I and my family were able to live in China as Chinese, using Chinese thought patterns to consider the problems of China or of the world, there might be no reason to leave. But I doubt that I could mold myself so, or that I would want to. My mental language was formed in America, and I want to think like an American. Other foreigners in China fail to make themselves a part of China as years go on; moreover, they lose touch with their homes and with the currents of thought there. This is unfortunate, since in their isolation the ideas they exchange with other foreigners and with the Chinese don't rest on a common tradition and mean different things to each person. We tend to believe that all the mind needs is a continual crop of new ideas. I have come to see that it also requires the stability of association with its own kind while it absorbs the new ideas. Our "one world" is beset by problems whose answers will affect each part of it. But the problems are not stated alike in all nations, nor are the answers found by the same methods. An entire nation may misstate the problem or arrive at the wrong answer; that is a contingency we are now having to face. But how much more easily can a lone individual, such as this missionary paleontologist, lacking full communication of ideas with those around him and thrown only on his own resources, go astray! He would be the better for a period of refertilization in his native soil. My own soil, in the States, is by no means free of the ideas and influences I considered harmful here; but tolerance of widely divergent thoughts and opinions is one of the things on which I was nourished. And, however divergent these ideas may be from my own, they are generally presented in my own mental language. I shall be glad to meet them again on my own home ground.

Dick

FROM DON KEENE IN SHANGHAI, JAPAN AND
HONOLULU TO TED DE BARY IN TOKYO
December 20, 1945

Dear Ted,

Since I last wrote I have been in Shanghai, just missed you in Japan, and have flown almost across the Pacific.

Shanghai, which I was prepared to hate as a loathsome port excrudescence, turned out to be a city of wonders, the realization of the name, Shanghai, with which romancers have familiarized us. I understood this the first night there when I went to an unpretentious restaurant, the only one on the street not lighted with neon. On entering I saw at once that it was a White Russian cafe. At one of the six or seven tables a small party sat laughing, celebrating. A young man stood near the door playing the balalaika, something extremely nostalgic which made me homesick in advance for the Shanghai to which I had come only a few hours before. One of the women in the party stood up, called out a few words to the musician and started to sing. Her voice was sweet and strong, with just enough of the quality of Nina Koshetz to intensify my acute longing for what I was actually enjoying—the White Russian restaurant, the balalaika, her voice, Mother Russia. I finished drinking my glass of tea and felt cheated that I could not throw a student's cape about my shoulders and stalk out moodily.

Walking through the streets of Shanghai one feels strongly the desire to share its wonders with some simpatico person—the singing peddlers, for example. One walks down the street to catch one tune after another, from the towel-seller to the candy merchant, or the coolies carrying a great weight on the ends of bamboo poles. I felt impressed by the intelligent appearance of even coolies in Shanghai in contrast to the doltish expression on the faces of the Shantung Chinese. The singing in the streets has the kind of charm at which Charpentier must have aimed in the street music in *Louise*. I hesitated a moment, fearing the scene too Chinese, and looked back over my shoulder wondering if it hadn't been a purposeful show for my sake.

After the degeneration of the Chinese restaurants in Tsingtao, Shanghai's presented fresh delights. I went into one and ordered a meal by pointing at the sign painted in front of the shop, being hard put to understand the Shanghai dialect of the waiter. While the food was being prepared, I asked the waiter if there was any place I could relieve myself. He shook his head and then asked if I meant that I wanted to urinate. I answered that I did, and he led me smiling through the back of the restaurant and numerous low-ceilinged passageways—out into the street where he pointed at a wooden fence that had obviously been used since time immemorial for that purpose. The neighborhood kids watched gravely until I finished my business. When I returned to the restaurant, the food was ready, a superb meal which I will not torment you by describing.

On leaving the restaurant I walked through the streets again, stopping to have a Chinese seal cut at one store and to buy some red sealing wax in another. Walking aimlessly, the thought came to me to visit the Japanese military. There is perhaps in me a subconscious conviction that the Japanese owe us something, a feeling which appears to be shared by the Japanese as a part of their real war guilt. They may also be motivated by kindness and, in the case of an interpreter like myself, gratitude at that rarity, a foreigner who can speak Japanese and who is interested in arguing with them about those matters of theory and ethics in which they are so passionately interested.

After finding Japanese navy headquarters, I made my request of them, one which was unusually difficult for them to satisfy—a hotel room. After much telephoning and trouble they apparently persuaded the proprietress of a Japanese restaurant to let me stay there that night. I didn't realize this, however, until after dinner. After the table had been taken out and the charcoal braziers refilled, the proprietress came in and started to apologize, "I am afraid that it will be cold sleeping tonight, but my daughters . . . we really aren't that sort of place." One of the Japanese officers interrupted, "But he is almost engaged and is going back soon; you needn't worry."

While we sat there shivering in the growing chilliness of the room, stirring the charcoal every now and then, another Japanese officer, Lieutenant Yamada appeared, looking astonishingly like

Henry Pu Yi at first glance. The conversation with him traveled over rather uncertain beginnings, but before we knew it, we were off on one of those discussions which have become the backbone of my Japanese language proficiency—the moral characteristics of the nation. The subject of the *banzai* attack came up inevitably. I pointed out that bravery in a Japanese is not the same as bravery in an American, because the low value placed on human life by the Japanese made sacrifice of their lives much less significant than the sacrifice of an American life.

I had made this statement before to Japanese and had hitherto been greeted with, "That's right, I guess"; or at worst, "That may well be true." Lieutenant Yamada protested violently, however, "There is no people which clings to life more than the Japanese. The Japanese individual is passionately desirous of remaining alive no matter what the circumstances of his life may be. The point is, though, that Japanese, as a result of Buddhist teachings, have learned to cultivate that part of man which is human as opposed to animal. Thus, if a man were to respond at once to hunger, desire, cold or the instinct for self-preservation by seeking to obtain satisfaction of his wants without other considerations, he would be purely animal. The Japanese, in common to a certain degree with other peoples who are disciples of Buddha, have sought to deny this animal incentive in order to show to what degree they are liberated from primitive unreasoning drives. There is nothing more painful to the Japanese than to give up his life, yet he will make even this sacrifice to show his superiority to the animal which knows nothing higher."

While I afterward could think of several convincing arguments to demolish Yamada's theory, at the time I was caught in rather a curious dilemma. I was not persuaded by what Yamada had said, but I was struck by the feeling that even though his interpretation were a mistaken one, it would be so much more noble if it were not. By that I mean that there is, after all, something wonderful about ideals, about any spirit which could move men to sacrifice what is most precious to them for an abstract good. Idealism, of course, leads to fanaticism or to the vacant Homerism that Rebecca West found in the Montenegrins. In a newspaper today I saw an article by an American colonel in which he compared the fighting on Corregidor in 1942 and on Iwo Jima this year. The colonel concluded that, for whatever reason (fanaticism or bravery, etc.), the Japanese fought much more determinedly and successfully as defenders than did the Americans. To my question, "Why didn't the Japanese on Iwo Jima give up when they realized they were hopelessly outnumbered and outclassed?" Yamada would have answered by pointing to this article as a proof of how Japanese idealism, at the cost of what was most dear, was able to overcome obstacles before which Americans flinched.

Later, when Yamada had gone, I was left with Ensign Sakurai who had taken little part in the conversation. He volunteered, "I agree with you, not Yamada. The Japanese soldier knows nothing of those high principles, but acts instead as part of a mass. If the mass goes on a suicide attack started by one determined officer, the soldier becomes intoxicated with the spirit and goes along. There is nothing abstract involved."

Sakurai, it turned out, had been delegated to spend the night in the same room with me so that I would have someone with whom to talk if I couldn't fall asleep. He is very young and is that extreme rarity among Japanese, a literature major, French literature at that. We spoke for a long time after we had turned out the lights. He told me of his term (in the spring of 1945) at the Tokyo Navy Supply School. "It was very strange there. We never talked about women or politics or other things that young men discuss, but only food and how to get enough of it so that we wouldn't feel hungry all the time. It seems ridiculous now, but we were all confident then that Japan would win somehow. It was a feeling that ran contrary to reason and certainly to our empty stomachs, but it was impossible to imagine a defeated Japan. One night there was a terrible fire-bombing of Tokyo and the flames came right up to the school. We fought the fire until four in the morning, went to bed for two or three hours, and then had crew races on the river as scheduled. It never occurred to us to despair."

After a few hours of talking I changed the subject to a new field, saying, "I've met a great many Japanese military here in China. All of them deplore the *gumbatsu*, Tōjō and the rest, and assure me that the defeat of Japan has proven a blessing in disguise. Aren't there any left who are still convinced that the *gumbatsu* was right?"

I scarcely hoped for more than an evasive answer, but Sakurai replied at once, "Yes, there are. Every night at the barracks we get together and talk, for want of something better to do. A number of the officers, possibly representing half the total number, actively hope for another war after twenty or so years and think that if there is one, Japan will be victorious."

"Against the United States?"

"Or China. Not everyone follows the same line of argument."

"Are the officers who hold that view regular navy as opposed to the reserves?"

"Until you asked me, I hadn't even thought of making that distinction. No, they are all mixed up."

Sakurai is certainly the frankest Japanese military man I have met, and I believe what he said. If conditions in Shanghai prevail elsewhere, we may have a serious problem. The Japanese army and navy in China are still unaware either of the meaning of defeat or its reason. I was unable to check on the report that the Japanese planned to fight on in China regardless of surrender action taken in Japan. Probably if the emperor had not made his proclamation, surrender would have been most difficult to ensure. When the news came that a rescript was to be read personally by the emperor over the radio, it was generally believed that it would be a rescript urging redoubled war efforts. Intense static prevented the message from being understood in China, and it was not for several days that the order was passed on generally to cease hostilities. I wonder how difficult a decision that was to make. In any case, the general attitude is, "The Chinese never beat us. The Americans beat other Japanese troops, but in China things might have turned out differently." I think that this attitude was probably shared by Japanese in the Indies, Indochina, Siam and, of course, Manchuria before the Russians crashed in. I do not suppose that such an attitude can long be preserved once the troops return to Japan and see the effects of bombing and the power of the Americans. For safety, though, I feel more strongly than ever that a ten-year occupation is a minimum essential for Japan.

After several days wandering through Shanghai, I managed to fly back by way of Japan and spent a short while there. There is little point in describing my reactions other than to note that I was not disappointed, nor did home acquaintance with the Japanese entirely persuade me of the more real virtues of the Chinese. I have long been one of those who sneered at Mussolini who "made the trains run on time" and at people who were worried senseless about uncleanliness in Chinese restaurants, but like novels about golden-hearted bandits and prostitutes, the mythology of irregular individualism palls. Honesty, cleanliness, promptness, courtesy and the rest turn out, after all, to be virtues and not bourgeois or fascist vices. They are not everything, but I no longer despise them, and I no longer can despise the Japanese whose diaries I used to read.

My chief accomplishment in Japan was meeting individuals either by design or chance. I visited Yamada's mother at his request. She lives in a beautiful suburb of Tokyo which has not been bombed out. We spoke together for a little while about her son and about the war. "My boy was always so much interested in America. He studied English and neglected everything else. What a terrible thing that war should have come about between two countries he loved." She asked about my experiences in the war and I told her a little about Okinawa. "Were you really on Okinawa? What a frightful place that must have been. They said that everyone, even the women and children, were killed, but now I read in the newspapers that there were prisoners taken. I imagine that the prisoners will be coming home soon. Once that would have been considered very disgraceful, but now it doesn't matter. It couldn't be helped."

I went to Nikko with Hisashi Kubota to see the famous temples, the red bridge and the waterfall. We became separated and I found myself a guide to show me the sights. He was a charming quiet boy, just out of high school and about to go into the service when the war ended. He had lived in Nikko all his life and knew everything about the temples. There is a name for everything, a name for each of the hundred dragons, for each lacquered pillar. Over a door was the carving of a cat, just a little one, but so famous in Japan that the "Sleeping Cat" stands for all that is wonderful in art. We walked in stockinged feet over the red lacquer floors and stopped to buy a fortune and a good-luck charm. As we left the Tōshōgu with its magnificent gold and white gate, my guide turned to me. "Before the war a wealthy American offered a great deal of money—a million dollars I think—for this gate, but it was declared a national treasure and not for sale. I suppose that it will go to America now anyway, won't it?"

Then, the day before the plane left from Kisarazu, I stood in a bookstore looking for something suitable to take back to the prisoners left in Hawaii. I could hear two old women talking. One was telling of her family. "My daughter lived in Yokosuka, right next to the navy yard. When the first American planes started to visit Japan, my son-in-law decided that it would be dangerous there in Yokosuka so she moved the family to Kōfu, which is in the mountains. There are no military installations there, so we thought she would be quite safe. But they bombed Kōfu often, almost every week, and her house was burned down, while they didn't bomb Yokosuka at all." She ended this with the nervous laugh that worries me so in Japanese. Hearing that, I had a double reaction—a reaction to the calmness in telling of disaster which makes it possible for a Japanese to relate with a laugh that his son was eaten by cannibals in Borneo or was starved to death on Guadalcanal; and a reaction which led me back to the officers' club on Guam. I had asked a B-29 navigator why they bombed Kōfu so often when there wasn't anything there of great importance. He answered with a little laugh, "Well, for one thing it's easy to find, right on the direct route over to Tokyo. For another, there isn't much AA there."

I left Kisarazu one morning and was in Honolulu the next. Now I feel like a ghost wandering through the buildings in which we used to work so feverishly. There is no one left at all. Everyone is in the Orient or else back home, where I hope to see you before long.

Don

FROM OTIS CARY IN TOKYO
TO DON KEENE IN HONOLULU

December 21, 1945

Dear Don,

It is too late to have this wish you a Merry Christmas. Perhaps it will get to you in time for New Year's. Sherry, and I'm sure the Shikibas, would want me to pass on the season's greetings.

This last week Doc Shikiba and I have been to see Prince Takamatsu a couple of times. He is the third brother of the royal family. Prince Chichibu, the second, is down at Hayama most of the time and is pretty much out of the picture on account of his tuberculosis. Prince Mikasa, the youngest, is rumored to be approaching fatherhood, which makes the first child by any of the emperor's brothers. Prince Takamatsu evidently has a wide variety of interests and has been known increasingly in the last few years for helping out his oldest brother, the emperor.

You know what my stand on the emperor is. I have no use for his position in its past or present form. The Japanese emperor institution must have an entirely different basis or it cannot be condoned at all and might as well be given up. I had expected considerable chaos in Japan once we got in here and started giving conflicting orders, in which case the emperor wouldn't matter much any more, and it would have been best to retire him then. But he, through his peculiar position, was able to maintain order well after the surrender because of defter handling of him than I thought us capable of and, it seemed, could do so indefinitely. In view of the way the occupation is working out, that is a very fortunate thing for both sides. However, he cannot be maintained in his present (and past) tradition forever. As long as he exists as their ruler, is not publicly humiliated, and is doing things of his own volition, the Japanese people will be perfectly happy, in fact feel deep obligation, to do anything he asks.

Within that framework, the task he would have to take in starting on a new tradition seemed obvious to me. In this, the greatest hour of need of his people—a people who had spent eight years dying for him because they didn't know what they were dying for—there was nothing left for him to do but become a "people's emperor" and expend his energies along that line. There are countless things (many of them little) he could do if this is what he thought, or if this is what is thought for him, that would be of great benefit to the Japanese people in spurring production, combating inflation, giving Japan a new sense of self-respect, making her people feel that they belong to an even greater nation, one which stands together with the rest of the nations rather than apart from them.

Aside from this unique force of the emperor lying practically latent, there is only one other force in Japan right now big enough to have anywhere near enough strength to pull the country and the people out of their plight and set them on some sort of a path where reeducation and reform is possible. That power is the occupation backed up by the Potsdam Declaration. Although the Japanese government is a potential third force in Japan capable of alleviating the people's present plight and should be the real force, it is so wrapped up in its own machinations and red tape that it is practically strangled. The occupation has a monopoly on Japan's foreign policy—or the field it used to cover—and holds virtually veto power on anything done within Japan by the government. However, the occupation policy so far is pretty clearly defined and is more of a negative, corrective force than a positive leading force. The theory is to have the Japanese government lead unless it completely breaks down. Although it has not completely broken down yet, it is having pretty tough sledding. In Italy things are somewhat stuck at this juncture with the people having to wait for new leadership before their government can do more for them. But the Japanese emperor holds a certain loyalty from almost every Japanese; he is the only force in Japan at the moment which can move quickly and effectively. Thus, whether considering it on its own merits or from the point of view of an occupied Japan, there seems no better time to make use of this force.

Countless times at the Shikibas', and elsewhere, talk had centered around this. With the military out of the way, the Imperial Household Ministry had had four months "behind the moat" to set a course. What had they been dreaming about, anyway?

What had they been doing? After all, what had the emperor done since the surrender? He had checked in at Ise's Grand Shrine and had passed the word up "the unbroken line for ages eternal" on the end of the war; he had seen MacArthur for a bit; he had opened and closed a (truly) Extraordinary Session of the Diet; he had gone up to the Tama Mausoleum. (The man on the street couldn't even tell you this much of what he had done since the surrender.) This was pretty meager considering what he could be doing, and Doc Shikiba was anxious to get that understood in the highest place he could reach.

As you know, Japanese society is such that the higher one goes the more difficult it is for a Japanese to speak his mind. By and large when you talk with people of higher stations, you speak when you are spoken to and then agree. This seems particularly true when one goes up into the royalty. However, in Japan it has always been easier for a foreigner to speak his mind, and he is listened to—in this present situation, heeded much more than he ever was—with no offense taken. He is excused because he is considered to be a product of a different society with different customs and so his frankness is not held against him whether he speaks in English or in Japanese.

Among the fourteen princes of the blood only Princes Takamatsu and Higashikuni are at all approachable. They are the only two who will meet commoners without their entire retinue present and will talk naturally and openly. Doc Shikiba, in his capacity as director of the Mingeikan (Folk Art Museum), had entertained Prince Takamatsu there before, for the prince is interested in such matters. Before I left for the Marshalls in October he had wanted to arrange a meeting, for I didn't know whether I'd get back up to Japan or not. I had put him off then. This time he didn't want to let me get away without speaking my mind—a piece no Japanese commoner could ever say to a Japanese prince. Always in the back of my mind are Yokota, Oyanagi, and the other POWs, and the terrific injustice they have been done, to say nothing of the complete hoodwinking job done on the Japanese people in this war. Doc Shikiba felt the same way. If he thought it would do any good I told him I'd go, but I warned him that

I wouldn't be prim, proper, and pussy-footing, but would speak my mind. He told me that that was the only reason he would try to arrange it, for we both agreed that things in Japan on any level were beyond a pussy-footing stage, especially on *this* level.

Doc Shikiba was duly informed after negotiations that the prince could give from 4:00 to 6:00 P.M. and that minor refreshments would be served. It happened to be the day that Prince Konoye committed suicide. Right across from our billet the *Asahi* had it up on posters as we went by on the way to the "audience." Also, the directives killing State Shinto came out earlier that same day. I made quick mental notes on all this, for the only problem that presented itself in my mind was how to turn the conversation smoothly to the emperor. It was hard to figure out what he'd think we'd come for, although I knew he was sure to ask me about American opinion on the occupation, on Japan, on the emperor, etc. I wonder whether he had any idea that we'd want to wade into the problem of the emperor and what he should be doing.

We arrived by weapons carrier and foot and wandered into the grounds of his palace. It was a large, not particularly unusual Western-style mansion of stone and concrete. No one was at the gatekeeper's building where there should be two or three policemen. (We were later told that the prince had ordered them into the back room some time ago, for "There's not much point in having them out front and they look sort of grim there anyway.") It looked so deserted that I began to wonder whether this were the right place. The front entrance with huge paneled doors had no doorknobs on the outside. It made me wonder whether the attempt was being made to present a forbidding front or whether it was really an extremely hospitable entrance which would be wide open and flanked by bowing servants for anyone who mattered. Eventually we managed to scare up somebody out back who informed the prince's secretary of our presence. The front entrance was opened for us. We walked into a front hall completely in Western-style with not too many rugs and some handsome ivory tusk decorations as the only unusual thing. There was no place to remove our shoes. After taking off our coats we were ushered into a front parlor where we met the manager of the estate and where we waited until the precise hour of 4:00 passing platitudes about my "wonderful Japanese," "where did you go to school?" etc. I wore my regular olive drabs for the occasion. This was an afternoon meeting and the ODs were the uniform of the day, so I saw no reason to do anything special. Just before 4:00 Mr. Yoshijima, his secretary, said he would see if they were ready. He informed us that the princess would also be present. He returned. They were ready. We entered the next room going through the hall. Doc Shikiba was asked to present me. Mr. Yoshijima knocked on the door and we went in. Prince Takamatsu, smiling, came forward immediately with extended hand which I shook as we told him between the two of us that I was Cary. Then I also shook hands with the princess, who was all smiles. Doc Shikiba bowed a little, which is very low for him. (We sat in a ten-foot square, with a little table each for the princess and me and a longer one between Doc Shikiba and the prince.) I sat across from the prince. The chairs were stiff, padded and armed, and the room was furnished peculiarly—a rather nineteenth-century room turned twentieth century. There was a rug of usual design on the floor and a colorful, unusual *kakemono* scroll over the fireplace. The ceilings were high. An electric heater warmed the room. Prince Takamatsu wore a single-breasted blue pinstripe suit of 1941 style with a blue V-neck sweater instead of a vest and a conservative tie. The princess was wearing a dark blue ski-suit sort of arrangement—perhaps the imperial *mompe*. She looked quite impromptu and attractive. The prince looks like the picture of his oldest brother around his chin and mouth though his hair and eyes are different.

Before I could catch my breath, or Doc Shikiba could get in any introductory dope usual to Japanese situations like this, the princess asked me, "Where have you been?" I didn't know whether she meant in Japan or America or what. We got leveled off though and I gave them a fill-in on my background: that I was born and raised in Japan and went to the first four years of Japanese primary school, etc. I said all this in a straight unadorned Japanese, for it was the way both of them talked. We continued on with much ordinary talk.

Then I asked them, "Have you heard the news?" They had not. I said, "Prince Konoye committed suicide early this morning rather than be apprehended as a war crimes suspect."

"We heard something about it, but I wonder if it's true," said the prince.

"We just came by the *Asahi* and *Mainichi*," I said. "Evidently he drank poison."

"Is that right?" they both said, the princess leaning forward.

"What a stupid thing to do at this time," I said. "This way, in spite of leaving his memoirs and record, he does nobody any good. If he were innocent, he could serve his people best by taking the stand and defending himself. If he were found guilty, that would be time enough to commit suicide and with much more reason, for he obviously considered himself innocent. The knowledge he has of the entire China Incident period is invaluable and it was his to bring out for the record. This way he proves nothing, vindicates neither the emperor nor himself. What a pitiful exhibition! Konoye has merely 'thrown in the towel again.'" (A plumber fixing a shower at our billet had said that very phrase only an hour previously when I had told him.) This was pretty strong talk right at the start. I wondered if the prince would explain how he really had vindicated the emperor and so open the topic of the day. Perhaps he didn't believe he had either. He gave no indication. We passed on to another topic.

"How did you become a full lieutenant so quickly?" asked the prince.

"All I did was stand and wait. Any good navy man who stands and waits gets his promotions in our navy, too." I said, for the prince was a naval captain during the war, attached to the naval general staff in Tokyo. He laughed.

"The Bombing Survey certainly is an all-inclusive organization, isn't it?" he said. "They seem to cover much more than a mere bombing survey."

I answered, "Everybody says that, but the mission of the bombing survey is to survey the entire influence that bombing had on Japan. As bombing affected all ramifications of life from economy to religion, we need to gain good background in all that."

Then Dr. Shikiba asked, "Your Highness, do you remember a Captain Yamaga?" He should have, for Captain Yamaga was the senior meteorologist in the Japanese navy and they must have rubbed elbows at navy headquarters. I had hoped to bring up the writing of a rescript exonerating all POWs of any blame for becoming POWs as one of the things that the emperor could do.

The prince said, "Yes. He became a prisoner, I understand. With things as they are now, certainly there would be no problem on POWs' return." That rather spiked my idea, but we looked at each other and let it pass.

Finally we got off on the middle ten days of August after I asked him, "What do you think of MacArthur and the occupation?"

He said, "It's going remarkably smoothly, but what good does it do to say much else about it." I waited for him to expand. He went on, "If America is going to go on ramming American democracy down the Japanese throat, you might as well go on. We can't stop you. That won't make a truly democratic Japan though."

I didn't answer directly, but added, "MacArthur has done most of the big things now. He has freed the press, abolished 'thought control,' freed political prisoners, instituted women's suffrage, declared the crushing of the *zaibatsu*, returned the land to the farmers. The test is ahead. How much of the detail work is he going to have foreign personnel do and how much is he going to allow the Japanese to do. That will be the deciding factor and if he expects any but the Japanese to do much of it, he is crazy." Then, starting to trace the course of things from the first sign of surrender, I sketched for him a little of the excitement in the States at that time and some stories I had heard in Japan since my arrival. Now it was with Sweden, now it was with the Swiss, now it was with Byrnes that negotiations were underway; then Dōmei News Agency said something.

The prince said, "Most of the listeners here in Japan were disappointed at the very poor reception." I told him we had had good reception on Iwo, for I'd heard an almost complete dictaphone record of the emperor's surrender broadcast in Hawaii.

"Hardly anyone understood it, anyway," Doc Shikiba rejoined, and we all agreed heartily with a smile. This gave me my opening.

"Everybody I've talked to," I said, "except those 'in the know,' if I'm not mistaken (I knew I wasn't), thought they'd been given the direct charge to do their utmost when they heard the broadcast ending the war, and so they went back to roll up their sleeves and work harder. I heard of some military commanders who went to hear the broadcast (asking them to cooperate fully with what the imperial will felt bound to do) in their dress uniforms with their units and trudged back to duty to redouble their efforts only to be overtaken by panting aides telling them that evidently what was meant was that the war was to end. Many people didn't find out that the war was over until the next morning when the newspapers came out. So the turnabout was made successfully, and with a saving in life to both sides. It's unbelievable that there hasn't been an incident so far."

"The problem of the emperor," the prince said, "seems entirely incomprehensible to the Americans and yet it is such an accepted thing in all Japanese minds."

At last I was able to light into it. "Yes," I said, "and what wonderful things he could be doing right now which would be understandable to the world in its present patient incomprehension and which would result in vast good for the Japanese people—things entirely apart and away from the political (which he should stay away from), which could be interpreted as definite steps in the right direction. If he doesn't start taking these steps pretty soon he may not be in any position to take them later. (From the first time I had to refer to the emperor I used the Japanese term *niisan*, "big brother." The first time the prince wasn't sure whose was meant, mine or Doc Shikiba's, although it was evident by the context of the sentence very shortly. The second time he understood right off and I got a definite, audible giggle out of the princess. It didn't bother either of them at all; of that I'm pretty sure—in fact I think they rather liked it.) The entire basis of war and peace and the governing of people takes on a different light with the advent of the atomic bomb, and an emperor such as still exists becomes that much more of an anachronism now. To anyone here it is obvious that Japan would be chaos without the stabilizing forces of the emperor on the people, but he should use this power for the people's sake in many more ways. If steps, and such little simple ones, are not taken soon, public opinion from abroad, which has been strong on this question all along and which knows nothing of the actual situation, may force something very unfortunate for the emperor."

Then he invited me to expound. He said, "But *concretely* just *what* can he do?"

What an invitation! What would you have said? I waited half a minute not to appear too eager. Then I started in.

I told him there were many things, for instance, those new Imperial Household uniforms which the emperor had just been "pleased to bless" before going to Ise. (Immediately the princess broke in and said, "And those awful decorations!" I heartily agree with her.) Uniforms have military connotations. They are designed to make a fellow feel he "belongs." The first step in cutting out individualism is creation of a uniform. To those of us in the occupation forces who aren't professional military men, which means over ninety percent, no promotion is as great as the one which allows us to take off our uniforms and regain our freedom. Japan has nobody at home who has to be in the army or navy any more. But then a new Imperial Household uniform has to be created and given publicity because the emperor passed on it. When he goes somewhere, to court or official functions, why can't he do one of two things: either wear the correct Western diplomatic dress to state and court functions, or wear the old proper Japanese white *montsuki* dress [old Japanese dress clothes with the family crest worked into them; only his are white]. But no more uniforms. Granted it's a step down from the Grand Marshall, Grand Fleet Admiral get-up of yore; but he's been promoted to civilian now. Just as distasteful are the Japanese military-style civilian uniforms and the visored military-style civilian caps which all males wear because there is nothing else sold. There is some excuse for the general public due to scarcity of material, but to create a new uniform for the Imperial Household now that the war is over is inexcusable.

Although the nobility is another story and should be resolved along with the problem of the House of Peers, all the decorations (Imperial Golden Kite, Second Class, etc.) that the more important

Japanese acquire in an increasing number and ascending scale as they work longer and longer in the services of the imperial government he could abolish if he had a mind to. They are meaningless now. Just yesterday Suzuki Kantarō, the ex-premier, was nominated to the post of president of the privy council and all over the front pages he was "Admiral Suzuki" plus all his court decorations. Military ranks certainly are passé now, with no army or navy, to say nothing of the fact that Suzuki had been retired for a dozen or more years. And why not get rid of all these old meaningless court decorations, too? If the emperor merely expressed an opinion designating all military ranks as distasteful and court decorations as meaningless and never to be used again, that would be all that would be necessary. They would never be used publicly or in the press again.

I reminded him we'd just been talking of the rescript which stopped the war. There is so much that can be done in the whole field of rescripts, simplicity first of all. Rare is the rescript that can be understood by the average Japanese even with a dictionary, for they don't know how to pronounce the words in order to look them up. Yet rescripts are the only means so far of making information from the emperor directly available to the people. Why not forget the Chinese style and the special imperial language and write them so that even I could understand them? I told him of the POWs interest in seeing in the local Hawaiian papers a photograph of the imperial credentials taken down to Manila by General Kawabe for the surrender negotiations. They were much imimpressed with the characters "Hiro-hito" on the document. Although they had never known before, they had come to understand who Hirohito was when the American press referred to him that way, but to actually see the characters, and by his own hand! They had had no idea what characters were used. All rescripts had *gyomei-gyoji*, which corresponds to our "s/ Harry S Truman," but means "honorable name, honorable seal." His name never appears in copies. Why couldn't he express a desire to allow his name to be printed at the end of all copies?

The prince rejoined here with the idea that photographs of the rescripts could be passed out instead of copies. I told him I was afraid that it would still be sent over the wire in the old way, because of the existing precedent, but that it could be tried. However, the main thing was simplicity.

I went on to the point of official pictures of the emperor. All Japanese schools have formal pictures of the emperor, and they are highly revered. Teachers in the schools have the duty in rotation of spending the night at school to guard it. Some teachers have been burned to death trying to save the thing in cases of fire. Little fireproof vaults were sometimes made for them. Everybody must bow before it. It is hardly ever shown and when displayed usually has dark curtains almost completely covering it. I knew that they had all been called in for a reissue which was about to come out. I suggested that the emperor "forget" to issue a new one. If the clamor grew too loud and schools sent in asking for them, then would be time enough to issue one to those schools. And if one must be issued—I told him I thought many schools would be glad to be rid of the responsibility—have it a good impromptu shot of him working in his marine biology laboratory. Why couldn't he make a statement that he hoped the students of Japan would spend the time they used to accord his picture in studying harder.

This brought us into the whole problem of pictures generally. I suggested that since informal pictures of the emperor or his family had never been released, some good ones be taken and given to the Japanese press. Any shots would be fine, but they must be candid, catching them in any part of their daily lives, attempting merely to show the Japanese people that the first family is not very different from any other Japanese family, probably not so lavish as some. Incidentally, interviews could be handled in the same way. It would be a great mistake, of course, to have a news conference by the emperor. That is the prime minister's pigeon, and the emperor should make no political remarks at all except in conjunction with the prime minister. However, rather than have canned handouts given to the Imperial Household Ministry reporters (of which statements the big papers get a certain quota and the little papers a smaller quota and which are worked up to by the newspapermen taking the job) whenever the emperor worships at such-and-such a shrine, why not have him meet the press (*any* accredited Japanese newspaper reporters) occasionally and put some matter-of-fact questions to them. "Is rationing tough?" or "Are things getting built up in your section pretty quickly?" or "What goods are in short supply?"; anything to show he is interested in those mundane things, is a person after all, and realizes the Japanese people are not without their problems. It would be a good idea in one of the first meetings for him to decry the terribly stilted language with which he himself is referred to in both the Japanese- and English-language press and suggest that it be toned down considerably.

At this point the refreshments were served by waitresses in *mompe* (those garments that are a cross between bloomers and long pants). Of course, we had Japanese tea right at the start, but the treat now was baked apples and Western-style tea. They were very good. I wondered if they thought me a boor because I like the skin, which I ate calmly, not realizing till I was through that perhaps I was distressing the princess. She looked at me when I got through in a surprised way.

Sherry had made an excellent suggestion the night before. Have the emperor merely by his wish officially change the country over from the 20th year of Shōwa to 1945 A.D. It would simplify many things. Since every other civilized country in the world uses A.D., why not Japan? He could make some pronouncement as to how he had started out his era as "enlightened peace," but it hadn't worked out that way unfortunately, and it's really best to stay in line with the rest of the world anyway. I thought I could see Prince Takamatsu making many mental notes.

I suggested further that by the emperor's wish the inner palace grounds be opened up to the Japanese public for certain hours every week. Here again the fact that the emperor *himself* had made the gesture would be important. What might happen very easily in Japan would be to have the palace opened to the occupation troops for certain hours, too. I begged him not to make the mistake of catering to the occupation troops. This would be a chance to give the Japanese people a feeling of partnership in what goes on "behind the moat." They need not show the emperor's bedroom, nor need there be visitors' hours every day. The value of the thing would be in the people's knowing that they *could* go, whether they actually went or not. Incidentally, he could also commission some surveyors to survey the palace grounds and put them on the maps from now on. Until now the palace grounds have always been a blank in maps of Tokyo, again setting him apart. Allowing the grounds to be mapped would again bring him and his family closer to his people.

Another point I brought up was about the Diet. I told the prince that I had recently visited the House of Peers in session. I was impressed by the plant but depressed by the attitude of the members. At this turning point in their nation's history these men should be more concerned. I had become friendly with the head of the guards while the session was going on. I noted particularly that, aside from the throne where the emperor reads the rescripts opening and closing the Diet, there was a box in the middle of the balcony for the royal family, should they wish to attend. It was curtained off, of course, but surprisingly open. I suggested that the emperor *unannounced* sometime attend the Diet for a half hour or so, just "to see what was going on" in his government. On his return he could make some simple statement to the press about the lack of attendance or the poor lighting or whatever occurred to him, but not about the political factors involved. This would be no political move, but merely an attempt to show to Japan that Japan's No. 1 citizen was trying to keep up with things. Since he has a box there for his family, why not use it once in a while? Incidentally the quality of the speeches and the attendance would be markedly improved for months to come and the amount of sleeping markedly decreased.

Turning to political fields, I went on. The only way to stop inflation was to increase food and production. It would be the emperor's duty to do whatever he could to increase either or both. I thought there were two things he could do. Right away, he should make a long, extensive, six-week tour of the four main islands, stressing industrial production and food production. While he is in Tokyo, he should make weekly unheralded trips to the outskirts of the city and get out of his car to inquire personally after the welfare of his people. But there should be a real attempt to cover the whole country. If it were cut down to a ten-day express train run to the main cities, it had better be left undone. I was advocating a long, tedious junket all over the country. It should be an unheralded trip with the train stopping as often as something interested him. He should get off and talk to farmers by the tracks, workers in the cities. He should, once underway, change his route a few times, visit the electric power plants, the coal mines of Ishikari and Kyushu in operation, schools, hospitals, everything. I even said I didn't believe that the emperor had seen as much of Japan as he had wanted to. Now would be a good time to let him plan his own route. Wherever he went, if he were to stress production, it would make a surprising difference to the total output of the country and would allow it to come closer to pulling itself out of its hole. This should be done as soon as possible but certainly before the next Diet was elected.

The other thing he could do would be to give a radio address before the next election asking that everybody eligible, both men and women, turn out to vote for candidates of integrity and character—those whom *they* thought best. He should use whatever type of language he usually uses with no 'royal we' or out of the ordinary verb endings. It should be short, intimate, warm, thanking the people for their attempts so far and asking them for further endeavor. Perhaps he could draw some simple illustration from something he'd seen which would stress the value of production. He should make a talk like this at least once a year.

The prince and princess were listening attentively through all this. I told them there was one more little thing that might be fun for the emperor to do, then I would stop. I said that all Japanese in all walks of life were coming in contact with occupation troops; they were in effect a segment of Japanese society now. The emperor, however, has yet to do so. It would be a mistake to invite a half-dozen GIs to a garden party and "meet" them in an attempt to be democratic. The thing just might not go over. But why not ask to be allowed to attend some GI show or sports contest, perhaps with his sons. Certainly a pavilion or box would be put up for him. No interpreters or "explainers" should be requested. He should go with a minimum of retinue and try to figure out with his sons what it all meant. On his return he might tell the Japanese press, for instance, "American football is too complicated. They are always in a huddle or out flat on the ground. I think I'd better stick to my microscope!" This would allow him to see and have a certain amount of contact with the GIs enjoying their own pastimes and, incidentally, it might prove somewhat amusing to him.

At the end of this harangue it was 6:30. We had been told the prince had till 6:00. They made no signs of wanting to have us leave, but not knowing what they had scheduled for the evening, I thought we had better start making our departure. Prince Takamatsu said more than once, "That's good advice," followed with a nod of the head, and Doc Shikiba told me later that he easily expected us to be invited to supper on the strength of how things were going. It is extremely unusual for them to deign to stay after the time previously quoted, but Doc Shikiba said they seemed to be enjoying it and must evidently have had something on the docket for that night. We excused ourselves from the parlor, exchanging routine words of parting, and shook hands again.

Doc Shikiba, once we'd been bowed out of the palace by the attendants, was delighted. He said that everything we had talked about so often seemed to find its way into the talk and that the prince, he thought, took everything to heart. He didn't think anyone had ever talked to him before in such a straight way with none of the unnatural politeness which Japanese have to assume. And he was sure nobody had ever talked to him like that about the emperor. We laughed over the kick they seemed to get out of referring to the emperor as "big brother." He was sure that nobody outside the family had ever said that to him before.

It is Japanese custom after such an audience to appear at the palace in formal dress the next day to thank one of the secretaries for the time the prince was able to give. Doc Shikiba didn't go for that very much, but he went to see the prince, if he could, to deliver some *Life*s I'd mentioned that I'd been able to get hold of and a copy of Grew's *Ten Years In Japan* and to pick up any reactions that might be forthcoming in a quick conversation. Although there were many people waiting, the prince took Doc Shikiba first as soon as he got back. He had been to the main palace, Mr. Yoshijima said. He was grateful for the *Life*s (there were at least fifteen—probably as complete a set as there is in Japan) and the Grew. He asked Doc Shikiba if we could all get together again. Since I had told Doc Shikiba that from my side I was seeking no audience, he emphasized to the prince that I was leaving soon after the 20th. Nevertheless, the prince was anxious to have another session. By the time Doc Shikiba got hold of me it was the 18th, and I had some time on the 20th, so another visit was arranged. Meantime I had contracted an infection of my gums in connection with my wisdom teeth that was extremely painful, but we went anyway. I figured that I had said my piece and it would be my turn to sit and listen, especially if he was anxious to see me. Besides I didn't feel like doing anything else but listening.

We arrived a little before 2:00 and at 2:00 were ushered in again. We shook hands this time, too. The princess wasn't there, although I had hoped that she would be and Doc Shikiba had mentioned it when he had been there to arrange the meeting. The prince commiserated over my teeth and asked when my orders were dated as we sat down. I told him that they had not been written yet, that there still was a possibility I would stay on. Then he came right to the point and said, "More concretely what can the emperor do right now?" I tried to trace for him a little of the feeling in the States toward Japan from the day of Pearl Harbor to the surrender, why MacArthur was so impatient when they asked for another week at Manila, etc. I used both barrels regularly, telling him just how bad the feeling was back in the States. We went over point by point again all the ideas that I had expounded four days previously.

I asked him if he had had a chance to look at Grew's *Ten Years* at all. He had just barely glanced at it. An idea came to me on the spur of the moment. I remembered how abruptly official relations were severed with Japan by Pearl Harbor and what an irreparable cleavage that produced in the minds of most Americans. To anyone looking over the records it was really rather insulting to have Roosevelt's letter, written in that typical grand Rooseveltian style, answered by the Pearl Harbor attack and the thirteen-page memo of December 8 (here), never mentioning war or its possibility nor even breaking off diplomatic relations, but merely ending the conversations. Why doesn't the emperor write a brief letter to Roosevelt's successor, Truman, through the proper channels, decrying the actions of his armies and navies and the tragedy they forced much of the world into? Include in it much humility and admission of guilt but still a hope that with the help of the rest of the United Nations they could eventually take their rightful place in the world. He could work in the change of year idea to good advantage saying he was changing the calendar of Japan to conform with that of the rest of the world, for his era of "enlightened peace" had not been very successful, and hoped that someday in all other things they could take their place beside other nations, not over. I told him I thought that might heal a little the huge wound Pearl Harbor had opened up. I tried to emphasize over again what a fantastic boner the Japanese had pulled at Pearl Harbor, that they had set themselves back fifty years by doing that.

We concluded the interview in about two and a half hours again. I was glad to get home to bed. I have written this in a somewhat feverish state; I hope it's adequate for your trained eye.

Otis

P.S. I forgot to mention what a help Sherry was through all this, of course. Many of these ideas were his and he was very patient in discussing over and over with me how to present them.

◆ ◆ ◆

FROM SHERRY MORAN IN TOKYO
TO TED DE BARY IN HONOLULU

December 23, 1945

Dear Ted,

"It is a portentous symbol. Blazing boldly at night in electric splendor, standing out by day in cheery crimson and green, and reflected at all times, whether he will or no, in Hirohito's own somber palace moat as the occupation's greeting to all who pass. It is the final invasion . . . etc."

No news story out of Tokyo on Christmas in Japan will fail to start out with a description of the elaborate business which has transformed the forbidding exterior of the Dai-ichi Insurance Building, MacArthur's headquarters, into as gala a promoter of Christmas good wishes as any department store in New York City. And no newsman trained in catching "significance" will fail to note that reflected MERRY XMAS and spend a paragraph on all it implies.

The day before yesterday as I was walking up toward the Dai-ichi Building from Radio Tokyo I fell in step with a press relations officer whom I know slightly. He was out for a breath of air, he sighed, before he went back to his office in the radio building to finish up a release he was getting up on GI Christmas activities in the city. It was almost finished, and he just needed a breather before he put it into final shape. His deadline was in forty-five minutes. It was dusk and, as we approached general headquarters, the still uncompleted decorations were visible from quite a distance. Especially, MERRY X stood out in electric lights that could be seen half a mile away. I asked him if he had written much in his article on the huge Christmas sign on MacArthur's headquarters.

"No, what have they got up there?" I pointed ahead. His interest was immediately aroused. "Say now, that's really something! When did they put that up?"

"They must have started about Monday," I suggested. "They've had poles and rope for scaffolding cluttering up the sidewalk and about fifty workmen running around putting it up for days."

"How many workmen? About fifty? How many days? About four? Say, this is interesting. I'm glad I ran into you. What does it say?"

I hastened to disclaim any detailed knowledge of GHQ's Christmas card. "All it says so far is MERRY X," I pointed out. "It looks as if they're working on the MAS now." We had reached Hibiya corner a scant two hundred yards from the display.

"MERRY XMAS, eh? Sure that's what it's going to say?" Apparently he had taken off his glasses when he left the office for the breather. There was no question of the lettering which was plainly visible. We stood on the corner until the traffic light turned.

I suggested that we cross the street and get a good look at the sign. "Oh, I haven't got time. Got to get that story out." He mused there on the corner for a moment. I started to go.

"Say! Does that sign reflect in the moat?"

"I'm sure it does. If you look at it from the right angle it would have to."

"Say, that's good!" He was exultant. Then he frowned. "You sure that you can see that MERRY XMAS in the moat? The palace moat?"

"Well, it stands to reason you can, but for Christ's sake, let's cross over and settle it."

"Oh, no, no, no! I have to get back and turn out that story. Just so long as you're sure. And you are, aren't you? It says MERRY XMAS and you can see it in the moat? Thanks a lot, Moran. Sure lucky I ran into you."

Pictures of GHQ in its Christmas wrappings will undoubtedly get into all the newspapers. It is a real spectacle. Four of the eight giant square granite columns of the facade have been sheathed in solid green cypress boughs to a height of about sixty feet. The greenery is spangled with stars, and across the top are the words I discussed with the public relations officer. To each side are giant Christmas trees, decorated and lighted with colored bulbs. The supreme sideshow touch occurs around the cornice, where painted wooden sections cut in festoon patterns and outlined at night with electric lights continue around three sides of the building. Crowning everything is another Christmas tree, brilliantly lighted, standing alone on the roof. The entire display uses about 2,100 light bulbs.

Christmas is a time to be charitable, so why take a swing at somebody's attempt to be Christmasy? I can't help speculating, however, on who is supposed to be impressed by so showy a greeting. Most Japanese are in a receptive mood; the way the Americans do it is the right way—they won the war, didn't they? "We must learn from them." Most soldier reaction I've encountered is summed up by, "Boy, oh boy! Isn't that something?" I ran into one guy who was more negative and more vocal. "Instead of wasting all this goodwill on the Japs, why don't they spend a little of it on us and get us home?" I think that the net GI reaction may be a mixture of such outbursts; Japanese reaction will be appreciative, even though it may be secretly wondered whether MERRY XMAS is a greeting or a directive.

Japanese have a lot of reason to be uncritically appreciative of American activities to celebrate the day. There is extensive evidence that a lot of the soldiers want to play Santa, especially to the children. A letter in the army newspaper of the 20th says, "Christmastime is near and it is a very good time to put over our ideas and win the friendship of the Japanese as a whole. I would like to see a campaign started to give the children of Japan a Merry Christmas. Give them parties with gifts of candy and gum and other small things that make kids happy. It will win a lot of the average citizens to our way of thinking." It was signed by a sergeant. I know of two such parties scheduled for next Tuesday, one in Tokyo at the Red Cross Club, where every man will bring a kid under ten years of age, another at the headquarters of the XIth Army Corps near Yokohama, where six hundred kids of laborers working for the corps will decorate a tree and receive small presents. The story of the Christian Chrismas will be told by the chaplain there.

All this is very heartwarming, of course. On the adult level, one of the most spectacular instances of joint celebration by Japanese and occupation troops will be the two-hundred-and-fifty-voice chorus and the Nippon Symphony Orchestra rendering Handel's *Messiah*. On Christmas Eve a Catholic High Mass will be celebrated, primarily for troops in the Tokyo area. The celebrant will be an army colonel, and the archbishop of Tokyo, Peter Takui Doi, will attend. Among Protestant services will be one addressed by Toyohiko Kagawa, the noted Japanese Christian leader.

All in all, Christmas in Tokyo will not be an unpleasant experience for a large part of the occupation troops. But pleasant as it may be otherwise, Christmas without home and family will be a substitute thing at best. There will be many soldiers for whom the gaiety, goodwill and home-likeness of this Christmas in Tokyo will serve primarily as reminders of even more complete Christmases in the past.

Sherry

FROM FRANK TURNER IN SHANGHAI
TO SHERRY MORAN IN TOKYO

January 2, 1946

Dear Sherry,

I am certainly glad that I spent three days in Shanghai because the visit revealed how impressionable I can be. In Japan I was constantly exposed to the more attractive aspects of Japanese character: children waved and women smiled at me; businessmen told me that the American occupation was a great blessing for Japan; the Japanese praised General MacArthur; I was courteously welcomed in stores and even in homes. I had the impression that the Japanese people were trying to accommodate me in every way. Thus when I left Japan, the more unattractive characteristics of the Japanese, ever in the public eye during the war, assumed a hazy unreality and faded from my consciousness. I would not classify my attitude as pro-Japanese in the usual sense, but I was, I am sorry to admit, forgetful of realities.

My father has spent his active lifetime working in China with the YMCA and, at times, helping to foster a unified central government as an advisor to Chiang Kai-shek. As a boy, I was constantly exposed to an antagonism toward the Japanese. When I arrived in Shanghai a week ago, after an absence of ten years, all the earlier emotionalism and prejudice against the Japanese in my thinking welled up once again, as the result of opinions expressed by almost everyone with whom I talked, including Chinese, White Russians, German Jews and an American lady who had spent the war years in Shanghai. In talking to these people, I sensed the opposition which was sure to flare up if I mentioned my entirely happy visit in Japan and the favorable impression I had gained of the Japanese people.

On arriving in Shanghai, I made immediate efforts to find an American lady named Mrs. Helen Ling. I had met Helen Ling in the early 1930s when she first arrived in China at about the age of twenty-two. She is one of the most impressive women I have ever met, fairly tall, beautiful, very forceful in presenting her ideas but always pleasant, firm in her convictions, which she is quick to support with careful reasoning. Her appearance had changed little in ten years except for a marked graying of her hair. She is devoted to her family and especially to her son, a bright boy of sixteen. An illustration of Helen Ling's independent thinking and self-reliance is the manner in which she decided to come to China about fifteen years ago. She was brought up in New Jersey in a moderately well-to-do family, attended an eastern college and took graduate work at Columbia Teachers' College. While at Columbia, she met a Chinese student chemist who asked her to marry him. She was ready to accept his proposal, but her Chinese fiancé pointed out that much unpleasantness might arise in China where his mother, as head of the family, might regard her as an unwanted interloper. Unsanitary conditions and a Chinese-style house might make her restless. Eurasian children might pose difficult problems. These and several other possible impediments to a successful marriage were raised by her fiancé. Helen Ling finally accepted his cautious attitude and decided to visit China and live there at first on an experimental basis. Despite opposition from friends and family, she persisted in the experiment, traveling to the native-style home of her fiancé in Soochow to meet his family. Despite language and cultural differences, Helen Ling was regarded favorably by the dowager mother. I suspect that Helen Ling's graciousness and sincerity made her endeared, as they do wherever she goes. The period of experimental living in China expired, and she married her fiancé and later had a son. Her husband succeeded in various industrial chemical enterprises, as might be expected of any Chinese possessing the benefit of American technical training. Never once in the years that I and my parents have known her has Mrs. Ling wavered in her determination to make a success of a venture which to a less forceful person would have appeared most unpromising.

When I visited Shanghai, Helen Ling and family were living in a Western-style house in the French concession. During the war years, she had lived there alone with her son; her husband was separated from her by force of circumstances and was working in Chungking and later in the United States. Thus alone, she underwent the harrowing experience of living under Japanese rule for almost four years. Living was difficult for everyone in

Shanghai, especially if one tried to maintain a standard of living comparable to that of normal times. For Helen Ling, an American woman, life itself was constantly endangered.

Like many Americans, she was unwilling to escape from Shanghai on an exchange ship because her work and loyalties were rooted in China. Unlike other Americans, however, she was able to evade the insistence of State Department officers because of her Chinese citizenship. She was determined to maintain her home in Shanghai, to continue the education of her son and, above all, to assist her Chinese friends through the crisis. To leave in the face of possible danger would have meant the selfish abandonment of her friends and relatives to sink or swim. Also it would have meant the abandonment of an ideal for which she came to China, namely to make a complete success of an international marriage, believing that such marriages can make a contribution to world peace, and, in her case, to the concept of interracial equality. After the Pearl Harbor attack, she realized for the first time what price she might have to pay for her determination, and then it was too late to escape even had she wanted to.

Helen Ling was American in every sense except citizenship. She dressed elegantly in Western style; her face would have been difficult to disguise; and her knowledge of the Chinese language, although good for a foreigner, still betrayed her. She had no choice but to be herself—a typically American woman—regardless of the omnipresent Japanese suspicion. She explained that from the Japanese viewpoint she possessed all the usual qualifications for being a spy suspect. Her husband was actively working for Chiang Kai-shek as a technician and traveling in the United States on official business. She had presumably been given an opportunity to leave Shanghai but had elected to remain—a most unusual choice for an American woman. She had many Chinese friends who could smuggle information out to the enemy.

Such suspicions existed in the minds of the Japanese *kempeitai* as the natural result of her mere physical presence in Shanghai. However, Helen Ling gave the Japanese even further provocation to suspect and even to convict her. She lived dangerously in an effort to feed herself and her son and to keep friends alive. During these years she exhibited a clever unscrupulousness which in peace time would be classed as crime, but which, under the circumstances, I would class as heroism. She bribed Japanese officials and guards at internment camps so that she might smuggle food and comforts to interned friends. She entertained Japanese officials at her home with an affected affability which was designed only to patronize them. She stored valuables and potentially incriminating papers in her attic for the benefit of refugees who had fled from the Japanese, and then on several occasions dissuaded the *kempeitai* from making a search of her house. "I stayed awake nights inventing ruses for evading the petty regulations which the Japanese called law," she explained. She even admitted reluctantly to having indulged in gold speculation—a practice condemned by the Japanese. In 1943, a friend had predicted a rise in the gold price and Helen Ling had invested some of her savings accordingly. The investment proved profitable enough to keep her household running and supplied for almost a year. She mentioned this when I inquired about her income during the war, knowing that her husband could not communicate with her or send funds.

She did these things despite frequent questioning by the ever-vigilant Japanese police. She had the fortitude to assume tremendous risks despite the inevitable question which sprang to her mind as she set out to perform any of her so-called crimes: "Is this worth a possible trip to Bridge House [Japanese military headquarters]? What will become of my son if they take me away?" She told of the pathetic cases of friends who sustained permanent injuries or were drowned when Japanese investigators poured kerosene or water down the nostrils of their strapped victims. She spoke also of cases of forced exposure to heat or cold and of beatings.

After hearing her account, I naturally wondered how she herself had escaped untouched. She explained that a friend of her husband's, whom the Japanese unwittingly trusted, had interceded on her behalf. I suspect, however, that her survival was largely due to an unswerving determination to save her son and to assist her Chinese friends.

Helen Ling recounted her experiences with no dramatics or special emphasis on her own hardships. She was emphatic, however, in describing her relief at seeing the nightmare come to an end. She described the moment of exhilaration when she heard American longwave broadcasts from Leyte and realized for the first time in the war that Americans were pushing the Japanese backward. She mentioned the joy of seeing Americans and the glorious sense of security engendered by the presence of Americans. She remarked, "It's a wonderful feeling to be no longer forced to resort to dishonesty and subterfuge just to stay alive."

I was never so moved as on Christmas night when some Chinese friends and I had supper at Helen Ling's home. There was steaming American coffee and sugar. Helen Ling's nine-year-old niece played on the piano, somewhat haltingly to be sure, but we all applauded generously. Mrs. Ling sat down beside her and guided her through the playing of "Silent Night." We all joined in singing, perhaps more loudly and happily than the conventional rendition of this particular carol. I thought I noticed Helen Ling's eyes glistening abnormally, but couldn't be sure because she placed her cheek against that of her Chinese niece, hiding her eyes in the little girl's hair. There was no longer a Bridge House, no need for dishonest affability and no *kempeitai* to play Peeping Tom around Helen Ling's house.

An anti-Japanese attitude different from Helen Ling's was expressed by a White Russian girl who worked in a cabaret called Ciro's, on Bubbling Well Road. She was about twenty-five years old and called herself "Kleo," an abbreviation of a much more complicated Russian name. Kleo was one of the many dancing partners at Ciro's. I ought to explain that Shanghai's dancing partners normally earn their living in two ways: first, by dancing with male patrons; and secondly, by having patrons purchase "cocktails" for them. The word "cocktail" in a Shanghai cabaret has a special meaning; it denotes a simulated alcoholic beverage made of tea or some other innocuous liquid. In the event that a patron does not care to dance, he must pay for the girl's conversation through the purchase of "cocktails," a record of which is kept by the waiter and the girl's account is credited accordingly. This sounds like a devious method of recompensing the girls, but it works out well in practice.

Kleo worked in a bakery during the day and made additional earnings at night by working at Ciro's cabaret. I was amazed at her dancing ability and asked how she kept in such good practice during the years under Japanese occupation. She explained that she was a professional acrobatic dancer but had been forced to discontinue her career as the result of a spinal injury. She elaborated on her experiences in broken English, saying that she had worked with a troupe of White Russian performers before the war, playing in nightclubs and theaters from Harbin to Singapore. She had married a colleague, expecting to settle in Tsingtao, but she and her husband proved incompatible and she had moved to Shanghai to live with her parents.

As she drank "cocktails" with me at a corner table, I began asking her about conditions under the Japanese. Her livelihood was largely dependent on the demand for evening entertainment, and suffered naturally because of the curfew which prevented cabarets and nightclubs from operating. The Japanese were strict in enforcing the regulation that no Chinese, and especially no white persons, were to be seen on the streets after eight P.M. Earlier in the war, "when the Japanese were winning," cabarets were allowed to operate, but as the American air raids occurred, blackout and curfew were rigidly enforced.

I had gained the impression from reading a book entitled *Bushidō*, dealing with the Japanese policy in Manchuria that the White Russians were treated in a patronizing way so as to elicit their support against the Red Russians. Kleo's statements indicated that the contrary was true in Shanghai. She maintained that the Japanese were never sure but that a so-called White Russian might not be a Red in disguise. Many White Russians were taken to Bridge House and internment camps, where, she insisted, they received worse treatment than Americans or British. I felt that her opinion was prejudiced by the treatment accorded a friend of hers—terrible treatment to be sure, but probably no worse than that experienced by persons of other nationalities. This friend of hers was a healthy six-foot White Russian in his early twenties, an employee of a grocery store who was entirely innocent of any political or subversive activity. One evening he remained at the residence of a friend until a little after curfew and was challenged by Japanese sentries as he proceeded homeward. He then disappeared, only to be found a week later, hobbling back to the French concession. Some friends took him home, but he died soon afterward as the result of internal injuries sustained from beatings on his back.

Aside from the mental discomfort of being under suspicion, Kleo asserted that White Russians suffered economically to a greater degree than other white groups in Shanghai. Many of them are employed in tailoring, grocery, baking, brewing and other trades which are dependent on the availability of materials. The Japanese enforced stringent rationing of food and clothing, and failed to see any raison d'être for bakeries and delicatessens. Supplies were therefore cut off and the establishments forced to close down.

Unlike the majority of Chinese who are used to a rice diet, the White Russians are accustomed to bread, meats and other occidental foods. It was therefore more difficult for them to maintain a normal standard of living, since the Japanese considered such foods as unnecessary luxuries. Kleo claimed that the French and German Nazis in Shanghai enjoyed the prestige of national identity and thus were granted the privilege of living on a higher level than the White Russians.

Kleo had hated the Japanese occupation because it brought an end to night life and professional entertainment. Also the occupation had meant living under constant suspicion and economic discrimination from which there was no visible hope for relief, as the White Russians are a nationless people.

Still another reaction to the Japanese occupation was given me by some German Jews who worked in a bar in the French concession. The bar was unusually small, consisting of a main room hardly forty feet long and fifteen feet wide. There were only two customers besides myself, a soldier and a sailor who were leaning over a tabletop utterly besotted. I wondered why a bar so small and apparently so little patronized should require the services of six persons: a manager, two bartenders and three "bar girls." (The bar girls, like Kleo at the cabaret, were supposed to drink "cocktails" as a means of livelihood.) I later learned that the bar was typical of businesses managed by German Jews in Shanghai, who frequently formed groups and pooled their meager capital in some joint enterprise.

I ordered a brandy and ice and began conversing with the manager. Several of the staff assembled within earshot to ask about my recent visit in Japan. The manager was a man of forty-odd years, while the two bartenders were boys of about seventeen or eighteen. The two boys exhibited a hang-dog obsequiousness which led me to believe that they had undergone a lot of brow-beating. If I had suddenly said "boo," they would probably have groveled on the floor. By contrast, the manager was extremely self-possessed. On hearing that I had just come from Japan, all three of them inquired about the Japanese reaction to the American occupation. Their questions were marked with caution at first, possibly a caution bred by many years of enforced dumbness on political matters. They were incredulous when I told them that the Japanese were reacting to the Americans with complete docility. "That is just a trick," one of the boys remarked. "It can't last long." Then one of the boys asked me about the treatment of German Jews in Japan. I know of only one instance, that of a Mr Reese, now employed by Mac-Arthur's headquarters. I told them how Reese had been tortured to obtain a spy confession. Reese had told me the steps in reasoning employed by the Japanese *kempeitai*: Reese was a German by birth, but a Jew. As an anti-Nazi he must have come to Japan only for the purpose of spying.

My audience of bar employees listened intently. The manager then remarked to my surprise that few such instances had occurred among Jews in Shanghai. He then proceeded to describe the treatment accorded by the Japanese to himself and others.

About ten thousand Jews had arrived in Shanghai from Europe by 1940, just at a time when American and British interests were evacuating the Orient. It was an ideal opportunity for them since they could step into recently vacated positions and businesses. They had a little capital, which was usually pooled by small groups. The capital was brought from Europe in such forms as jewelry, watches, gold and cameras (one reason for the abundance of Leica cameras then available in Shanghai). Thus the Jews were just beginning to establish themselves solidly when the Japanese occupation began in 1941, and the promised land, which Shanghai had become for them, soon lost its fertility.

The Japanese established a ghetto in the predominantly Chinese quarter of Honkew. German Jews were not permitted to live outside the ghetto or to visit other areas of Shanghai without special permission and had to wear identifying armbands at all times. The restriction of their movements meant economic ruin in many cases. If a Jew owned a cabaret or jewelry store in the French concession, where most of them had settled incidentally, he had to give up the business. Terrific overcrowding occurred in Honkew, one of the most densely populated areas of Shanghai to begin with. (It is interesting that the Chinese authorities in Shanghai have now established a "ghetto" for the Japanese in the very same Honkew district.)

Having heard Reese's experience in Japan, I had expected that the Japanese would have been similarly brutal to German Jews in Shanghai. Aside from economic discrimination, however, the Jews were not badly treated. None of the three men talking with me offered a satisfactory explanation for this apparent leniency; they did not seem to expect persecution anywhere but in Nazi Europe. The manager felt that they were indeed fortunate to have escaped from Europe. Publicity regarding Nazi death camps had just been released, and he told me that such institutions were in active operation as early as 1935 when he left Hamburg. I pressed him further for an explanation of the difference in the Japanese and German treatment of Jews. He had little to say except that the Japanese were unable in most cases to distinguish between Jew and Gentile, and even if they succeeded in doing so, the distinction meant very little. He also felt that the Jews had come to occupy a fairly important position in the local economy and to eliminate them entirely might have jeopardized Shanghai's commercial welfare.

Turning from the three men, I began conversing with one of the bar girls, who seemed very alert and intelligent. She told me that she had been a chiropractor in peacetime, in preparation for which she had attended medical school in Vienna. She spoke phenomenally good English, and I had the impression that her comments on the status of Jews in Shanghai were reliable. I asked her why she had abandoned her profession. She claimed that it was hopeless to start up in it again because of business uncertainty. She was biding her time until the American authorities would grant her a visa to go to Oregon where her uncle was.

Life in Shanghai had been uncertain since the coming of the Japanese and continued to be so even after they had gone. The Japanese had forced her to live in Honkew thus necessitating the relinquishment of her office and practice in the French concession. She felt that even her life was in danger because the Japanese regulations were notoriously changeable and became more so as the threat of American bombing raids increased. Also the existence of factories around Honkew led the Jews to believe that their ghetto would be leveled at any moment by American incendiary bombs. The American forces finally came, bringing with them temporary prosperity but no less uncertainty. The Chinese were immediately given jurisdiction over the nationless Jews, and, as a final blow, were taking active steps to have the entire Jewish population of Shanghai deported. She asked me wistfully if the Americans were likely to intercede. I said that I thought they would, especially if the American public were informed of the true state of affairs.

I then asked her why the Chinese authorities were seeking to deport Shanghai's Jewish population. I had made previous inquiries of non-Jews and was told that the Jews had become conspicuous racketeers and public leeches. The more logical explanation of the former chiropractor ran as follows: The Chinese government was beginning to test its strength, now that extra-territorial rights had been relinquished by the Western powers. Many Chinese had opposed the immigration of Jews in the first place, but had lacked sufficient influence in the Shanghai Municipal Council to enact an immigration ban. Now that the Chinese were supreme, there was little to stop them from deporting the Jews if they desired to do so.

The Jews were more unpopular now than ever before, she claimed. Whereas many of them had once engaged in legitimate businesses and professions, the Japanese had dislocated them, forcing them to take advantage of money-making opportunities to be found in the inflationary tendency and the rapid fluctuation of exchange rates. This meant that the Jews had turned to the sale and resale of property, to hoarding and to currency manipulation.

She cited her own case: "I would like to resume my original profession as a chiropractor, but I would first have to reestablish myself in an office. This would take a fortune in 'key money' and the rent would be prohibitive. I would have to obtain a license from capricious Chinese officials who would probably not grant me one without special payments. All this would take me months and would cost more than I can afford. I am now obliged to make a living in any way that I can. Being a bar girl is as good a business as any these days. Like many Jews, I am forced to do a kind of work which most people regard as degraded and unproductive. I therefore contribute to the already unfortunate reputation of others of my race."

I wished her the best of luck in getting to America and she thanked me perfunctorily. America seemed like an untouchable, but nonetheless glorious land, where a person is appreciated for his own merits and where at last predictability might be found.

Frank

◆ ◆ ◆

FROM SHERRY MORAN IN TOKYO
TO TED DE BARY IN HONOLULU

January 3, 1946

Dear Ted,

Christmas Day in Tokyo did not have an auspicious beginning for me. Last night Otis and I were sitting in the ground-floor lobby of the building in which I am living, listening to phonograph records when, about eleven o'clock, an unnerving incident occurred that left us with an unwelcome feeling of bitterness and resentment. Halfway through a record—I don't recall what it was, but it was light and noisy—the doors of the room swung open and three enlisted soldiers walked slowly in, supporting a young Japanese woman by the arms. She had on a green kimono and a *haori* [top kimono] of rich red. She seemed about four and a half feet tall and might have been pretty. But she was in terrible agony; her face was twisted with pain. It was impossible to guess what had happened to her. I thought that it might have been an auto accident. The men eased her onto a davenport inside the door, where she sank, burying her head in the cushion beside her, hardly breathing, refusing to look up.

The men were boiling mad. One of them said, "You should'a taken off after the guy, Bill. What was the matter with you?" Bill didn't make any reply that I remember. They kept their attention on the girl. As we gathered around, the story came out. "It was a Jap hit her," Bill said. "Son of a bitch came up behind us while we was walking along in the street just now. Hit her hard right below the ribs then ran. I should'a gone after him, but by the time I knew what happened, he'd beat it. Damn, she crumbled up on the sidewalk like a silk stocking." Eventually somebody got a doctor and procured transportation which took her to a hospital.

I do not think that attacks like these are common, but they do happen often enough to mar an otherwise very placid record of mutual acceptance of one another between Americans and Japanese.

Christmas Day was uneventful and would have passed like any other holiday had it not been for a stirring presentation of Handel's *Messiah* which I heard that evening. The performance was given at one of the big downtown public halls. It was sung by an American and Japanese Christian chorus, accompanied by the Nippon Symphony Orchestra. About a hundred and eighty Japanese men and women made up the bulk of the chorus. The Americans were soldiers, about seventy of them, distributed equally between the tenor and bass sections. The orchestra was entirely Japanese and Japanese-conducted. The soloists were two Japanese women singing soprano and alto and two Americans singing tenor and bass.

It was an impressive performance. Without making allowance for the *Messiah* being sung in a language foreign to most of them, without making the mental note that this kind of work had not been given in Japan for over five years, and even without making excuses for the chilling cold of the unheated auditorium that night, I thought that the presentation was an unusually fine one. The singers stood for almost three hours in a tight, ten-banked horse-shoe with the orchestra seated in front. The black-haired soprano and alto sections were in white surplices, the Japanese men in threadbare dark business suits, the blond American soldiers in olive drab and sweaters. I saw no gloves, but there might well have been. Many in the audience wore theirs.

The GI tenor was the best of the soloists. You probably remember the very difficult air at the beginning, "Every valley shall be exalted," in which it is necessary to exalt the word "exalted" for about thirty seconds. He did it very well, and throughout had a good clear tone that is often lacking in other tenors singing this part. The other three soloists were good, but seemed to lack his firmness. It was especially interesting to me to note how the women pronounced the words of the solos. They weren't perfect, but except for a few obvious slips, I doubt if the ordinary listener would have caught those places where the Japanese have trouble with English. One of the alto parts, for instance, tended to come out something like, "O zou zat terrest goodsu tidingsu tsu Zion" for "O thou that tellest good tidings to Zion," but the th's and l's were generally under good control. Again, it was the alto, a stately woman in a formal Japanese blue silk kimono who gave the soberest, most grief-filled rendition I have ever heard of, "He was despised and rejected of men; a man of sorrows and acquainted with grief."

The chorus of two hundred and fifty stood, as I said, throughout the entire performance. It was a feat of endurance which I have never seen equalled under similar conditions of crowded space and of temperature. A great deal was gained by so doing. By not sitting during the solo airs, as is commonly done, the chorus was thus ready as soon as the cue was given to burst out with full effect. The usual distracting rustle of papers and the noise of getting in and out of chairs between choral portions of the work were thus eliminated. It seemed to me, too, that the cold accidentally contributed to their impressive singing, for with no other bodily motion permissible during the performance, the singers appeared to fight the cold with the volume and energy of their notes. The net effect was overwhelming, quite drowning out the orchestra. I could not attempt to say which section sounded best to me. They went through the exciting, "For unto us a Child is born" with wonderful pep, the sopranos and the basses tossing it back and forth like a volleyball. The full chorus singing at the top of their lungs, "Glory to God in the highest and peace on earth, goodwill toward men," produced a tingle in the spine like an electric shock.

I think that the audience of one thousand five hundred, mostly soldiers, sailors, WACs and nurses, was unprepared for the impact this presentation had on them. I know that many shared my feelings as we stood up in traditional fashion for the stirring Hallelujah Chorus that there was something being displayed that transcended the music. It was a promise, perhaps no more than that, of something outside the realm of art. I was not prepared, as I said, to be moved by this performance more than the familiar music itself could move me, but I was, and so were the two men sitting in front of me. One of them said to the other as we filed out of the hall, and without a trace of humor in his face, "Those black Japanese heads! A year ago I was heaving mortar shells into formations like that." The other said simply, "Yeah."

Sherry

❖ ❖ ❖

FROM OTIS CARY IN TOKYO
TO DON KEENE AND TED DE BARY IN HONOLULU

January 6, 1946

Dear Don and Ted,

You have been in the dark again over your allotted time, but I am happy to be able to tell you that for my silence I at least have the disappearance of my "teethaches" to show. They hung on for almost a week, spoiling for me a Christmas that the Shikibas had planned and leaving me the most un-Christmaslike fellow. When I finally got up and around I found that dispatches (prompted by chasers) requesting to have me stay on, which should have got through weeks before, had finally come through, so I'll be here for a while yet. I refused to stay after February 20 though, so I should be in the land of my wife and the free before too long.

When did you first see the New Year's Day rescript? Sherry and I didn't see any papers till the morning of the second. I was amazed when I read the full translation in the *Nippon Times*, but I wanted to see the original Japanese version. It seemed too much like a wonderful translation of a not-so impressive document. If the translator is good enough, a translation can be an improvement on the original. I particularly wanted to know whether it actually said "people" in the Japanese, as it did in the English, or still "subjects." I was also keen to find out whether "defeat" had been rendered actually as defeat or the usual phrase *shūsen*, "termination of hostilities," which, after the "hundred years' war" propaganda campaign Tōjō had waged, could very easily be used twenty years hence as a rallying point for a group of militarists. ("Come on, there's eighty years to go!") If the actual words in the emperor's rescript had been "defeat," it could never be said by the jingoists that the supposed unconditional surrender was really just a clever *bushidō* tactic to maneuver into position to beat the Western heathens—Japan has never been beaten at arms, etc. I also wanted to check the whole thing and see whether a picture of it had appeared. I got hold of a Japanese paper and checked especially those two words. The Japanese word "defeat" (*haiboku*) was in there big as life, a word with no secondary meanings, only defeat. Although the rescript was still signed "honorable name, honorable imperial seal," I felt that the Japanese document was blunter than the English as I plowed through it with a dictionary; and I was amazed that even I could read it with a little help and discussion with some grade-school kids. They continually were calling my attention to and discussing among each other the pictures on the front page: one, a big close-up of the emperor in mufti, stick in hand, walking with one of his daughters; the other of the empress sewing for relief with some of the other children at her side helping. They were tickled about that, never having seen such pictures of the imperial family before. I think the paper I looked at was the *Mainichi*. I didn't have any idea what was in store for me when I saw the *Asahi* out at the Shikibas' that night.

I got out there in time for supper as usual and soon we were talking of the rescript and the favorable comment it was drawing from abroad already. We went over it point by point also remarking on the unprecedented pictures. Then Doc Shikiba said, "You saw Prince Takamatsu's article and the imperial interview, didn't you?" I hadn't, of course. The prince's article was headlined "My Big Brother, the Emperor." I was somewhat disappointed in reading it. It maintained the superpolite language and was fairly stock stuff, although, of course, it contained things the Japanese public had never heard. Did the reporter himself put in all the special language, because "one always does when writing about His Imperial Highness?" He wouldn't have, had the prince asked him specifically to leave it in the simple language he had probably used. Didn't he realize that unless he practically commanded that it be done simply, it would automatically be rendered in this superpolite form, no matter how he had said it? It contained many points of which we had talked: his present pastimes of planting various types of grasses, his not playing golf these days although he likes to, his concern over the crown prince's education, the mention of "peace" in all his rescripts. Then the imperial interview was also featured on the front page with the pictures. The emperor, it reported, had casually met the Imperial Household reporters as they were going the rounds and said a few things, "You've been around a very long time"; "Are you having trouble getting enough to eat?"; "Did your houses burn down?"; all of which created quite a stir among the Japanese. They were both attempts, but they certainly were mild. Perhaps the headline on the prince's interview was as striking as anything in the article, although it too was in formal polite language.

After this, for them, auspicious beginning I was a little disappointed over some well-substantiated information to the effect that abdication papers were being prepared at the Home Ministry. They were at it full tilt two days after my last talk with Prince Takamatsu. A more recent piece of information from the same source said that all the work had been gathered up and was tight in the home minister's safe, evidently completed. If abdication was being contemplated, the February 11 "Empire Day" would be the logical time. I couldn't figure why they had gone to all the trouble of putting out this New Year's Day rescript if they were going to retire him off. Indeed, I felt that it would be quite like pulling another Konoye. If he were to abdicate, right after the surrender would have been the time. To abdicate now merely complicates the situation and destroys many chances of ever being able to help out the Japanese people. Doc Shikiba wanted to arrange an interview again. We thought it would be more conducive to talk—more informal, and more fun—for the prince and princess if they would come out to the Shikibas' home, in which case I agreed to participate. When Doc Shikiba got in touch with Mr. Yoshijima, however, he found that the prince didn't think he could afford the time till later, but that he was really anxious to have a talk as soon as possible. He arranged another afternoon audience. We went, bound to find out about this business of possible abdication.

We were about fifteen minutes early, but this time we were announced as soon as we got there and ushered right in. There was a *hibachi* [charcoal brazier] in the middle of the room this time which made things more informal, allowing us to cross and recross our legs without so much attention being drawn to it, and it gave the prince something with which to play. I wondered if the formula read that the third time formality can be broken down a little.

I said to the prince as we shook hands and sat down, "This is a New Year's on which to really wish you well."

"Yes," he surprised me by replying, "but we must not sit back and rest now; we must go on, mustn't we?" The way he said this seemed to indicate that abdication was not contemplated after all.

After asking about my teeth, he said, "Isn't it fine that Mac-Arthur endorsed the rescript the way he did? That really makes us feel that we've got some basis to work on now." He said this many times during the interview.

"We have felt that there was a difference in point of view between the younger officers of GHQ and older, higher-ranking officers.

The younger ones are difficult to understand. They seem to want to get rid of the emperor, and they appear defiant without knowing very much about the situation. This endorsement by MacArthur should unify the GHQ point of view so that there is no internal difference in GHQ attitude." Even here I could see Japanese thinking clearly. He was figuring that we were like the Japanese: if a Japanese commander says something, it automatically becomes the public and private point of view of all men below him. It did not occur to him that such was not the case in America or its army. The mere fact that the senior commander says it's a good idea to buy war bonds doesn't mean that they are bought. And the mere fact that he endorses a rescript of the emperor doesn't mean that all the young officers (do we have a young officers' group, too?) under him are never going to have their own attitudes and express private opinions about the emperor institution.

I answered him, "It would be a mistake to construe MacArthur's statement as anything but an expression of approval on an excellent, rational, and sound rescript. The young officers may have some reason to be impatient, too. Only this morning (the day commemorating the founding of the line unbroken through ages eternal) one lieutenant, looking at an article in the *Nippon Times* said to me, 'What good does it do to get out directives dissolving State Shinto, or for a superficially fine rescript like that of New Year's Day to come out, when we get this right back again?' "

The prince said, "Those things should have no more fuss made about them than the announcement of some service at some cathedral." I thought he got the point nicely.

The talk drifted off to the rescript. I told him the words "people" and "defeat" were especially pleasing, as was the citing of the Five Articles of the Charter Oath of his grandfather. The entire paragraph,

> We stand by the people and We wish always to share with them in their moments of joys and sorrows. The ties between Us and Our people have always stood upon mutual trust and affection. They do not depend upon mere legends and myths. They are not predicated on the false conception that the

Emperor is divine, and that the Japanese people are superior to other races and fated to rule the world,

was well put. But above all the simplicity of the thing was fine; even I could plow through it with a dictionary and a little help!

Just then the princess came in through the door directly behind me. Prince Takamatsu looked up and then back at me again and went on talking, so I thought it was a servant. Little did I realize it was she till she got over into the circle to sit down—after shaking hands, of course. I felt rather stupid not rising when she came in, but the prince didn't, nor did he give me the cue. She was made to understand that we were talking about the rescript and that even I could plow through it with a dictionary. She was amazed. So was I!

Then I asked him point-blank about abdication and the papers in the home minister's safe. He replied, "I don't see how he can now. The papers are kept up to date for any emergency." Talk swung around to the newspaper interview he had given the *Asahi*. I told him I got a big kick out of the headline "My Big Brother, the Emperor." He had a chance to say where that idea came from, but he didn't take it. I'd like to claim an assist on that one, at least!

We went on to the rescript. He said that preparing rescripts was a cabinet function, but to get all those points included—simplicity of style, to the "people," he was not divine nor they a fated people, "defeat," etc.—the emperor would have had to designate them specifically. I asked whether the pictures of the imperial family had been taken at the time of the imperial interview. He said, "No, they were taken a few days before Christmas." I remarked that the imperial interview, the pictures, the prince's interview and the rescript were a start at least. Then Prince Takamatsu said, "That's where you had quite a bit of influence." I felt he was still talking about the informal pictures of the imperial family, but Doc Shikiba felt that he meant all of those things. He went out of his way to say this later, and who am I to argue with a Japanese about his own language!

I had brought some literature along that I wanted both of them to read and pass on. Included were Japanese translations written out in longhand of the chapters on the emperor (as Man, as God, as High Priest, as Symbol, as Emperor) from Hugh Byas's *Government by Assassination*, and the whole set of galley proofs of Johnstone's *The Future of Japan*, which had a full chapter devoted to the emperor question, as well as the special Japan number of *Fortune*, Lamott's *Durable Peace in Eastern Asia*, Wallace's *Far Eastern Peace* and John Foster Dulles' *Post-War Treatment of Japan*, sponsored by the National Council of Churches. I was able to muster these five from people who were good enough to send them on from the States to me. I felt they depicted some of the more progressive wartime thinking in America about the general problem of Japan. They were delighted to get these, and Doc Shikiba asked him to make sure they got to the top.

I planted a gag here. "Considering the shortness of time, they must have taken the pictures and had the interviews in a hurry. Didn't the emperor get a bit of a kick out of it all because it was hurried and had to be squeezed in? He must be bored with his usual pre-announced routine." The princess laughed heartily and the prince looked quite sheepish.

Doc Shikiba and I urged them to come out to the Shikibas' home sometime, telling them it would do them good to get away from all this! We made our exit with that.

I've written you a couple of pretty factual letters but there are some conclusions I want to draw soon which are getting more and more confirmation from many quarters. I hope you'll find time to listen.

Otis

◆ ◆ ◆

FROM OTIS CARY IN TOKYO
TO TED DE BARY IN HONOLULU

January 24, 1946

Dear Ted,

I found out some very interesting dope the other day from an unimpeachable source. I had occasion to meet and have a couple of hours to talk with a Mr. Fukushima, Prime Minister Shidehara's secretary. It came out in the talk that the first draft of the New

Year's Day rescript was written in English. The premier got the emperor's ideas on what he wanted included and wrote the thing off in English. When he took it back to check it, the emperor thought it would be a good idea to include the Five Articles of the Charter Oath of his grandfather, the Meiji emperor. This was done. Then the document was put into Japanese and routed around the cabinet for any additions, corrections and comments. At this point Prime Minister Shidehara became ill and it was rushed to completion in the final Japanese form without his supervision. The released English version is still not an exact translation of the Japanese, and they are expecting to turn out an official English text.

This accounts for some of the fine English in the released English version. Mr. Fukushima said that Shidehara has an excellent command of English, as does Fukushima himself, so he ought to know. On the corner of the prime minister's desk are always a Webster and a Shakespeare. He said he is especially strong in his classics—Milton, Bunyan, Bacon, Shakespeare, etc. It is easy to see from where "the slough of despond" and like phrases came. Mr. Fukushima doubted that there was any other Japanese that knew the great English literature as well as Premier Shidehara or took such joy in it. Judging by this, I think he insists on editing, if not writing, his own foreign press releases, too, for certainly the flavor of translation is lacking in them, and they are written in fine English—quite a contrast to some of the releases of Prince Higashikuni's cabinet.

I was speaking to Mr. Fukushima just at the time when it was doubtful whether the Shidehara Cabinet could stay in power after the January "purge" directives. He said that whether it survives or not Shidehara will always be close to the throne, indeed very close, for there is no one else in the whole Japanese reservoir upon whom the emperor could draw with his experience or knowledge of English and the West. He spoke of all the pictures (close to two hundred) of the imperial family which had been taken. He said they had been given to *Life*, with one exception, but *Life* wanted to wait for an interview to go along with them before printing them. The exception was the photograph showing the bust of Lincoln in his study. It was felt that that would be misinterpreted. [I noticed that that picture nevertheless got into *Life* and *Time*. Probably *Life* talked them out of it.] He also said that when the crown prince reaches high school age in two years, they are thinking of sending him to prep school in America. When he said that I almost choked. It would certainly be a terrible responsibility for any school in our country. Of course, the attempt, as he said, would be to show him something of democracy and how it really worked. He should pick up his English pretty quickly, but once he does just how much of democracy is he going to learn at Groton or Deerfield or Andover? He should be sent to a New York City high school for two years, to a Midwestern high school for a year and to a California high school for his last year. Then his college should certainly not be Harvard or Amherst, but a small coeducational college that puts the maximum on scholarship, perhaps like Swarthmore or Oberlin, or else a large state university. Even then it would be hard to say how much he would see of democracy. However, they probably would want to send him to Oxford or Cambridge to take his college work, just to "round him off and give him the fine points of that culture, you know." As an old friend of mine used to say, "It's a problem!"

Evidently I've received some reputation around here as a man who knew many POWs, probably because of an article Doc Shikiba wrote about my first visit to his home and the eventual realization that came to them all of Yokota's good health and continued long life and happiness. Princess Takamatsu, who was formerly a Tokugawa, directed her younger sister to me. The younger sister had become a Matsudaira and her husband had not been heard from in the Philippines since June. He was a naval lieutenant and code officer on the staff of one of the air fleets that had been dispatched to the P.I. I missed connections with her, but she left me as much information as she had. I didn't know how I could find out anything for her, but one doesn't turn down a request like that, ever. Perhaps some P.I. POW had heard of a captured Matsudaira, a name not easy to overlook. I knew a few returned P.I. POWs. It was too bad he hadn't been in the Central Pacific, I thought.

I later had a chance to meet her at the Takamatsus' when we

were invited there for dinner one night. I was very much interested to see whether it would be Japanese or Western-style. Mrs. Matsudaira, young and very attractive, was in a delightful kimono, but the prince was sharp in his blue pinstripe. When the princess came in, however, she was resplendent in kimono, too. After cocktails, which none of us seemed to do much with, we went into the banquet hall—I hope it's not where they always eat. It was a large room with a large table in the middle and little around the sides. A screen covered the doorway from which the servants—still in *mompe*—came and went. It was a Western-style dinner of eight courses, although we didn't get close to using up all the silver in front of us. I sat across from the prince, beside the princess. Doc Shikiba was at the "head" of the table between the prince and myself, and Mrs. Matsudaira was across from the princess to the right of the prince. The seating arrangement seemed to follow no particular custom, either Japanese or Western.

We talked small talk all through the dinner and most of the evening, Mrs. Matsudaira and I comparing our short, even if blissful, married lives. She had over two months to show for my twenty-seven days. Not to be abashed, I followed the prince's lead on the asparagus salad course and plunged in with my fingers, but we were the only ones. It was a cold night, and we all huddled around the *hibachi* when we returned to the parlor. The two sisters and I continued to small-talk, with Doc Shikiba joining in once in a while, but the prince stayed out of the conversation till about the last half hour or so.

The princess dispelled the problem we faced all through the war in translating documents of whether Tōjō's first name is Hideki or Eiki, the readings for the characters making either possible. She blithely characterized Mrs. Tōjō on the occasion when she came to their palace as always talking of "Hideki this" and "Hideki that." This reminded me of the nickname Tōbirei that evidently had come to be applied to her before the Tōjō Cabinet fell. Long after the China war had begun, Japanese women continued to have great admiration for Mme. Chiang, whom they knew as Sōbirei, the Japanese reading of the characters in her Chinese name, Soong Mayling. Mrs. Tōjō had had much publicity wafted around her. Many of Mrs. Tōjō's days had been publicized in the press, as well as her latest recipes, and how well she got along on just her ration. So skeptical were the women of this, and it was in such contrast to Mme. Chiang, that the nickname Tōbirei (Tō for Tōjō) got started, as a takeoff on Sōbirei, and gained wide acclaim. The sisters were amazed I knew this; I was amazed they knew it.

The princess mentioned to Doc Shikiba, while I was talking to her sister, that she had just seen the empress, who wanted special thanks passed on for the *Life*s I had been able to gather. She and the emperor had spent a long time looking through them together. I offered to drive Mrs. Matsudaira home in my jeep, for she had never ridden in one. She was delighted. The princess even came out to the front door to see us off and seemed anxious to ride in one. I offered to drive her out to the Shikibas' in one when she came out.

One of the interesting points of the evening to me was the suddenly formal leave Mrs. Matsudaira took of the prince and then of her sister, the princess, when she left the room to get her wraps. We had been on a completely informal basis all evening, nudging each other after jokes and laughing freely, but then when she left the room, she took humble leave not only of the prince but of her older sister. She did this when we left the parlor after she had come back with her wraps on, too. Not with just a nod but with a bow and another bow at the door.

Later Doc Shikiba was able to return the gesture by inviting all three of them out to his home. We planned a good feed, but otherwise were going to try to be as natural as possible—sitting in the sitting room, dining in the dining room, etc. It was, of course, a great occasion for the Shikiba household to be able to entertain a prince. There was much running around in preparation in spite of the fact that the attempt was to be as natural as possible.

They arrived at the appointed time and were ushered into the living room, where there was a blazing fire. A big heavy table was too close to the fire to allow us all to sit around it, so I started to move the thing with the princess and her sister jumping to my assistance. We sat around the fire for a while, passing pleasantries. MacArthur's review of the Yamashita case had just come out, and the prince asked me what I thought about it. I told him that I was rather disgusted by the identification of the "profession of arms" with religious classifications of a "faith," a "cult," a "sacred trust," etc. I rather felt that MacArthur had tried to write another Gettysburg address and failed miserably. He said he had given up trying to read the original English after plowing halfway through it with a dictionary.

We started to look at the various fascinating pictures and curios which are around Doc Shikiba's sitting room. Dinner was announced. The princess said, "Evidently it's to be served in the next room." The prince and I were left alone in the room talking about a picture. I didn't know whether he was going to make his entrée after everyone else or had not heard the princess and was expecting to be served in that room. I recalled having heard that wherever people of such station go visiting they are always put into the best room in the house, where everything is brought to them. Of course, that is Japanese style—only the best, meager though it is, is suitable for their eyes. But even in Western-style Japanese homes that is done. I spoke up and said, "I think we're eating next door." The prince looked surprised, and we went to the dining room. There we were seated helter-skelter. We had an ample but definitely home-cooked type meal with much small-talk. Mrs. Shikiba started and got away with one story I almost choked on a couple of times. Evidently it carried no offense in Japan.

Doc Shikiba runs a mental disease hospital, and talk turned to various interesting types of insanity—Napoleon was back in style again, Tōjō wasn't too popular with the schizophrenics either, etc. Doc Shikiba told of one young, attractive college girl who claimed that Prince Chichibu (Prince Takamatsu's next older brother) was in love with her because of a certain look he had given her when visiting her school. Indeed she said that that was why Prince Chichibu had had no children. Then Mrs. Shikiba chimed in and said she thought that the girl had insisted it was

Prince Takamatsu (who has no children either). When the dates were checked, it was found that Prince Takamatsu had been the one to visit her school. Mrs. Shikiba then told the whole story in great detail. Everybody seemed to get a big bang out of it—so I laughed heartily, too, but I thought that when people are thirty-five or so and don't have children yet, you don't rub it in.

I had mustered a couple of each of the different types of candy and K-rations I could find for them to have the fun of opening. We spent much time opening them with explanations by Cary on how everything worked and how scientifically they were all prepared. It is always a great wonder to the Japanese how scientifically we go at problems like eating—even our candy (tropical chocolate, etc.). The incidental advertising that makers put on wrappers, in spite of it being a product made for and on contract with the military, amuses them. In their military they would seek to stamp out the homesickness that a N.Y. GI might feel on seeing a cube of sugar with a Waldorf wrapper on it. We recognize and attempt to take care of it. It baffles them. Yet for us it just raises the fighting efficiency of the men in the organization. I think there in miniature is the whole problem they are up against. They must see that problems are going to exist till they compensate for them. They cannot be eliminated by officially declaring they don't exist. The lower levels of Japan are beginning to see that, and the upper must, too.

I gave the prince a number of other *Life*s I had been able to gather together and showed him several books I had just received from the States on the Far East, most of them written during wartime. He took down many of their titles. I was able to give him Roth's *Dilemma In Japan*, which he had mentioned before, but I had no other duplicates. He told me that the copy of Grew's *Ten Years in Japan* was down at Hayama with the Chichibus, "They're better at English down there!" I also passed on a set of unopened K-rations for him to take to his older brother and family. He seemed pleased.

Of course, before breaking up we had to have a photograph taken. The prince seemed to take it in his stride. It always seems rather out of place to me to pull out a camera suddenly to take a picture of the assemblage—sort of proof that such a personage actually came to "our house." The party broke up later than planned and was a great success.

Later: I find this letter still unfinished. Let me complete it now. Doc Shikiba in a conversation he had with the prince sometime after the dinner out at his home told him that I was to leave soon. The prince was very busy during the next few days, but wanted to do something for me. They put their heads together and figured out that a visit to the Imperial Household might be a good idea.

I duly received a fancy invitation delivered by messenger on the day before the only day I could possibly go. I checked with the headquarters of the cavalry outfit that does guard duty around the Imperial Palace and they gave me their pass. The prince had said there was something for me there. Doc Shikiba was good enough to come along, for I certainly didn't want to go alone to a thing like this. We met Mr. Kinoshita, the vice grand chamberlain. The retinue was out with the emperor on some inspection trip just at that time (as suggested by me?). Mr. Kinoshita was very hospitable to us and even took us to see the emperor's laboratory. His chief assistant there does some fine drawing of various marine specimens that the emperor picks out, and he showed us many of them. He would turn every page for me and then bounce back four paces to the left and rear. I was obviously sitting in the emperor's chair. Considering the terrific honorific language he was using and the care he exercised not to allow me to even turn a page, I almost wondered if he didn't have me confused with the emperor, but I guess one just gets into a rut after a while. It was interesting to watch the faces of the guards as I went by. The vice grand chamberlain was wearing the Imperial Household uniform and there were salutes for him, which he returned very methodically as though he had had to salute everybody always. I ventured forth without my hat or coat and in good navy tradition was not saluting when uncovered. Doubtless they thought me a strutting conqueror although I tried to smile.

Coming out of the laboratory a guard stopped us and asked us who we were. Mr. Kinoshita replied humbly, I must say, that he was the vice grand chamberlain, producing his name card, mind you, and asked if there were any questions. Of course there were none. I wondered how that guard would have been told off six months earlier by any lieutenant colonel or better in the Japanese forces if asked for identification. But the resigned almost apologetic way in which Mr. Kinoshita answered seemed to me typical of the attitude on the part of all the people in the Imperial Household from the secretary that delivered me the invitation to the cops at the gates. I got the idea that they had been used to being pushed around and stepped on, even more than the usual Japanese flunkies, for so long that now most of the burden had been removed, they didn't know which way to turn. Here they were the guardians and direct servants of the emperor, and they were at a loss as to what to do with the controlling forces removed.

Mr. Kinoshita showed me all the pictures that had been taken of the imperial family recently. He said he had been told that I was to be offered any and all I wanted. I picked out a number, and he said that he would see that copies were delivered to me. I wasn't exactly sure what I was supposed to do with them or what I would do with them, but I accepted them. (The nice old messenger that came to deliver them was again a man who it seemed had been walked all over. Although he had been told that he should get a receipt he was sure that it was all right to give them to me "who spoke such good Japanese, wasn't it?") We took our leave and walked out of the palace grounds. The grounds were in bad condition— not enough gravel on the driveways, broken-down fire engines and other vehicles in open garages right on the main thoroughfare, etc. The whole visit to the Imperial Household Ministry, although they were extremely cordial and hospitable, was a revelation to me.

Many ideas had been floating around my mind with regard to the fitness of the very upper classes of Japan to be in their present position. This trip to the Imperial Household seemed to crystallize my point of view toward all the fêting that I had undergone from many *zaibatsu* families (as well as the Takamatsus). The Japanese upper classes, and I know much of ours, have failed to understand that this was more a war of ideologies and of people than any war of modern history. As a group they fail completely to know what their position should be now or what it actually is. There are exceptions, such as Prince Takamatsu, who are trying to do something, but they only look worse because of the apathy of the rest of the uppermost class. Doubtless, not a little of it is planned apathy, but I am convinced much of it is lack of any idea of what direction they do want to take. I think now, just as in the 1930s, they are suffering as the result of errors of omission rather than commission. In the 1930s they had to follow the lead of their reactionist elements, for they could not afford to split up the group. For a while they were winning by default: now they are losing by default for they have nobody to lead them actively in the opposite direction. This does not warrant the perpetuation of the system for a minute longer than it is needed to save the country from complete breakdown and chaos. But that will not be till a more educated public and a group of new leaders emerge.

Many examples illustrated for me the failure on the part of this class to understand what this war had meant in terms of civilization. Six men were recently elected to receive the Imperial Cultural Medal. How could any responsible person who had put any thought into it elect these six old men to receive this medal at this juncture in the fate of their country? For two of the six men there may have been some excuse: Dr. Nishina, Japan's foremost cyclotron man, and Mr. Iwanami, publisher and originator of the Iwanami book series, rather like our pocket books. But nothing either of them had done could be measured by any world standards as especially worthy of note, nor could anything they had done be considered as having especial value to the Japanese people in their past and present plight. Only twenty-odd of these medals have been given out so far. I suppose it is an attempt to combine the idea of the Nobel Prize, the Pulitzer Prize and the British Royal Academies of Arts and Science into one Japanese Imperial Cultural Academy. If there were Japanese of enough stature in absolute world terms to be recognized now before the world, it might be worthwhile, but certainly this choice cannot be condoned. It looks strongly to me like a case of trying to get back to what they think the rest of the world is doing.

I could sense the same thing in the many imperial duck hunts thrown for heads of SCAP sections, etc., of which Prince and Princess Takamatsu often spoke and to which they went probably as senior hosts; or the way he would wonder often out loud, "What does MacArthur do for recreation anyway? He can't just sit in the embassy (his quarters) and his office all day, all week, or can he?" There was no attempt to try and win over the occupation bigwigs and so lull us into complacency here, although many correspondents would happily interpret it that way. There is an element of oriental hospitality there—no matter what your plight, be hospitable to your guests and do all you can for them. But there was basically a complete failure to understand the job of the occupation and why we felt that the entire cause for Japan's aggression and militarism must be wiped out, that merely leaving her impotent and blocking her economically from ever being able to rise again was not enough unless we got clear down to the roots of the problem, which the Japanese themselves fail to see at all.

The reason for this failure, I think, is an inexperience in Japanese life on the part of the highest brackets. Japanese superformality (what is usually interpreted as "You can't trust 'em!" or "You can never tell what they are thinking!") is bad enough anyway, but the entire isolated upbringing of the upper brackets of Japan leaves them completely in the dark about what their own country really is. I find with uneasiness that because I went to Japanese grade school in the sticks, and associated with all types of POWs during the war and Japanese since I've been back here after the surrender, I may easily know more about the Japanese people and what they feel and think than these upper-bracket Japanese.

Probably many of the upper, moneyed families cared little whether they knew the people or not, but the emperor at last has been released to the point where he can. Also, he feels he should. Can he, even with the help of the people he has around him? Indications are not favorable. He lacks the vital knowledge of how much respect he commands, what sacrifice he can call forth from his people, and what he is bound by responsibility—after a war like this—to do with it. Further, as a result of such an upbringing, he doesn't know that if he wants to do something enough and insists on it, no Japanese can stand in his way. It is a matter of complete reeducation. I keep remembering what Yukio Ozaki (the eighty-seven-year-old gentleman who has been a member of every Japanese Diet and who is one of the few true Japanese liberals) said to me about the emperor: "With that kind of an upbringing, I don't know what he *can* do."

You have heard me enough on this score now. I hope I can see you before you see this letter. The way airmail service is now, it shouldn't be difficult.

Otis